The studies in this volume explore the relationship between state taxation and economic development, and attempt to provide a framework for a more coherent, responsible state-level tax policy. Michael Barker's "Introduction" places the essays in contemporary context. In part I, "State Taxation and Economic Development," Roger Vaughan shows that tax policy is only one of many factors influencing economic growth, and by no means the most important. He provides detailed guidelines for policymakers interested in the reform of state/local taxation, always stressing three principal criteria: equity, efficiency, and administrative simplicity. Michael Kieschnick's "Taxes and Growth: Business Incentives and Economic Development," part II, analyzes the impact of state business tax levels on a state's rate of economic growth. Kieschnick also provides the first empirical analysis of the impact of state-level business tax incentives on corporate investment decisions. These studies were originally published by The Council of State Planning Agencies.

Books of related interest

Duke Press Policy Studies

Rebuilding America's Infrastructure
An Agenda for the 1980s
Edited by Michael Barker

State Employment Policy in Hard Times
Edited by Michael Barker

Financing State and Local Economic Development
Edited by Michael Barker

What Role for Government?
Lessons from Policy Research
Edited by Richard J. Zeckhauser *and* Derek Leebaert

Being Governor
The View from the Office
Edited by Thad Beyle *and* Lynn Muchmore

Duke Press Paperbacks

America in Ruins
The Decaying Infrastructure
Pat Choate *and* Susan Walter

Published in cooperation with
The Council of State Planning Agencies

STATE TAXATION POLICY

Edited by
Michael Barker

Foreword by
Robert N. Wise

Duke Press Policy Studies   Durham, N.C.   1983

Library of Congress Cataloging in Publication Data
Main entry under title:

State taxation policy.

  (Duke Press policy studies)
  "Published in cooperation with the Council of State
Planning Agencies."
  Includes bibliographies and index.
  1. Taxation, State—Addresses, essays, lectures.
I. Barker, Michael, 1951- . II. Kieschnick,
Michael. III. Vaughan, Roger J. IV. Council of State
Planning Agencies. V. Series.
HJ2385.S69 1983 336.2′013′73   83-1551
ISBN 0-8223-0535-6

CONTENTS

FIGURES AND TABLES

Part I. Figures

Part I. Tables

Part II. Tables

Tables in Appendices

r

FOREWORD

President Reagan's proposal to "return to the states" the responsibility for a wide spectrum of domestic policy matters has drawn a decidedly mixed reaction—not only from Congressional committee barons unwilling to relinquish their patronage powers, but also from activist groups and others who see greater state involvement in domestic policy as tantamount to a retreat from the social contract of the American welfare state and as a positive attack on the poor, on minorities, on the quality of the environment, and on the safety of the workplace. Conservative and New Right activists, by contrast, have tended to view the Reagan "New Federalism" proposal as a happy means of minimizing the public sector's meddling with the American economy and of reducing the governmental role in societal and community life—apparently hoping that many states will "localize" their treatment of this or that national malady in a prescription for benign neglect. Somewhere between these two extremes are the majority of state officials, who are desperately eager to control the allocation of federal program dollars but quite unwilling to assume the political risks associated with raising those dollars through local tax sources.

For all these reasons and more, Reagan's New Federalism, in and of itself, seems unlikely to have many far reaching effects on federal-state relations.

Nevertheless, there are a growing number of people who believe that state and local governments have a larger role to play in our public life, and that this role can only grow through a diminished federal presence in certain domestic affairs. They are people who hold with Justice Brandeis the belief that state governments have always provided the nation with a margin for innovation and experiment in its public life.

The studies that are republished in this volume grew out of the efforts of the Council of State Planning Agencies to explore this "margin for innovation." They were the most tangible product of a four-year economic development project directed by Michael Barker, who was then the Council's Director of Policy Studies. He commissioned the studies and shaped the final reports, of which more than thirty-six were issued over the years 1978–81. At the same time, he assembled a small group of economic policy consultants, including many of the authors whose work Duke University Press is now republishing, to provide detailed assistance to state officials on the implementation of the recommendations contained in the Council's published research. Much of the current interest in small business development, the investment of public pension funds, the decay of the nation's infrastructure, and national industrial policy grew out of the formal and informal work of this select group.

Robert N. Wise
Executive Director
The Council of State Planning Agencies

INTRODUCTION

Michael Barker

Not long before the November 1982 elections, *The New York Times* ran a lengthy article entitled, "The States Look at Supply Side, Tax Cutting is Out of Favor in Washington, but it's a Big Issue in Many State Capitals." The article suggested that many of the same economists and pamphleteers responsible for the Reagan tax program were successfully working the corridors of the nation's statehouses, persuading both incumbent and aspiring officials to sponsor massive cuts in state level taxes as a spur to economic renewal. Jude Wanniski, who, as an editorial writer for *The Wall Street Journal,* was an early advocate of supply-side economics, and who now heads his own New Jersey based consulting firm, attributed this state level success to the absence of Keynesian advisers surrounding the nation's governors. Arthur Laffer, who first drew his famous curve illustrating the effect of marginal tax rates on the back of a cocktail napkin in a Washington restaurant, claimed that the supply-side program had worked well in every state in which it had been tried, and took particular note of Alaska, Massachusetts, New York, and California. Both men appeared to relish the opportunity to market their ideas in the relative obscurity of a state capital, free of the media glare— and academic scrutiny—that accompanies work in Washington. As Wanniski put it in an interview with *Business Week* magazine, "Supply-side economics is making a millionaire out of Art Laffer, and making rich men out of the rest of us."[1]

In virtually every state, businesses and their trade associations make an annual pilgrimage to the state capital, pleading for additional tax reductions or the creation of special investment incentives. Armed with studies and charts, they attempt to show why the state is suddenly in danger of losing jobs to other, more attractive areas. Usually, they stress that the tax reductions being advocated pose no long term threat to the state's treasury and that prompt action on tax reductions will provide such a stimulus to private taxable activities that the changes will pay for themselves, producing no net loss in state or local revenues. But the alternative is always clear. Without action, disaster looms. The state's business climate will be severely damaged. Investment capital will flow elsewhere. Existing businesses will wither and die. Workers will go jobless. Tax *xiii* revenues will fall as industry stagnates. Business interests will support other, more responsive candidates. A blight will move across the face of the land.

That such efforts continue to prove successful in the complete absence of any empirical evidence that state or local taxes play an important role in guiding business investment decisions is not surprising. Business lobbies are powerful in state capitals. What very few numbers do exist concerning the impact of taxes on business investment decisions have usually been furnished by the very people seeking tax relief.

More than ten states have enacted major reductions in personal taxation since 1981. Corporate taxes were reduced in five more. Sales taxes fell in three. In Massachusetts, one of the supply-side success stories cited by Laffer, this reduction came at considerable cost. It eliminated the opportunity for increased state aid to cities and towns—the only means of major property tax reform in the state—and continued the state's reckless practice of not funding its multibillion dollar pension liability. With a FY1984 revenue shortfall estimated in excess of $250 million, the state once again faces a fiscal situation in which it will be forced not only to raise taxes, but to continue to reduce funding for basic services. The old slogan of "Taxachusetts" seems likely to be revived. In California, the birthplace of the modern tax revolt, the new governor, George Deukmejian, pledged not to increase taxes during his term of office; he now faces a budget deficit well in excess of two billion dollars, with few palatable opportunities for new revenue. In New York, a bidding war between the legislative and executive branches of state government produced a tax reduction package so costly to the state that a billion dollar deficit seems a virtual certainty. The state has already been forced to return to the short term bond market to finance continuing operations for the first time since its 1975 fiscal crisis. Only Alaska, still sleek with oil revenues, has escaped immediate damage. Yet even there, troubles are threatening. By retreating from a commitment to accumulate and preserve revenues in a trust fund against the day, not far off, when Alaska's oil wells run dry, the state has assured that it will ultimately be unable to sustain the many services it now rushes to provide its citizenry. Indeed, its far flung infrastructure and widely dispersed population create service demands already in excess of what the state's own economy is capable of sustaining.

Do tax reductions really provide a stimulus to economic growth? In California, 461,000 new jobs were created in the year following the passage of Proposition 13—an impressive total often cited in defense of supply-side theory. The number pales, however, against the 634,000 jobs created in the year *before* Proposition 13 was enacted.

In Massachusetts, business lobbyists claim a direct link between the tax cuts of the administration of former Governor Edward J. King and the emergence of the state's high technology sector. Yet the state had begun to emerge from a long period of structural adjustment as much as ten years before, and made the most dramatic improvements in its position relative to national and regional averages during the administration of King's predecessor, former Governor Michael Dukakis. Dukakis, who inherited a $600 million deficit from his predecessor, had slashed state programs dramatically, alienating many of the liberal groups which had supported his candidacy. He also raised taxes by the largest amount in the state's modern history. Yet business flourished, and the state's unemployment rate fell from 11.2 percent in January 1975 to a mere 5.5 percent in January 1979. New business starts approached record levels. During the administration of his tax-cutting successor, however, business investment sagged, and unemployment rose upwards toward national averages, exceeding it by as much as 10 percent in many of the state's older cities. Although the King tax program found much favor in the editorial columns of *The Wall Street Journal*, making King a popular figure among the state's industrialists, it contributed heavily to his electoral defeat.

In 1978, popular Minnesota congressman Albert H. Quie rode the burgeoning tax revolt to the governor's chair, and promptly pushed for enactment of a $700 million tax cut. Quie, too, was hailed by *The Wall Street Journal* as an example of the new breed of supply-siders coming to power throughout the nation, impatient with the old state house habits of spend and tax, tax and spend. Minnesota now faces a budget deficit of more that $1 billion. Although state spending was reduced by $625 million in 1981 and $402 million in 1982, and despite major increases in state taxes subsequently enacted, the state's fiscal affairs continue to unravel. During one remarkable period in 1981, the state issued three substantially different revenue projections in almost as many months. The voters took all this badly, and Quie chose not to stand for reelection, Like his tax-cutting colleague, Ed King, Quie was succeeded by the very man he had defeated with his program for massive tax cuts.

In New York, the new Democratic governor Mario Cuomo made a point of endorsing the substantial tax cuts instituted during the term of his predecessor, Hugh Carey—a reduction in the corporate tax rate from 14 percent to 10 percent, a 9 percent cap on personal income taxes, a reduction in the capital gains rate, and the creation of a number of costly new investment incentives. He also pledged not to increase the state's income, sales, or business taxes. In light of the state's onrushing fiscal crisis, however, one must hope that the public viewed his statements as a purely political gesture required by the campaign rhetoric of his opponent, Lewis Lehrman, and not as a commitment to policy.

The studies in this volume explore the relationship between state taxation and economic development, and attempt to provide a framework for a more coherent, responsible state-level tax policy. In "State Taxation *xv* and Economic Development," Roger Vaughan attempts to show that tax policy is only one of many factors influencing economic growth, and by no means the most important. He provides detailed guidelines for policymakers interested in the reform of state/local taxation, always stressing three principal criteria: equity, efficiency, and administrative simplicity. Michael Kieschnick's "Taxes and Growth: Business Incentives and Economic Development" analyzes the impact of state business tax levels on a state's rate of economic growth. Kieschnick also provides the first empirical analysis of the impact of state-level business tax incentives on corporate investment decisions. Each study deserves a word of introduction.

If it were being written today, with the benefit of research conducted in the past two years, Vaughan's study would doubtless give greater weight to the following two issues: the impact of the state/local tax structure on the birth rate of new businesses, and the potential of user fees as a source of needed capital for infrastructure financing.

New business formation. Although a state's tax structure exerts a negligible influence on the location decisions of entrepreneurs, it can influence the rate of new business formation in several ways. On a small scale, it can influence the amount of research and development activity conducted by the state's businesses and universities, accelerating the rate at which new ideas are transformed into new products and businesses. A frequent example of this effort: Providing tax incentives to corporations making contributions of cash or equipment to university research facilities, and targeting this activity to specific areas of generic technology identified by policymakers as important to the creation of new businesses. (California recently enacted a variant of this approach, directed at the state's microelectronics industry. The state matches, on a one-to-one basis, industry contributions to university research and graduate education in microelectronics technology.) A second method of stimulating research and development spending would be for the state to offer tax exempt financing of university-based research facilities, backed by the university's endowment or by user fees, and linked to the extent of private sector support of the facility. A third would entail providing refundable tax incentives to new and small businesses engaged in targeted areas of importance (such as nondefense-related research).

Another means of influencing the rate of new business formation is to offer *refundable* tax credits. This option attempts to shape the after-tax cash flow of young businesses, and thereby their ability to leverage debt capital. New firms frequently have minimal tax obligations, and derive little benefit from nonrefundable credits during their important early years.

A final means of stimulating the rate of business formation would come from the more sophisticated treatment of unincorporated businesses through the personal and business tax codes. One commonly advocated

xvi

approach is to establish a Subchapter S election for corporate taxpayers in conformance with federal law. Essentially, Subchapter S offers closely held corporations, including virtually all new businesses, the option of being taxed as a partnership while still retaining the limited tax liability of a corporation. Under Subchapter S, a corporation pays no corporate tax on its income; instead, the net taxable income is paid directly to shareholders, where it is taxed as personal income. This permits developing businesses to retain more of their earnings for reinvestment at a time when the company may be unable to raise capital from external sources.

A state could also influence *investor* behavior by providing more favorable treatment of capital gains, thus improving, however marginally, the accessibility of equity capital. In New York, for example, the state provides special treatment of capital gains realized through investments in new businesses located within the state. (A new business is defined as any business which has filed a New York State tax return for three years or less.) The goal is to provide investors with an incentive not only to leave their money in developing businesses for longer periods of time but also to take the risk of investing in a business that is not yet able to provide a return on investment in the form of dividend income. California has also enacted a targeted capital gains reform which reduces the tax benefits associated with speculative investments in nonproductive assets, such as collectibles, while increasing tax benefits for investors who put their capital at risk in small business development. (In California, a small business is defined, for the purposes of this legislation, as one which has 500 employees or less, is headquartered within the state, and which has securities that are not publicly traded.)[2]

User fees for infrastructure financing. User fees are essential to the development of a rational, effective system for financing and managing public works. Not only do they provide a source of revenue to back bond issues and pay maintenance and operational expenses, they also ensure the more efficient use of public facilities and encourage a more efficient delivery of public services. For example, if consumers pay a price for water equal to the marginal cost of supplying it, the use of water will be weighed against its conservation. This will produce a more efficient allocation of water among users. At the same time, those responsible for supplying water will be able to use the change in water revenues over time as a measure of whether an increase in supply would be cost-effective.

Critics of user fees frequently argue that such charges are unable to encompass external benefits provided by public facilities and services. The users of mass transit contribute to a lesser degree of traffic congestion and lower air pollution—benefits which accrue to automobile drivers as well. Those graduating from an employment training program are less prone to go on welfare or commit crimes—benefits enjoyed by the entire community. Yet these are still benefits which can be captured through a *xvii* system of charges. Using a portion of the gasoline tax to support mass transit is an obvious example.

By one estimate, a well-structured system of user fees—consisting of increased gasoline taxes and automobile registration fees, utility hook-up charges and water rates, and other lesser charges—could raise as much as $30 billion for state and local governments to use in infrastructure construction and repair.[3]

Michael Kieschnick's "Taxes and Growth: Business Incentives and Economic Development" represents the first effort to measure empirically the impact of business taxes and special investment incentives on three different types of firms: new business start-ups, single-plant firms considering expansion, and large, multiplant firms. Kieschnick reaches the following conclusions:

■ Most firms making new investments never even consider investing in more than one state, seldom know about available incentive programs, and where they do, rarely attribute any importance to them.

■ In virtually all industries, the overall level of general state business taxation exerts an *undetectable* impact on the rate or level of private investment.

■ Overall reductions in business taxation on the state level, even if targeted to industries thought to be particularly burdened by taxation, are unlikely to stimulate added levels of investment.

■ State governments are foregoing substantial amounts of revenue— perhaps billions of dollars—through special tax incentive programs that are demonstrably useless in creating new jobs or increased private capital investment. Moreover, there is virtually no legislative oversight of such programs nor any attempt to estimate the annual cost of such tax expenditures to state governments.

Whether the fulsome praise Kieschnick's book has received from tax analysts will ensure that policymakers themselves, always under pressure to do something about their state's economic performance, take note of these findings is still to be seen.

NOTES

I thank Michael Kieschnick and Roger Vaughan, colleagues at The Gallatin Institute, for contributions to this introduction.

1. When the history of the nation's flirtation with supply-side economics is written, the supply-side program of the past two years will be seen to have passed through several stages. In the first stage, dominated by the ardent advocates of radical tax cutting who now ply their wares to state governments, it was argued that all that was needed to avoid a looming "Economic Dunkirk" was for the new administration to merely announce its program of tax cuts, regulatory relief, monetary restraint, and spending limitations; then, it was argued, through the simple alchemy of anticipation alone, the stock market would surge, interest rates

would fall, investors would invest, workers would work harder. The economy would be restored to greatness with no pain, no hardship. The second stage grew out of the rejection of the supply-side program by Wall Street analysts, who saw disturbing contradictions between a tight money policy, unprecedented increases in military spending, and substantial cuts in both business and personal taxes. Their refusal to believe that supply-side economics would work the miracles claimed for it produced a sharp contraction in the stock market and a rapid resurgence of high interest rates. The third stage of the supply-side program began on October 1, 1981, when the new tax program went into effect. The economy, in the words of more than one market observer, "fell off a cliff," and every leading economic indicator pointed to an increasingly severe recession. Advocates of the supply-side miracle were reduced to arguing that a recession was needed to wring out of the economic system the excesses wrought by twenty years of loose money and free spending—that inflation, after all, could only be fought with unemployment. The fourth chapter in the history of supply-side economics was one of increasing dissension among the theory's own advocates. Some worried openly that the supply-side program would lead the nation down the same path taken by Britain under the Thatcher government. Others, more concerned with their place in political history, took to arguing openly about the proper content of a supply-side program. Most, however, began to abandon ship. Arthur Laffer was quoted as saying that he regretted ever drawing his famous curve, that what he really meant was that the economy needed to be returned to the gold standard. The fifth and final stage, leading up to the midterm elections in 1982, was one of internal confusion among those few supply-side advocates remaining in important policy positions; with the recession deepening and no sure sign of recovery in sight, the challenge was to blame someone other than the architects of the program for the subsequent collapse of the monument they had designed.

2. Another means of stimulating the flow of equity capital to smaller businesses involves the relaxation of the often archaic legal restrictions which impede the ability of public pension funds to make certain forms of equity investment. See another volume in this series— *Financing State and Local Economic Development*—for more detail.

3. For an extensive discussion of user charges, see another volume in this series, *Rebuilding America's Infrastructure: An Agenda for the 1980s*.

Part I

STATE TAXATION AND ECONOMIC DEVELOPMENT

Roger J. Vaughan

INTRODUCTION

The 1970s have been anything but kind to state governments. Major metropolitan areas, traditionally both engines of growth and major sources of tax revenues, have lost jobs and veered toward fiscal insolvency. Mayors and federal officials have blamed states for not caring. Social programs, grown as a result of local political pressures and federal mandate, have inflated expenditures. Swollen federal grant programs have by-passed states and gone directly to local jurisdictions. The rise of the "New South" at the expense of the "Old North" has pitted Sunbelt states against Snowbelt states. The national economy, apparently recession-proof during the 1960s, has faltered, straining unemployment insurance funds, swelling welfare rolls, and leading the jobless to demand aggressive state economic development programs. Taxpayers, whose rising incomes and property values provided localities with annual fiscal dividends, have finally rebelled.

State governments have, for the most part, fallen into a reactive role. Their functions have proliferated, often unwillingly. They are forced to work through a bewildering number of regional organizations and special districts. Federal red tape has multiplied. States must compete with cities for federal funds.

These changes necessitate a rethinking of the role of the states within our intergovernmental system. This paper examines a part of this complex puzzle—how can the state/local tax structure be modified in order to be an effective economic development tool? In the past, state involvement in economic development has been principally concentrated on physical development. After nearly a year of monitoring state community assistance programs, the Advisory Commission on Intergovernmental Relations concluded that: "Although broadly based structural and fiscal reforms have been widely endorsed as mechanisms by which states might ameliorate local development patterns, the adoption of such reforms has been relatively limited (*Information Bulletin,* January 1979)." To encourage a more radical approach, we must ask a number of very basic questions. How do state business and personal taxes influence state economic development? What will the impact of the fiscal limitation movement be? How do federal programs and policies affect state fiscal actions? How can the structure of state taxes be changed to improve efficiency and equity?

The following chapter defines overall state economic development goals, both in responding to local development problems and in the way they interact, or conflict, with federal and local goals. Chapter   *3*

2 outlines the factors that influence the process of economic growth. This allows us to place in perspective the role played by taxes, and to identify the direct and indirect links between tax policy and growth. Chapter 3 sets out the guidelines to apply when developing state tax systems—efficiency, equity, and administrative ease. It also outlines existing constraints on state fiscal policy, including the fiscal federal structure, the degree of fiscal strain in different states, and our lack of knowledge concerning tax incidence and impacts.

Chapter 4 discusses the problems inherent in the present state/local fiscal structure, including inequity, the dwindling availability of federal funds, and the problems associated with reliance on the property tax at the local level. Alternative ways to improve the structure are outlined.

Chapters 5 and 6 analyze the effectiveness, equity, and administrative ease of business taxes and special business tax incentives. They also suggest ways in which present policies could be improved. The discussion encompasses the effects of inter- and intrastate differences on the overall tax level, the effectiveness of targeted fiscal incentives on business, and alternatives to the corporate income tax and the local property tax. The examination of personal taxes in Chapter 7 describes how property and income taxes affect household migration and property investment and outlines ways to improve the present system. The origins and impact of the fiscal limitation movement are described in Chapter 8, together with some recommendations on how the states may avoid its more disruptive consequences. An annotated bibliography is provided at the end of this report; it will allow those interested to pursue the topics covered in more detail.

1
WHAT IS ECONOMIC DEVELOPMENT POLICY?

Economic development remains remarkably difficult to define positively. Specialists debate target rates of growth and unemployment, and unacceptable rates of inflation, but leave the central definition nebulous. In fact, this omission is understandable, at least from the viewpoint of public policy analysis. *Economic development policy, at all levels of government, is best understood as the response to perceived problems, not as an attempt to meet targets.*

The effectiveness of state and local development policies must be judged on the basis of their ability to redress those problems they have been developed to resolve. Tax policies are but one set of weapons in the armory of state economic development policy.

ECONOMIC DEVELOPMENT PROBLEMS Economic development involves structural change in response to both market forces—technological change, rising incomes, changing international and national growth patterns—and changes in federal, state and local policies. This adaptation is not without cost, nor is it borne equally by all geographic areas, firms, or population groups.

The costs of adjustment include the redevelopment of existing public and private capital, building new facilities, relocating firms and households, and acquiring new skills. These adjustments are not made instantly because employers and employees make decisions with imperfect knowledge about what opportunities are available now and what will happen in the future. Responsibility does not rest solely with workers—to move and to learn new skills—nor with firms—to incorporate new techniques and build new facilities—nor with local governments—to provide new services and adjust local taxes. Adjustment encompasses all these factors. The symptoms of imperfect adjustment are familiar: high local unemployment; the outmigration of firms and households; vacant buildings; low labor force participation rates; and declining income. Faced with these symptoms, the state government may respond in one of three ways: take no action, provide relief or compensation to those affected, or implement a corrective strategy. How it responds depends on its diagnosis of the causes of the problem. Inaction is appropriate if the problem is either not serious or better dealt with at the federal or local level. Relief, in the form of income transfers or municipal grants, is appropriate where the 5 problem is temporary (a cyclical downturn), or is not susceptible to state policy action. A corrective strategy should be undertaken when public policies can effectively address a problem that will not rapidly disappear of its own accord. The focus of this paper is on the last type of response, and in particular, on how tax policies can address local development problems.

In designing a corrective strategy, the state must identify the causes of the economic problem. Why is the local unemployment rate so high? From the state's viewpoint, three classes of problems can be identified:

■ **Places.** Local unemployment may be high because the area has lost its comparative advantage as a place to do business—its infrastructure may be obsolete, or its work force may be concentrated in declining industries.

■ **People.** High unemployment may also reflect the characteristics of the local labor force. The young, ill-educated, or unskilled may experience high unemployment rates.

■ **Jurisdictions.**[1] A local jurisdiction may be unable to provide the population or services necessary for development. High local taxes resulting from a dependent local population, or a small per capita tax base, may slow growth.

Of course, these classes of problems are neither exhaustive nor exclusive. While all areas suffer some degree of economic distress for all of these reasons, the relative severity of distress differs among areas. A steel town in Ohio suffers primarily from a problem of place— its infrastructure is not suitable for modern steel production. High unemployment in the South Bronx may be caused by a lack of training for its residents, while Cleveland's fiscal problems are a jurisdictional problem. Nor are these reasons independent. A concentration of the hard-to-employ in a neighborhood will strain local government resources.

These classes of problems require different types of state policy response. Place problems are normally tackled by state public works projects—new industrial parks, expanded transportation links, and renovated buildings. People problems are addressed through training, work experience programs, and subsidized jobs. Jurisdictional problems have led to expanded grants to local areas and state assumption of local expenditures. Tax policies are part of each type of strategy: tax incentives are offered to firms moving into industrial parks; tax breaks are given to private firms training their workers; and tax sharing is used to help local jurisdictions. The goals of state tax policy are, therefore, interwoven with the more general goals of state economic development policy.

STATE ECONOMIC DEVELOPMENT GOALS   A state's economic development goals are to avoid, or at least lessen, local economic development problems. However, the achievement of these goals is complicated by the imprecise allocation of both fiscal and administrative responsibilities among federal, state and local governments in the "layer cake" structure of fiscal federalism. This section discusses state development goals and the ways in which they may conflict with national and local goals.

National Goals   In addition to pursuing their own goals, states are called upon—sometimes even compelled—to assist the federal government in meeting national objectives. Under the Federal Highway Act, states were called upon to contribute to the construction of a national highway network. States have also been nudged into improving income distribution, administering employment and training programs, abating pollution and enforcing equal rights legislation. Recently, they have been asked to help the Carter Administration in its fight against inflation. What can a state be reasonably expected to do to further national economic goals? How do national goals conflict with state goals?

The following considerations should guide state policy makers in attempting to comply with Washington's wishes:

National Goal	*State Actions*
Stable Prices	There is little, if anything, that states can do to stabilize the rate of inflation. Reducing sales taxes during a period of inflation would have the *cosmetic* effect of reducing the rate of price increases during the month in which the cut was effected. However, prices would continue to rise during the ensuing months as reduced retail prices led to a greater demand for goods and services.
Income Redistribution	States can assist a little in redistributing resources from the affluent to the poor with direct cash transfers and the provision of special services—education, training, health, and housing. States are limited in what they can do about interstate differences in income. (If poor states could export some of their tax burden and rich states import some of theirs,

7

then some shifting of the tax burden could be achieved.)[2] However, intrastate income distribution can be influenced by:

■ the progressivity of the state tax structure;
■ interjurisdictional revenue sharing;
■ state financing of property tax circuit breakers; and
■ state assumption of the cost of services for the poor.

Economic Stabilization

States can participate, in a moderate way, in an effort to reduce economic fluctuations. This is especially useful in view of the fact that states vary considerably in their timing and response to national economic cycles, which makes national expansionary or restrictive policies often inappropriate to state needs. Although states, with two exceptions, are legally prevented from deficit spending during recessions, they can accumulate surpluses during periods of rapid expansion, cutting down consumer demand, and reduce surpluses during recessions.[3] This can lead to some countercyclical impact. Other stabilizing policies by state governments include:

■ adoption of a progressive tax structure;
■ increasing expenditures on automatic stabilizers such as unemployment insurance payments and premiums; and welfare benefits; and
■ tying capital project expenditures to prevailing local economic conditions—delaying construction during booms and expanding activity during recessions. (States do face political pressure to spend surpluses which limit this role.)

Overall, with the exception of income redistribution, the ability of state economic policy to assist in the achievement of national macroeconomic goals is limited.

State Goals   The most obvious purpose of state taxation is to raise revenue to cover state expenditures. However, other criteria are also considered in the process of deciding the structure and level of state taxes, and a state's policy toward local governments.

State Goal	*State Actions*
Maximize State Growth	To encourage state development, expanding firms, or firms moving in, are offered public infrastructure, tax breaks, low interest loans, and other incentives.
Income Redistribution	State goals are similar to federal goals in this respect, and the relevant policies are outlined above. However, states are limited in their ability to redistribute income because households and businesses unwilling to pay for redistributive programs can move to less progressive states.
Economic Stabilization	Again, state goals correspond to national goals, but may differ markedly in their timing and intensity. Even during the recent, deep national recession, some states experienced only a shallow recession, and differed in the timing of their downturns and troughs. For example, while the construction industry experienced a deep recession nationally, the construction slump was, proportionately, less significant in growing areas such as Texas and Southern California. Thus countercyclical needs, both in timing and volume, differed among states. The federal response—the Local Public Works Program—took little account of these differences, and often created local construction bottlenecks (Vernez and Vaughan, 1978).
Intrastate Distribution of Economic Activity	States are also concerned with the distribution of economic activity *within* their borders. They attempt to encourage the

9

industry in distressed areas. Throughout the 1960s these efforts tended to be oriented toward rural areas, although the recent emphasis has been on central cities. To target expansion, states may offer fiscal assistance to distressed jurisdictions, locate state facilities where unemployment is high, build industrial parks, offer tax incentives, provide training programs, give low interest loans, or even prohibit local tax incentives in rapidly growing areas.

There are some obvious conflicts between state and national goals. First, and perhaps most important, the state goal of encouraging local growth may conflict with the national goal of balanced regional growth. Successful attempts by states to entice businesses away from other states may exacerbate interstate growth differentials. One state's gain is frequently another's loss. However, to the extent that a relocation allows a company to construct a more efficient plant and take advantage of better public infrastructure, national productivity may be enhanced. Overall, interstate competition is not productive. States in the Northeast have suffered under federal policies designed to raise the level of economic development in the low-income South. In fact, any federal regional strategy is bound to affect adversely economic development in non-target states unless the federal strategy addresses real market failure problems and succeeds in increasing total investment and employment so that all areas can gain.

A second conflict revolves around stabilization policy. The federal emphasis during the recent recession on construction activity—typified by the $6 billion Local Public Works Program—ran up against relatively tight construction markets in some states. Even in upstate New York, scarcely a booming construction area, there are reports that the construction schedule for the 1980 Winter Olympics facilities at Lake Placid was jeopardized by a lack of heavy construction firms able to bid as a result of their participation in a number of Local Public Works projects.

A third conflict is less obvious but just as important. Federal programs aimed at social goals may inadvertently slow development in some states. There is some evidence to suggest that abating pollution or enforcing safety and health conditions slow growth more in older central cities, where it is difficult to modify plant and equipment, than in faster growing areas. State officials must always be aware that a federal policy may have very different regional impacts, even though it is enforced nationwide.

Local Goals   Local jurisdictions have a set of goals similar to states, although applicable to their own smaller boundaries.

The most important area of potential conflict between states and local jurisdictions is between the state goal of balanced growth and the desire of many jurisdictions to maximize their own growth rate. Local jurisdictions can offer business tax incentives that attract businesses from distressed urban centers within the state.[4] City/suburban tax differentials have played an important role in encouraging the suburbanization of jobs and households. This process is not necessarily desirable, for it can force a state government into the contradictory position of helping its suburban areas to accommodate business expansion and its central cities to redevelop abandoned facilities.

A second area of potential conflict is between the state's goal of assisting the poor and the desire of more affluent local jurisdictions to avoid redistributive taxes. The suburbanization of the nation's urban population has been accomplished through the proliferation of relatively homogeneous suburban communities that offer residents respite from central city tax burdens. These communities may not welcome increased state taxes that are channeled back into central cities. Until the last few years, this conflict has resulted in a marked unwillingness by state governments to involve themselves in the plight of central cities.

Another point of potential conflict occurs over the use of federal categorical and formula grants. Now that local areas are recipients of substantial amounts of federal funds for capital projects, the state can no longer ensure that local plans are coordinated—either with each other or with the state's own overall plan for state-funded projects. For example, a UDAG-financed shopping mall may not be effectively sited within the context of state transportation plans.

IMPLICATIONS   Two major conclusions can be drawn from this discussion. First, state economic development programs are undertaken in response to perceived problems—problems of place, people, or jurisdiction. The diagnosis of the causes of economic development problems—reflected in slow growth, high unemployment, and other familiar symptoms—affects the type of strategy implemented, and tax policy has a role within strategies aimed at each class of problems. But tax policy is only one weapon in an extensive armory of development policies. Other state actions include shifting program priorities, redesigning the geographic distribution of expenditures, and regulation of economic activity and local fiscal practices. The following chapter outlines the basic considerations that should guide state development policy makers in the design of their tax policies.   *11*

The second, more obvious conclusion is that there are clear conflicts between federal, state and local economic development goals. The principal conflicts between federal and state goals occur in the areas of balanced growth, income redistribution, and the inadvertent effects of broad federal social programs on local economies. State/local conflicts occur over interjurisdictional competition for growth, and in coordinating state and local development plans. As we shall see, these conflicts extend into the design and implementation of state tax policies.

FOOTNOTES TO CHAPTER 1

1. A major distinction between the problems of jurisdiction and the problems of place is that the severity of the former would be affected by changes in jurisdictional boundaries, while the latter would not.

2. Poor states well-endowed with such natural resources as lumber, iron ore, oil, natural gas, or coal have the best opportunity for this through severance taxes. But so do states with a substantial tourist trade or many out-of-state commuters.

3. A great deal has been written about state surpluses. Gramlich (1978) has argued that the rapid build up of surpluses since 1976 has acted to frustrate federal expansionary economic policy. However, as Stanfield (1978) has pointed out, it is difficult to determine the size of these surpluses from national income accounts published in the *Survey of Current Business*. Some surpluses represent offsets against pension obligations.

4. The discussion of business taxes in Chapter 5 suggests that intrastate variations are greater than interstate variations, and that tax differences have affected interstate business relocations more than interstate moves.

2
WHAT FACTORS INFLUENCE ECONOMIC DEVELOPMENT?

In trying to unravel the complex process of economic development to identify how state and local taxes may be influential, two facts stand out. First, *state and local taxes are only one factor among many that directly influence development, and, in fact, are not a major factor.* The role of taxes is not discussed in this chapter, but is discussed in detail in the following chapters. The discussion in this chapter provides a context in which to view the role of taxes. Second, *many of the ways in which taxes shape the development process are indirect.* For example, taxes affect residential location decisions which, in turn, affect the local demand for goods and services. A tax policy that attracted middle- and upper-income households would contribute to local development.

COMPONENTS OF EMPLOYMENT CHANGE[1]

Areas suffering from high unemployment often blame their difficulties on the out-migration of firms, and regard as a panacea an aggressive promotional campaign to attract new footloose firms. The myth of a rich vein of large, non-polluting firms that can be mined by state development officials offering free land and access roads, subsidized buildings, and tax abatements, has distorted state development efforts for years. A rational economic development policy cannot be developed until this myth is dispelled and the true components of employment change are identified. Recent studies on the location of industrial firms has revealed the following:

■ Interregional migration of firms is the least important component of employment change.[2] Differences in birth rates and the rate of expansion of existing firms are much more important. There is very little regional variation in the rate at which jobs are lost through firm contractions or closures.
■ Firm moves are slightly more important in determining central city/suburban growth differences, but are still less important than other components.
■ The birth rate of new firms is much higher in suburban locations than in central cities. Central cities do *not* tend to act as incubators. *13*

■ New, closing, and locally moving firms are smaller than stationary firms.

■ Most new jobs in an area are created by the expansion of employment in relatively small, young, and independent firms.

What are the implications of these findings for development policy? Unfortunately, we don't yet know what factors affect each of the components of employment change, so it is difficult to target policies. Obviously, research in this crucial area should continue. We can say that any continued effort to chase smokestacks is probably misplaced, and that greater effort should be devoted to ensuring that the overall economic environment is as attractive as possible, rather than simply providing benefits to a few large firms. The remainder of this chapter examines the factors that influence development.

Factors that influence growth and development may be separated into three types: those that affect the demand for output; those that affect the cost of production at a particular location; and a less tangible group of amenities that may affect the attractiveness of a particular location as a place to live and do business, such as air quality, recreation facilities, and the crime rate. The last group may affect the local market and local costs, but they do so less directly than the other factors.

Demand
Consumer market: population and income
Intermediate market: interindustry linkages

Input Costs and Availability
Transportation
Labor: size of force, skill level, wages, productivity, unionization
Land
Raw materials
Energy
Finance
Taxes and municipal services
External economies: scale and agglomeration

Local Characteristics
Amenities
Leadership

It is extremely difficult to separate the effects of these different factors and weigh them according to their relative impact on changing patterns of economic activity. For example, it seems probable that one factor in the rapid expansion of manufacturing activity in the South was the extension of the federal highway system into areas of declining agricultural employment where there was a ready pool of surplus labor. Should the rapid growth in that region be attributed to reduced transportation costs or to low-cost labor? The introduction of air conditioning for manufacturing plants may also have stimulated economic development in the South. How should the Southern growth rate be attributed among these three factors?

Another problem is that it is difficult to measure the factors themselves. For example, wages do not measure the skill of the labor force or the hiring and training costs a firm must incur.

Since state economic development policy is concerned with both aggregate economic growth and its distribution within the state, the following discussion analyzes how these determinants have influenced *interregional and intraregional* growth patterns.

CONSUMER MARKET

There is considerable evidence that market considerations are the most important single factor in explaining interstate differences in economic development, and that growth in employment follows rather than leads growth in population.[3]

Separating the influence of the level of demand on employment in an area is difficult. The size of the local population, often used as an index of demand, also measures the availability of labor. Demand, output and employment interact in a complex way, as shown in Figure 1. Growth in local population leads to an increase in both labor supply and the demand for output, leading to an increase in demand for labor. The growth in labor demand stimulates the increase in population as migrants arrive seeking jobs. As employment increases, so does local income, which stimulates a further increase in demand (the multiplier effect). Within this dynamic system it is difficult to determine whether growth in market demand stimulates the growth in employment or whether the growth in employment opportunities attracts people. Undoubtedly, the relative strength of the two effects differs from place to place. Retired persons seeking the sun in Phoenix or Miami are little interested in jobs, although their purchasing power has attracted businesses to these cities. Auto workers were attracted to Detroit by job opportunities.

There is some consensus that the expansion of local markets through population and income growth is the single most important factor in encouraging employment growth.

There is also some evidence that jobs have followed people to the suburbs. Using pooled cross-sectional and time series data for 15 SMSAs, Steinnes (1977, p. 76) found that, for both manufacturing and service jobs, businesses followed household location rather than the reverse. In fact, he found that people tended to move away from *15*

Figure 1
The Relationship Between Population, Labor Force, and Employment in a Local Area.

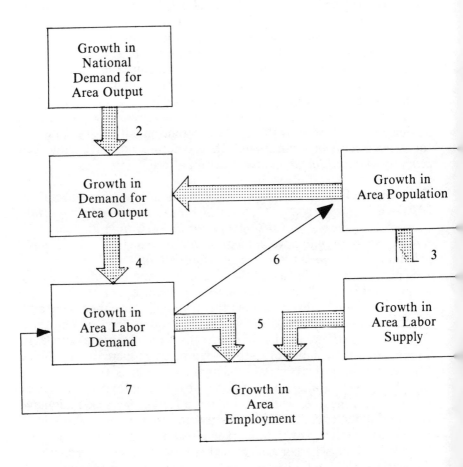

LINKAGES:
1. Population growth leads to expanded local market for goods a
services and increased size leads to increased import substitution.
2. National growth leads to expanded local market for goods and servic
3. Population growth leads to increased local labor supply.
4. Increased demand for local goods and services leads to increased dem;
for labor.
5. Increased labor demand and supply lead to increased output.
6. Growth in demand for labor encourages population inmigration.
7. Increased output leads to increased local income causing an incr
in local demand.

16

manufacturing jobs, presumably because of pollution or other dis-amenities. He concluded that "the efforts of central cities to attract and retain manufacturing may be accelerating, not retarding, the flight of residents from the city."

INTERMEDIATE MARKETS

The level of employment in their principal buyers is an important locational determinant for industries whose chief market is other industries. In addition, the presence of industries that provide vital inputs will make an area attractive to some industries. In a detailed analysis of output growth in 84 industries, Harris and Hopkins (1972) found that 32 industries were significantly influenced by the output growth of major customers. For example, the petroleum refining industry tended to locate close to the petroleum extraction industry (a major supplier), and the metal containers industry tended to locate near the beverages industry (a major buyer). Overall, evidence suggests that reduced transportation costs have reduced the necessity of locating near supplying industries and have made firms more footloose. The present gasoline shortage may reverse this tendency.

TRANSPORTATION

Transportation costs affect both the revenue a firm receives from its sales and the prices it must pay for its inputs. It is difficult to separate these two components in most of the studies that have been conducted. Lichtenberg (1960) estimated that 51 percent of manufacturing industries were sensitive to changes in transportation costs. Of these, 84 percent were sensitive to the costs of transporting commodities to consumers, and only 16 percent were sensitive to the costs of transporting inputs. Harris and Hopkins (1972) also found that more firms were sensitive to output transportation costs than to input costs.

Costs of transporting commodities to consumers have been affected by the rapid growth of trucking. The share of trucking in total freight transportation rose from 9.5 percent in 1940 to 21.3 percent in 1970, the increase coming almost entirely at the expense of the railroads. Truck transportation reduces the cost of small-load, short-haul freight movements relative to large-load, long-haul movements (Chinitz and Vernon, 1960) and has led to decentralization of industry as firms moved toward highway linkages and away from railroads. The growth of trucking has also increased the tendency for firms to locate near the market for their products. Cities with businesses using short-haul, small-load transportation[4] and able to relocate wherever there are trucking facilities will experience a more rapid loss of employment than cities whose industries rely on heavy-load, long-haul transportation.[5]

Many older cities that developed around rail terminals are ill-equipped to make the transition to truck transportation. Building densities are high and access inadequate. Congestion is heavy and parking spaces and truck terminals too few and too small. Firms may have moved away from older cities to escape these problems. Boston, New York, Baltimore, and Philadelphia—which have traditionally housed a large number of small firms whose products are fairly transportation-intensive—have been unable to compete with newer, truck-oriented cities.

In addition, the rapid growth in the use of private automobiles for commuting has increased the cost of transporting labor to work relative to the cost of transporting materials (Moses and Williamson, 1967). When the transportation costs of materials were of prime importance, companies located on railroad spurs in the central city. With the increase in labor force commuting costs, companies have tended to relocate closer to their labor supply.[6] For companies requiring skilled labor, this means a move to the suburbs. Companies requiring unskilled labor, which is less mobile than skilled labor, tend to remain or relocate within the city because of the availability of public transportation for their work force.

LABOR   Labor is the most important single factor of production. Nearly half of the value added in manufacturing in 1972 was spent on payrolls. Two-thirds of these payrolls were for production workers. Among the many dimensions of the labor input into the production process that are relevant to industrial growth process and location decisions are:

■ *The size of the unskilled labor market pool.* A company that experiences considerable seasonal or cyclical fluctuations in demand needs to be located in an area with a large labor pool that will allow it to hire easily in times of need (the apparel industry in New York is one example). Companies tend to lay off unskilled workers during a recession more readily than skilled workers.

■ *The skill level of the labor force.* Training labor can be expensive, so an area that already has a supply of skilled labor will be an attractive location. Labor priced low relative to its skill has been a major factor in the development of manfacturing in the South. To some extent, low wages in the South reflect low local taxes. However, rapid development in the South and slow growth in the North has narrowed wage differences and absorbed much of the surplus labor in the South. Future regional growth differentials are unlikely to be as pronounced as those in the past.

■ *Unionization.* It has been argued that companies move to avoid high wages and expensive working conditions imposed by powerful unions.

18

Evidence suggests that the main influence of unionization is on wages and not on any induced labor negotiation problems or work stoppages. Regional growth differences have been associated with a reduction in private sector unionization in the North and an increase in the South.

■ *Racial composition of labor force.* It has been argued that companies relocate to avoid having to hire minority employees—a business parallel to residential "white flight." There is no evidence to support this allegation.

LAND

Although a shortage of low-price land in central cities and in the Northeastern states in general has often been advanced as a reason for the decline in manufacturing activity in those areas, there is little evidence to substantiate this view (Harrison, 1974). Measuring the availability of land in an urban area is a difficult task. Land embodies many locational factors that may or may not be important to a company, depending upon its factor requirements. Square footage is not the only consideration in the purchase or lease of land. The purchaser is interested in the availability of transportation linkages, the ease with which trucks can make deliveries and collections, and the proximity of a railroad spur or a shipping pier. He is also concerned with the safety of the neighborhood, what precautions must be taken to minimize losses due to theft and vandalism, and the security necessary to protect his work force. The local red tape involved in site assembly may be a much greater investment barrier than either the quantity or price of land.

RAW MATERIALS

Proximity to raw materials, once a major determinant of the location of several manufacturing sectors, has declined in importance. As Niedercorn and Kain (1963, p. 130) explain:

> This is an inevitable concomitant to the later stages of economic development because value added by labor and capital becomes a larger and larger proportion of the total value of output. Today's complex products require much more processing per unit of raw material than those of a generation ago. So, location near the source of raw materials no longer gives an area a decisive advantage in many branches of manufacturing, because raw material costs have become a smaller fraction of total costs.

Raw materials may affect location within urban areas in a different way. Handling raw materials encourages firms that use them extensively to seek a suburban rather than a central city location so as to minimize the costs of constructing land-intensive truck-loading **19** facilities and warehousing. Although the effect is weak, the tendency is perceptible (Kemper, 1974).

ENERGY Recent international developments have made the energy sector and the effects of federal energy policy areas of considerable importance. In 1974, manufacturing used one-third of all energy consumed in the United States.

Energy costs vary regionally; the most expensive energy is in the Northeast, the cheapest in the West. Research has indicated that energy prices do influence growth (Huntington and Kahn, 1976).

Probably of greater importance than interstate variations in energy prices has been the impact of federal regulations that have placed producing states at a distinct advantage over non-producing states. Jones (1975, p. 1) summarizes:

> Constraints on gas supply, brought about by price regulation, have discouraged any expansion in regional gas consumption, however, and the Northeast has experienced extensive curtailment of industrial and commercial customers.

FINANCE The availability and cost of finance are important factors in economic development. There has been very little research into the effects that differences in regional capital markets may have on different growth rates. It is usually assumed that the capital market is a national market and that all borrowers face similar interest rates and loan availability. The banking industry, however, is heavily regulated at both the state and federal levels (Gardner, 1973). This regulation may influence interest rate differentials, which in turn influence local growth rates. For example, mortgage usury ceilings have exacerbated cycles in residential construction during inflationary periods. Also, federal regulation of pension funds and of venture capital corporations has reduced the supply of equity capital. Recent changes have ameliorated— but not cured—this problem.

Other aspects of bank credit deserve attention. The interest rate alone does not reflect the availability of credit. Entry into the banking field is quite severely restricted. Peltzman (1965) estimated that there were 50 percent fewer new banks than there would have been in the absence of such regulation. Pakonen (1971) found that the entry rates were reduced even further in unit-banking states. Restricted entry allows banks to discriminate among loan applications so as to minimize risk. Gardner (1973) found that banks in St. Louis behave much more conservatively than they would in the presence of more competition. Clearly, this risk-averse behavior can dampen growth by

20

causing new companies to shift to more congenial areas.

MUNICIPAL SERVICES

The role of public services in industrial location is more difficult to assess than the role of taxes. The effectiveness of municipal services can influence the crime rate, the level of amenities, the overall atmosphere in which business is conducted, the quality of neighborhood schools, and the quality of the air. The only insight into the role of the quality of municipal services has come from questionnaires and surveys. The Economic Development Administration (1971) found that fire and police protection were the two community attributes most frequently cited by business as being of prime importance in location decisions. In the survey conducted by Hartnett (1972), services were ranked thirteenth (out of 23) among *vitally important* factors and tenth among *important* factors. Several public service-related factors were also listed, including "the condition of the neighborhood" and "zoning."

An interesting insight into another aspect of municipal services and the role of local government emerges from Hartnett's survey. He asked firms what they felt the city could do to improve the business climate. There were 117 responses. The city should: train labor (10), offer financial incentives (9), purchase its supplies from industries located in the city (3), reduce taxes (31), reduce the number of rules and regulations (8), cut red tape (10), end harassment by city inspectors (21), reduce time lost from inspection visits (6), and improve its attitude (11). The fact that regulations, red tape, harassment, inspection time, and attitude accounted for 56 of the responses, compared with 40 concerning taxes and financial incentives, shows the potential importance of aspects of municipal behavior that have received little attention.

EXTERNAL ECONOMIES

Urban researchers have long hypothesized that companies may receive certain advantages by locating in a large urban area, advantages that result from processes external to the individual company but that can reduce the cost or improve the productivity of labor when the company does business there. Highly industrialized states, with diverse bases and large labor forces, may offer advantages to some industries that cannot be found in less urban states. By identifying those industries or even types of firms that seem to be especially attracted by agglomeration economies, state urban development policies can be tailored to them and be made more effective. Further, substantial agglomeration economies imply that the process of decline in employment in some urban areas will be self-sustaining. If firms move out of the city or substantially reduce their level of *21* employment, then the economies of agglomeration, and, therefore, the competitive position of remaining companies, will be impaired.

AMENITIES   The quality of life—the availability of recreational and cultural facilities, the cleanliness of the environment, the freedom from congestion and crime, and the quality of local schools—is an important consideration in the location decisions of some companies. If a firm is not tied to a large labor pool, raw materials, or rail or water linkages, then the attractiveness of a location as a place to live may play an important role.

The most important effect of differential levels of amenities is on the migration patterns of households. Executives may encourage the relocation of their company to an area they find attractive as a place to live. Amenities may also provide a small monetary incentive for relocation. Workers who live in pleasant, unpolluted, and uncongested surroundings will accept lower wages (Izraeli, 1973). Thus state environmental, cultural and recreational programs can be an influential economic development tool.

In one study, Burns and Pang (1977) separately analyzed factors that had influenced the movement of corporate headquarters between cities and from central cities to suburbs. Their conclusion is that suburban moves are influenced by major expense factors, while intercity moves reflect a desire to improve the level of community amenities. There is little, if these results are to be believed, that states or localities can do to influence overall state development through fiscal inducements, *although they may be able to influence intrastate development patterns through targeted inducements.*

LEADERSHIP   Leadership, both civic and entrepreneurial, is one of the most nebulous, yet also one of the most important, factors in explaining shifting patterns of economic development. The topic has been an issue among economic historians for many years. Thompson (1965), in an anecdotal description of the fates of three cities, provides an excellent introduction to the subject. He describes the adjustment of Boston to the loss of employment in the footwear industry, once a major industry. Leadership, civic and private, he surmises, may have been important in developing the research industry as a substitute. He also discusses the importance of leadership in the emergence of Chicago, rather than St. Louis, as the dominant Midwestern city.

The importance of individuals, as city leaders or as leaders of private institutions, in the adaptation of a city to changing economic conditions is difficult to assess. Was it far-sighted administrators in municipal government and local universities who led Boston to recovery from the extensive unemployment it faced at the end of World War II? Has the failure of some cities to diversify and capture growth industries resulted from their inadequate pool of natural endowments, from a failure of civic leaders to pursue an effective economic development policy, or from the failure of the policies themselves? In informal surveys, the attitude of local officials appears quite frequently as an important determinant of locational choice.

IMPLICATIONS[7]   This brief discussion of the factors that shape economic development has provided a number of important lessons that should be borne in mind when shaping state tax policies for economic development. The basic links between some of these factors, state development policies, and taxes are shown in Table 1. The major guidelines for a state economic development policy are:

■ *Combine improvements to the residential environment with improvements to the business climate.* The artificial distinction between community development and economic development ignores the symbiotic relationship between population growth and employment growth. Unless skilled workers, scientists and entrepreneurs can provide both a market and a supply of labor, an economic development program is bound to be ineffectual. Thus personal taxes are as much a development tool as business taxes.

■ *The future cannot be extrapolated from the past.* The very factors that give a particular state a comparative advantage during one period are eroded by differential rates of development. Wages and prices have climbed faster in the rapidly growing Sunbelt than in the slowly growing North. Home prices in booming Southern California make a move from Baltimore to Los Angeles, even at a substantial salary increase, a difficult proposition. Over time, the market system will come to the aid of declining areas, if state and federal policies allow it.

■ *Concentrate upon developing an attractive business environment, not upon offering special favors to a few companies.* Most employment growth must come from the expansion of existing companies, particularly relatively small ones, and from new births. These companies are often immune to the benefits of a personalized development program.

■ *Concentrate upon developing an equitable tax system that is tailored neither to the special interests of the existing structure nor to attracting a special class of footloose industries.* There are few footloose industries upon which to draw, and location decisions are based upon many factors, among which taxes play only a small role.

■ *Tax incentives do not define the business climate.* An economic   23

Table 1
Factors Influencing State Development,
Related State Development Policies, and the Role of Taxes

Factor	State Development Policies	State Tax Policy
Consumer Markets	• Residential amenities • Public service delivery • Housing programs	• Personal income and property taxes • Distressed areas can be aided by increased fiscal equalization efforts by the states • Tax treatment of out-of-state sales and production
Labor	• Public employment and training programs • Right-to-Work laws • Wage regulation	• Payroll and personal taxes affect wages • Tax incentives for training • Personal income taxes influencing labor force participation
Transportation	• Highway, road, and rail programs • Freight regulation • Mass transit subsidies	• Property taxes on transportation facilities
Land	• Land assembly grants • Land use regulations	• Depreciation provisions • Capital gains taxes • Property tax rates
Energy	• Public Utility Commissions • Public ownership • Land use regulation • Environmental regulation	• Utility sales taxes • Property taxes • Severance taxes • Depletion allowances
Capital	• Banking regulation • Public finance corporations	• Tax exempt bonds • Depreciation allowances • Corporate income taxes
Amenities	• Environmental regulation • Recreational programs • Subsidies to the arts	• Tax exempt pollution abatement bonds • Tax deductible business expenses • Tax treatment of not-for profit institutions

development policy must proceed on a number of coordinated fronts. Upgrading the quality of the labor force, ensuring adequate transportation links, adequate public infrastructure, facilitating land assembly, and reducing local red tape are much more important components, and much more influential when offered in combination, than tax holidays.

FOOTNOTES TO CHAPTER 2

1. For a review of the studies of employment change, see Allaman and Birch, 1975; Birch, 1978; Ledebur, 1978; and an excellent synthesis by Wolman, 1978.

2. This is very different from population growth. Although interarea differences in births and deaths explain a small part of interarea differences in population growth, *migration explains most of these differences.*

3. See Vaughan, 1977; and Vaughan and Vogel, 1979.

4. These industries may include apparel, food processing, printing and publishing, and specialized durable goods.

5. These industries may include primary metals and heavy equipment.

6. The incentive to do so comes from the fact that a company moving to the suburbs may offer its workers lower wages since the work force will spend less time traveling. If the work force is unionized so that wages are equalized throughout the metropolitan area, no such savings will be enjoyed though the company may find it easier to hire in the suburbs).

7. These implications anticipate some of the conclusions from the following chapters.

3
GUIDELINES FOR DEVELOPING A STATE TAX POLICY

What should guide the development of state tax policies? Three basic considerations must shape the way we evaluate existing tax policies: efficiency, equity, and administrative cost. This chapter explores these three concepts and discusses how they can provide a basis for selecting an appropriate tax structure. It also explores the constraints upon state tax policy imposed by: 1) the role of the state in the federal fiscal structure; 2) the problem of fiscal strain; and 3) our lack of knowledge concerning the impacts and incidence of taxes.

EFFICIENCY In trying to construct an *efficient* tax system we are concerned with minimizing the disruptive effects of raising revenues to support state services. How can a tax system be disruptive? First, and at present the most fashionable of fiscal concerns, the *level* of taxation may be too high, and stifle economic expansion. Broadly speaking, this means that the value of additional state supported services tends to be valued well below their cost in terms of the necessary local tax payments. Second, the *structure* of the tax system may cause inefficient behavior on the part of taxpayers. For example, a personal income tax, because it taxes wages, leads to reduced labor force participation, an efficiency loss. A property tax may discourage the upgrading of real property. The tax structure may also lead to spatial inefficiencies—failure to treat land as a depreciable asset leads firms to select sites in urban fringe areas where values can be expected to appreciate, encouraging urban sprawl. What characteristics must a state tax system have in order to achieve the greatest efficiency?

First, the level of taxes should be consonant with the local preference for state-provided public services. This does not mean that taxes must be as low as possible. The residents of some states, such as New York and Massachusetts, have long shown a preference for more public services than residents of other states. However, public officials have too long taken an annual increase in state public employment and activities as a matter of course, and the budgeting review procedure has been far too soft. The result has been a steady deterioration in fiscal conditions that the mid-1970s recession cast in stark relief. States should question proposed increases much more severely than they are

26

used to, and should avoid a tax system whose levels are way out of line with those in neighboring states.

Second, the structure of state taxes should not actively discriminate against actions which benefit economic development. Unfortunately, most taxes cause some loss of economic efficiency. A tax on earned income discourages labor force participation, and a tax on the income from capital discourages investment. A tax increase in one jurisdiction may cause businesses to move elsewhere, although the move yields no real efficiency gain. The only tax that avoids any efficiency loss is a lump sum head tax, and that violates all considerations of equity. We cannot hope, therefore, to build a perfectly efficient state tax system. But we can hope to improve on the level of efficiency of the present system.

EQUITY

The desire to make a state's tax structure as fair as possible yields three principles. *First, all other factors being equal, the greater a household or firm's resources, the greater the amount of taxes it should pay.* This is referred to as vertical equity. Resources may refer either to a stock— *wealth*—or to the flow of *income* generated by that stock. Whether the amount of taxes should increase proportionately to resources is a major and recurring fiscal issue. But we should note that those who advocate a progressive tax on income or wealth are not necessarily advocating that the tax burden increase more than proportionately to resources. They often argue that non-taxed resources are greater for those with high incomes than for those less well-off, and, therefore, a progressive income tax leads to an increase in tax burden proportional to the increase in resources.

Second, those with similar resources should pay similar amounts of tax. This is referred to as horizontal equity. All other things being equal, the tax burdens for similarly endowed households should not differ according to location, race, age or other characteristics. This does not imply that any geographical variation in tax rates is inequitable. One jurisdiction may offer a lower level of public services—fewer parks and libraries, or less police protection. The fact that taxes in these areas are lower than in a jurisdiction with extensive public services is not inequitable.

The final equity criterion is that, all other things being equal, *the greater the volume of public services received by a taxpayer, the greater the amount of taxes he should pay.* A firm taking intensive advantage of locally provided roads, water supply, and sewers, should pay more in taxes and fees than a similarly endowed firm that uses less truck transportation, uses little water, and discharges no waste.

ADMINISTRATIVE COST

Collecting taxes is not without cost. Taxpayers are all too familiar with the burden of completing the alphabet soup of tax forms, or paying an accountant to do it for them. States must process these tax statements and identify and prosecute those illegally avoiding taxes. But there are other costs as well. A tax that fails to yield an expected revenue necessitates hasty service cut-backs at considerable human and administrative cost. A tax whose revenue does not grow as service demand expands must constantly be readjusted, inducing uncertainty and expensive political deliberations. And finally, a tax should exert some countercyclical influence. Revenues should fall as economic activity declines, and grow as it grows. There are, therefore, four administrative principles, summarized in Table 2, together with efficiency and equity criteria.

It is apparent that these criteria are not necessarily mutually consistent. Efficiency may be improved at the expense of equity. A predictable tax revenue may not be cyclically stabilizing. However, these contradictions may be resolvable because the criteria in Table 2 are those desired of the tax system as a whole—all taxes taken together. An inequitable but efficient tax may be balanced by another less efficient but more equitable tax.

CONSTRAINTS ON STATE TAX POLICY: FISCAL FEDERALISM

Unfortunately, we cannot simply apply these criteria to current state fiscal practices. States operate within a federal fiscal structure that determines both how state taxes act upon firms and households, and the public service responsibilities that the state must meet.

The Federal Role

Federal influence over state and local fiscal matters has advanced on six fronts. First, public revenue collection is increasingly a federal function. Thus states acting alone are less able to shape the overall tax system. In 1902, Washington collected only 19 percent of revenues for civil functions, and made only 18.5 percent of all civil expenditures. By 1977, over 50 percent of civil revenues were collected in Washington, although less than one quarter of civil expenditures were made by federal agencies. The federal fiscal structure originally allocated to each layer of government a different tax base and different responsibilities. The federal government claimed personal income taxes and business taxes, and was responsible for national defense and major internal development issues. The state government collected sales taxes and governed state issues such as transportation and criminal justice. Local governments relied upon the property tax and administered education, health and local roads. The rapid growth of the public sector, reces-

28

Table 2
Criteria for Designing State Tax Policy

Efficiency
- The overall burden of taxes should reflect local preferences for public services.
- The tax structure should not lead to undesirable actions by taxpayers such as firm and household relocation.

Equity
- The greater a taxpayer's resources, the greater the tax burden (vertical equity).
- Taxpayers with similar resources should pay similar tax burdens, all other things being equal (horizontal equity).
- The tax burden for taxpayers with similar resources should be related to the value of public services received.

Administrative Ease
- The tax should be simple to collect and enforce.
- The tax revenue should be predictable.
- The tax revenue should grow secularly with the local demand for public services and the level of economic activity.
- The tax revenue should be cyclically stabilizing.

---

sions, and wars have melted the layer cake of fiscal federalism, blurring distinctions of revenue sources and responsibilities. Table 3 shows the source of funding for selected state and local functions. State governments are dominant in education, highways and health. Local government efforts are concentrated on criminal justice, education and health. And federal responsibility is for welfare and highways.

Second, the federal government shapes the way state taxes are collected. For example, the federal tax code allows local taxes to be deducted from federal taxable income. This has discouraged state and local governments from relying on fees and charges which are not deductible. In addition, Internal Revenue Service practices—the definitions of gross and taxable income, for example—provide a model that is difficult for state tax collectors to avoid.

Third, by distributing more and more resources through intergovernmental grants—grants that carry powerful, behavior modifying strings—the federal government, increasingly, is controlling how state and local expenditures are made. The way formula grants are   *29*

Table 3
Source of Funding for Selected Major Functions of
State and Local Governments
(FY 1977)

Function	State and Local Expenditures ($ Billions)	Federal Aid	Percentage from State Government	Local Government
Education	102.8	9.9	52.5	37.6
Public Welfare	34.5	56.5	38.3	5.2
Highways	23.1	26.4	49.4	24.2
Health & Hospitals	22.5	10.7	44.0	45.3
Police Protection	11.7	7.2	29.1	63.7

SOURCE: U.S. Bureau of the Census, *Governmental Finances 1976-77,* Washington, D.C. 1978.

distributed affects local actions. General Revenue Sharing allocations are based, in part, on local tax efforts, and Community Development Block Grant allocations are tied to efforts to provide local public housing. The result is that no discussion of state taxation policies is complete without reference to federal policies.

Fourth, the proportion of federal aid that bypasses states and flows directly to local government units has increased dramatically. The Housing Act of 1937 was the first that enabled the federal government to give funds directly to local governments. Recently, CETA funds, now totalling $5 billion per annum, and the massive $6 billion counter-recessionary Local Public Works Program, as well as General and Antirecessionary Revenue Sharing, have also, in large part, bypassed the states. These flows of federal funds affect state and local tax rates, the degree to which local service needs can be met, and the power of the state to influence local conditions.

Fifth, federal legislation has mandated programs that range from clean drinking water to assistance for the disabled. Meeting federal standards often necessitates considerable local expenditures and, therefore, increases in local tax rates. Complying with federal requirements leaves state and local governments with less and less discretionary power over their own expenditures.

A final avenue of federal influence has been through court decisions affirming civil rights and equality of opportunity. Most significant among these was the *Serrano vs. Priest* decision in California, and its repercussions in other states.[1] Courts have found that reliance on the local property tax for the bulk of support of public education is discriminatory, and that current state education aid denies equal protection of the law to local school children. A massive shift in the tax burden from jurisdictions to the state will be required to comply with these decisions. This will probably necessitate a reduced reliance on the property tax.

State/Local Relations In judging the effectiveness of state tax policy we must be aware that states differ markedly in their relations with local jurisdictions. For example, in New York, the state government collects only 48 percent of the total state/local tax revenues and makes only a quarter of the direct expenditures. By contrast, the state of Hawaii collects 78.6 percent of the tax revenues and makes 76.6 percent of the expenditures. Table 4 shows tax revenues and direct expenditures by state and local governments in FY 1977. All other things being equal, the lower the share of total state/local spending by the state government, the less influence on economic development that government can exert through tax and expenditure programs without the cooperation of local units.

As well as paying directly for some part of local services, state governments help local areas meet their fiscal objectives in four ways: (1) they issue grants to equalize fiscal capacity; (2) they authorize locally administered taxes; (3) they authorize local supplements to state taxes; and (4) they implement tax sharing. The effectiveness of these actions in improving the state/local fiscal structure is examined in the following chapter.

CONSTRAINTS ON STATE TAX POLICY: FISCAL CONDITIONS[2] The fiscal actions of state governments are not limited only by the structure of fiscal federalism, but also by the resources and preferences of their residents. The unwillingness of many taxpayers to finance ever-growing state and local budgets has compelled local politicians to make unpopular decisions to cut back local services. An inability to balance budgets and the unacceptability of massive layoffs and service cuts has confronted many troubled cities with "fiscal crises," crises that are often quickly transmitted to the state government. A definition of "fiscal crisis" has remained elusive.

The fiscal strength of a state or local area, in both absolute and relative terms, is an important concept. Fiscal strength affects the ease with which the state may enter the bond market, and the way in which federal funds are distributed. The fiscal strength of the state of California, measured by its large surplus in FY 1978, encouraged the pas-

Table 4
Selected Items of State and Local Government Finances by Level of Government: 1976-77
(Dollar amounts in millions)

State	Tax revenue			Direct general expenditure			State government percentage of	
	Total	State govern- ment	Local govern- ments	Total	State govern- ment	Local govern- ments	Tax revenue	Di gen◦ exp di◦
United States	175 878.7	101 084.6	74 794.0	273 001.8	103 535.0	169 466.7	57.5	
Alabama.......	1 870.7	1 403.7	467.0	3 696.3	1 862.1	1 834.2	75.0	
Alaska.........	934.4	773.5	160.9	1 333.1	793.8	539.2	82.8	
Arizona........	1 897.8	1 160.1	737.8	2 853.4	964.4	1 889.0	61.1	
Arkansas	1 059.3	802.9	256.4	1 878.6	947.5	931.0	75.8	
California......	23 842.9	12 589.1	11 253.8	32 532.1	9 942.0	22 590.1	52.8	
Colorado	2 157.6	1 077.3	1 060.3	3 524.6	1 268.6	2 256.0	49.9	
Connecticut ...	2 750.0	1 457.1	1 293.8	3 579.3	1 607.0	1 972.3	53.9	
Delaware	482.7	390.9	91.8	848.7	474.4	374.3	81.0	
D.C.	738.7	(X)	738.7	1 424.0	(X)	1 424.0	(X)	
Florida	5 309.2	3 274.8	2 034.4	9 287.5	2 886.0	6 401.5	61.7	
Georgia........	3 074.7	1 906.5	1 168.2	5 060.9	2 121.3	2 939.6	62.0	
Hawaii	872.1	685.7	186.4	1 714.1	1 313.5	400.6	78.6	
Idaho	547.9	367.8	180.1	977.7	464.1	513.6	67.1	
Illinois.........	9 674.0	5 319.5	4 354.4	14 237.0	5 703.8	8 533.1	55.0	
Indiana	3 477.6	2 162.9	1 314.7	5 080.1	1 851.5	3 228.6	62.2	
Iowa	2 155.2	1 292.5	862.7	3 556.3	1 391.8	2 164.4	60.0	
Kansas	1 692.3	969.0	723.3	2 775.5	1 143.1	1 632.4	57.3	
Kentucky	2 079.1	1 560.4	518.8	3 479.5	1 986.2	1 493.2	75.0	
Louisiana	2 494.0	1 718.7	775.4	4 733.5	2 294.1	2 439.4	68.9	
Maine	714.1	468.5	245.6	1 214.9	578.4	636.6	65.6	
Maryland	3 691.8	2 127.7	1 564.1	6 013.0	2 112.8	3 900.2	57.6	
Massachusetts ..	5 792.8	2 934.3	2 858.5	7 968.4	3 394.9	4 573.5	50.7	
Michigan	8 016.8	4 843.7	3 173.1	12 687.3	4 800.9	7 886.5	60.4	
Minnesota	3 601.7	2 485.6	1 116.2	5 803.2	2 023.7	3 779.5	69.0	
Mississippi	1 260.1	969.3	290.9	2 431.6	1 135.4	1 296.2	76.9	
Missouri	2 923.5	1 598.1	1 325.4	4 523.6	1 740.8	2 782.7	54.7	
Montana.......	582.7	312.4	270.3	1 072.3	498.4	573.9	53.6	
Nebraska	1 208.1	612.9	595.1	1 799.1	680.1	1 119.0	50.7	
Nevada	564.8	329.1	235.7	930.4	353.4	577.0	58.3	
New Hampshire	525.0	200.2	324.8	947.9	454.9	493.0	38.1	
New Jersey.....	6 826.6	3 103.7	3 722.9	9 722.8	3 423.8	6 299.0	45.5	
New Mexico ...	743.2	597.6	145.6	1 400.3	653.6	736.7	80.4	
New York......	22 444.8	10 743.2	11 701.5	32 177.9	8 175.2	24 002.7	47.9	
North Carolina .	3 275.2	2 384.8	890.4	5 426.0	2 148.3	3 277.7	72.8	
North Dakota ..	445.1	296.3	148.8	854.3	465.5	388.8	66.5	
Ohio	6 856.6	3 570.8	3 285.8	11 871.5	3 943.7	7 927.8	52.1	
Oklahoma	1 681.8	1 139.0	542.8	2 937.0	1 400.4	1 536.5	67.7	
Oregon	1 884.5	973.1	911.3	3 359.7	1 396.8	1 962.9	51.6	
Pennsylvania ...	9 074.6	5 590.8	3 483.7	13 746.5	6 180.7	7 565.8	61.6	
Rhode Island ...	741.3	438.8	302.4	1 199.7	641.5	558.2	59.2	
South Carolina .	1 578.6	1 187.6	391.1	2 814.3	1 559.7	1 254.6	75.2	
South Dakota ..	433.6	200.1	233.5	813.3	429.6	383.8	46.1	
Tennessee......	2 425.0	1 529.5	895.5	4 266.1	1 833.3	2 432.8	63.1	
Texas	8 178.3	4 750.1	3 428.2	12 873.1	5 133.2	7 739.9	58.1	
Utah	827.0	531.3	295.7	1 523.0	750.9	772.1	64.2	
Vermont	391.3	229.8	161.5	618.0	374.5	243.4	58.7	
Virginia........	3 468.1	2 053.8	1 414.3	5 671.8	2 456.3	3 215.5	59.2	
Washington	3 004.0	2 100.0	904.0	4 963.9	2 267.5	2 696.3	69.9	
West Virginia...	1 157.1	903.4	253.6	2 013.6	1 129.2	884.4	78.1	
Wisconsin......	4 048.3	2 733.3	1 315.0	6 147.0	2 088.7	4 058.3	67.5	
Wyoming	401.3	233.3	168.0	638.3	283.7	354.7	58.1	

SOURCE: Bureau of the Census, *Governmental Finances in 1976-77*, U.S. Department of Commerce, Wash▌ ton, D.C. 1978.

sage of Proposition 13. Public finance experts point out that a high degree of "local fiscal strain" will be reflected, in the long run, by the outmigration of businesses and households. At the extreme, proponents of the "Laffer curve" argue that many states and local jurisdictions are already taxed to such an extent that they could increase revenues by reducing tax rates.

Our measures of fiscal conditions are primitive. Commentators focus upon such readily available measures as taxes paid per capita or per $1000 of personal income. These measures ignore several facts. Some states are able to export a substantial portion of their tax burdens.[3] Others have extensive local manufacturing and commercial activity and so residents need pay only a low tax rate. States also differ in their need for social services. A state with relatively large and young families will face high per capita education costs. A large share of poor and elderly will raise a state's health costs. Thus some states can provide high quality public services at low tax rates, while others must impose high taxes and suffer inferior services.

A true comparison of state fiscal conditions would be based upon a comparison of both revenue sources and expenditure demand factors. Unfortunately, while the conceptual model for this type of analysis has been laid out (Barro, 1978), the necessary empirical work has yet to be performed. We can only provide conceptual discussion.

Revenue Base States gain revenue from their own revenue base and external aid from the federal government. A state's revenue base is a measure of the total resources it can draw upon to raise public revenues. It includes the income and wealth of residents, and non-residents who may work in the area, sales by business, business property, corporate income, and mineral rights. Total revenue is simply revenue base multiplied by fiscal effort. State fiscal capacity is a measure of the revenues that can be raised from a state's own sources. Personal income is the simplest measure, since it is related to the ability to pay. It is used by some federal grant programs, such as General Revenue Sharing, that attempt to redistribute from rich to poor jurisdictions. But income is inadequate as a measure for several reasons: (1) it does not reflect personal wealth —holdings of both financial and non-financial assets; (2) it does not reflect business income and assets; (3) it ignores interstate spillovers;[4] and (4) it ignores price differences among states that may reduce money income differences.

Expenditure Demand Factors A given level of per capita revenues does not support the same level of per capita services in each state. Demands for state services are determined by four factors: **33**

1. *Demographic Characteristics.* States with large numbers of dependent people—children, the elderly and the poor—will have to spend more per capita than other states to provide equal levels of services to those in need. Also, interstate differences in demand-related factors, such as population density, climate, terrain, and age of the public capital stock, will lead to different expenditure needs.

2. *Costs.* Industrial and highly urbanized states face higher prices for goods, services and wages than other states, and thus will have to spend more per capita to achieve a given level of services.

3. *Scope of Responsibility.* The greater the responsibility of the state relative to local governments and the broader the eligibility for program participation, the more the state will have to pay per capita to support those services.

4. *Other Factors.* Inherited obligations—pensions, mandated programs such as air and water pollution abatement, and services to non-residents—will all lead to interstate differences in expenditures need.

Taken together, per capita needs provide a picture of local fiscal conditions. Although a full analysis of this sort has not been completed, several partial studies have been performed.

One approach has been to develop a weighted measure of the tax base for interstate comparisons. States are compared by the amount of revenue they could raise if they applied an average (of all states) tax rate to each component of their tax base.[5] Recently, the Advisory Commission on Intergovernmental Relations has computed the fiscal capacity of states during 1964-1975 using this method. They were able to characterize both the present level and the current direction of recent trends in local fiscal capacities.

States were ranked both on their "pressure" in 1975, expressed as their own source taxes as a percentage of "adjusted income" (U.S. state median - 100), and on the annual average percent rate of change in adjusted tax effort, 1964-1975 (U.S. state median - 100) (Table 5 and Figure 2). New York, for example, at 171 over 537, had a tax effort 71 percent above that of the median state, and this effort had grown more than five times faster than the median state since 1964.

Summing up these findings, the Advisory Commission noted that rates of change in fiscal pressure are far from uniform, and some states, such as New York and Massachusetts, are now under relatively extreme pressure. As a result, it is certainly much easier to make a case for federal aid for central cities (New York and Boston) located in states already under extreme fiscal pressure than for central cities, such as St. Louis and Cleveland, located in low pressure states. In general, the Northeast and Midwest are experiencing rising fiscal 34 pressure, while the Sunbelt states are in the falling pressure category.

Table 5
A Two-Dimensional Measure of Relative State-Local Fiscal Pressure Using the Representative Tax Method to Estimate Fiscal Capacity: Dividing the States Into Quadrants: 1964-75
(Indexed on Median)

High and Falling		High and Rising	
Hawaii	130[1]/ 99[2]	New York	171/537
Wisconsin	126/ 29	Massachusetts	146/381
Vermont	119/ 20	California	132/310
Washington	109/ 95	Minnesota	127/173
Utah	103/ 65	Rhode Island	124/281
North Dakota	102/ -3	Maryland	121/347
Indiana	101/ 98	Michigan	118/241
		Maine	114/143
		New Jersey	113/324
		Pennsylvania	112/244
		Illinois	111/362
		Arizona	108/102
		West Virginia	106/242
		Mississippi	106/163
		Connecticut	106/149
		Virginia	102/396
		District of Columbia	101/419
		Delaware	101/377

Low and Falling		Low and Rising	
Colorado	100/-37	South Carolina	99/169
Iowa	99/-16	New Mexico	98/105
Oregon	98/ 66	Kentucky	96/205
Louisiana	98/ 62	Ohio	95/196
South Dakota	97/-94	Missouri	94/186
Kansas	96/-18	Nebraska	88/195
North Carolina	94/ 76	Wyoming	86/130
Idaho	94/ 12		
Montana	93/ 4		
Georgia	92/ 92		
Alabama	90/ 71		
Tennessee	89/ 14		
Nevada	86/100		
Alaska	88/-95		
Texas	84/ 41		
Florida	80/ 24		
Arkansas	79/ 68		
Oklahoma	79/ -3		
New Hampshire	79/-27		

[1]Fiscal pressure for 1975.　　　　[2]The index of change is from 1964-75.

SOURCE: Advisory Commission on Intergovernmental Relations, *Measuring the Fiscal Blood Pressure of the States*, M-111, Washington, D.C. February 1977.

Figure 2
A Two-Dimensional Measure of Relative State-Local Fiscal Pressure Using the Representative Tax Method to Estimate Fiscal Capacity: State-Local Systems More than One Standard Deviation from the Median: 1964-1975

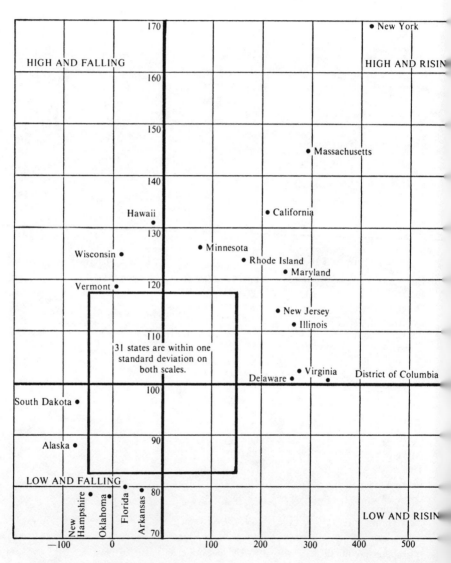

SOURCE: Same as Table 5.

However, regional location is not always an accurate predictor. Even in the Northeast and Midwest, state and local policymakers have been able to alter significantly the size and composition of their public sectors—compare the fiscal pressure of Vermont and New Hampshire, Michigan and Ohio. This diversity, ACIR concluded, makes it difficult to obtain widespread agreement about either the severity of the problem or the best way to resolve it.

The ACIR methodology is not without its critics. Akin (1973) argues that the concept of a "national average tax rate" is misleading, and instead relates per capita revenues to the whole array of tax bases through regression analysis. However, the ACIR analysis does show that states differ in their local fiscal efforts. Although differences in effort are not necessarily an indication of anything amiss, such large and rapidly growing differentials have left the "high and rising" states with little padding in the face of economic slowdowns that reduce their tax base and require increased expenditures.

CONSTRAINTS ON STATE FISCAL POLICY: IGNORANCE

Fiscal policy debates invariably circle around the question of incidence—who pays and how much? For those anxious for a definitive answer, we must conclude that few tax questions have received as much attention, and as little resolution, as tax incidence. Further, we believe that future academic research on the subject of incidence is unlikely to provide information that is truly useful for state and local policy makers. Two hundred years ago, Edward Gibbon observed that all taxes must eventually fall on agriculture, and his insight remains one of the surest in judging who pays for taxes. *The less the mobility of a factor of production, the greater the share of the tax burden that factor bears.* The most important implication of this fact is that it matters whether we are discussing tax incidence from the national or local perspective,[6] and in the long run or the short run.

From a national perspective, few factors are mobile. Thus the burden of the property tax, on average, falls on capital. But from the local perspective, capital and some segments of the labor force are mobile—they can move to another city or to the suburbs—and, therefore, the burden of interjurisdictional differences in taxes falls on land and relatively immobile low income labor. In a high taxing area, land prices are bid down, and consumer product prices driven up, relative to lower taxing areas. A local grocery store cannot move out of town and maintain its customers, so it must pass on part of the tax burden in terms of higher prices if it is to stay in business. Local households who cannot easily find employment elsewhere must shoulder the extra costs.

Similarly, factors are much less mobile in the short run than in the *37* long run. If a state increases corporate income taxes, a firm will not immediately leave. If it competes in the national market with many other firms, it cannot raise its prices. In the long run, it can move, expand activity in out-of-state branches, and gradually reduce its ongoing tax costs, although it will have suffered a capital loss on the value of the site it owns. Office firms that lease space will not even suffer this loss. There will be a tendency, therefore, for landowners in high taxing locales to experience a decline in property values relative to those elsewhere. The process will apply to industrial, commercial and residential property in the long run.

To summarize, inter area variations in property tax rates are borne by landowners, local consumers and immobile capital. The average national property tax burden is borne by capital.

Similar considerations apply to personal income taxes. Skilled and relatively affluent households operating in a national market require compensation for taxes in the form of higher wages, shifting the burden onto business, consumers and landowners. The burden thus falls onto less mobile segments of the labor force.

Another point is that the overall impact of fiscal actions depends not only on who pays the taxes but also on who benefits from the services for which the taxes pay. A state which used the receipts from a progressive tax system to pay for roads and parks in high income areas and a subsidized local opera would be less progressive in overall incidence than a state which spent the revenues generated by a similar tax system on social services for the poor. The difficulty in tracking the incidence of public expenditures has precluded such a broad based study. In fact, there are no overall studies of the incidence of expenditures on a comparative basis, although a few studies have examined the incidence of particular expenditure programs.

The results of the complex operation of the tax system is that incidence studies are rendered almost impossible. In fact, trying to ascertain who pays how much is not a fruitful exercise for state agencies. We should instead try to understand the direction of the impacts—how local taxes affect household and business migration, for example—rather than calculate the dollar burden.

CONCLUSIONS

Before beginning our analysis of the efficiency, equity, and administrative convenience of alternative business and personal taxes, three general observations should be stressed. The first point that must be made, and it will, regrettably, be repeated throughout this paper, is that there is a great deal that we do not know about the impact of taxation.

Second, it is difficult to arrive at any universal prescription concerning tax policy. A tax that is relatively efficient and equitable in one 38 place may be inefficient and inequitable elsewhere. The impacts of a tax depend heavily upon the local economic and social structure—the type of businesses, prevailing wages, energy costs, local labor skills, transportation linkages, and so forth.

Finally, we should note that it is difficult to "prove" that one tax is superior to another, not only because evidence is inconclusive and local factors must be taken into account, but also because the application of our criteria does not lead to unambiguous conclusions. Tax A may score higher on some criteria, and worse on others, than Tax B. Which is chosen depends upon the importance attached to each criterion. The primary purpose of this discussion is to assess· how taxes perform relative to each criterion in order to allow for a more informed local choice. Specific recommendations, based upon the author's judgment, are a purely secondary purpose.

FOOTNOTES TO CHAPTER 3

1. *Robinson v. Cahill* in New Jersey; *Horton v. Meskill* in Connecticut; and *Levittown Board of Education v. the State of New York.*

2. This discussion rests upon the excellent recent analysis by Barro (1978).

3. A state may export a part of its tax load by taxing firms that sell their products in other states, by taxing the extraction of minerals, or by taxing tourist-related industries, providing it enjoys some monopoly power.

4. Commuters from New Jersey that work in New York City form a part of New York's tax base. But the District of Columbia—another area with a substantial number of "out-of-state" commuters—is constitutionally proscribed from directly taxing commuters.

5. See ACIR (1971 and 1977) and Mandel (1971).

6. This point is argued by McLure (1977) in an important article reconciling the two views of property tax incidence, the "old" view that it falls on land and consumers, and the "new" view that it falls on capital.

4
WHAT SHOULD STATES DO ABOUT STATE/LOCAL FISCAL RELATIONS?

The division of fiscal responsibility among the federal, state and local governments has been compared to a layer cake, with each layer relying on a different tax and responsible for different functions. This structure is failing to address effectively the development problems that beset many states and local areas. This chapter analyzes what steps can be taken to improve the structure.

Since World War II, the federal government has relied primarily upon income taxes, state governments have relied upon sales taxes, and local government have used property taxes. However, this neat division has buckled in the face of rapid growth in both federal and local expenditures.

States still rely primarily on sales taxes—both general sales taxes, and selective taxes on such items as gasoline, liquor, and cigarettes. However, the postwar growth in revenue has stemmed largely from the expansion of state personal income taxes, which grew from only 7.4 percent of total revenues in 1948 to 21 percent in 1977 (Table 6).

States differ widely in their revenue systems.[1] There are also wide differences among states in the taxes that local government units are allowed to levy. While the property tax still predominates, twenty-six states now allow local sales taxes, and eleven allow local income and payroll taxes. The latter are either levied at a flat rate on all earned income originating in the jurisdiction,[2] or at a flat rate on all earned and unearned income.[3] A third type of local income tax is a graduated income tax on earned and unearned income, authorized by the state of New York and enacted by New York City in 1966.

In some states, local taxes are collected as supplements to state taxes. Local supplements to state taxes have three essential characteristics: they are optional; they are administered by a state agency; and the tax base is uniformly defined for all jurisdictions. Two states, Indiana and Maryland, have authorized local supplements to their income taxes.[4]

Table 6
Share of Total State Tax Revenue of Selected State Taxes,
1922, 1948, 1977

Type of Tax	Percentage of State General Revenue from Own Sources		
	1922	1948	1977
Sales and Gross Receipts	14.1	59.9	43.2
General	-	21.9	25.4
Selective	14.1	38.0	17.8
Motor Fuel	1.4	18.7	7.5
Tobacco	-	5.0	2.9
Other	12.8	8.0	7.4
Income	10.7	16.1	28.6
Individual	4.5	7.4	21.0
Corporate	6.1	8.7	7.6
License	31.5	14.5	3.8
Other*	43.7	9.6	24.4

*Includes fees and charges.

SOURCE: James A. Maxwell and J. Richard Aronson, *Financing State and Local Governments*, The Brookings Institution, Washington, D.C., 1977, p. 42; and Bureau of the Census, *Government Finances in 1976-77*, U.S. Department of Commerce, Washington, D.C., 1978.

WHAT'S WRONG WITH THE PRESENT SYSTEM?

The present structure of state/local fiscal relations contains several problems:

■ First, the system is inequitable. Poor jurisdictions face growing service demands but inadequate reserves. State aid is not effectively redistributive.

■ Second, local reliance on the highly visible and politically unpopular property tax will have to be reduced over time. Court decisions concerning school financing are likely to hasten this process.

■ Third, there is growing resentment against paying for redistributive public services and grants through local taxes.

■ Fourth, local jurisdictions have come to rely upon a massive increase in federal funds to survive the mid-1970s recession. This aid is unlikely to continue. States will have to assume increased fiscal responsibility for local jurisdictions.

■ Finally, the exemption of certain classes of property from property taxes places a heavy burden on occupants of non-exempt property. *41*

Table 7
Equity Characteristics of State Fiscal Policy

State	Incidence Classification[2] Prog.	Incidence Classification[2] Reg.	State and Local Tax Burden, Family Income $10,000	State and Local Tax Burden, Family Income $50,000	Tax[3] Redist. Index	P.C. State Equal. Outlays	Outlays as a % of Personal Income Percent	Outlays as a % of Personal Income Index[5]	Sales Tax	Pers. Income Tax	Bus. Tax	Prop. Tax	Gen. Tax Admin.	Overall Rank
Alabama	X		8.2	6.4	78	183.59	4.0	111	47	40	51	48	35	51
Alaska	—		N.A.	N.A.	—	859.05	9.0	259	13	8	19	25	20	10
Arizona	X		7.7	6.9	89	233.03	4.4	122	7	38	11	21	35	22
Arkansas		X	7.0	7.4	106	76.67	1.7	47	21	19	24	40	13	27
California		X	8.8	10.8	123	126.37	2.7	75	44	3	2	8	1	4
Colorado	X		9.5	8.4	88	189.06	3.2	89	9	21	19	28	6	8
Connecticut	X		12.3	7.6	62	122.58	1.8	50	51	43	11	32	20	35
Delaware	X		8.3	8.6	104	421.33	6.5	181	13	4	31	43	46	29
D.C.	—		N.A.	N.A.	—	—	—	—	28	15	11	17	32	17
Florida		X	4.9	2.6	53	209.65	3.8	106	25	43	38	5	35	33
Georgia		X	7.8	8.0	103	181.10	3.6	100	31	20	11	2	27	13
Hawaii	—		N.A.	N.A.	N.A.	491.49	7.4	265	3	10	28	22	18	7
Idaho	X		7.8	9.0	115	170.18	3.3	92	4	11	3	45	17	6
Illinois	X		10.7	7.6	71	273.68	4.0	111	49	37	40	14	27	42
Indiana	X		9.6	6.8	71	141.72	2.5	69	29	42	38	27	35	44
Iowa	X		12.1	9.5	79	208.28	3.5	97	10	26	11	7	46	16
Kansas	X		10.5	8.5	81	169.28	2.8	78	27	23	40	34	20	31
Kentucky	X		9.0	7.7	86	171.24	3.5	97	42	34	50	9	35	43
Louisiana	X		4.6	3.6	78	247.01	5.1	142	8	41	40	51	35	46
Maine	X		9.7	7.8	80	215.59	4.5	125	36	5	11	11	20	8
Maryland	X		12.8	11.7	91	158.09	2.5	69	34	29	35	5	11	23
Massachusetts		X	13.9	11.6	83	291.64	4.8	133	4	16	8	40	20	11
Michigan	X		8.8	8.7	99	297.29	5.0	139	29	7	6	4	2	2
Minnesota	X		12.1	11.8	98	260.34	4.5	125	12	2	19	15	18	5
Mississippi	X		6.6	4.5	68	178.95	4.4	122	48	27	40	46	46	50
Missouri	X		9.3	7.9	85	140.89	2.6	72	39	33	35	35	20	39

Income Redistribution Power[1] of the State — Local Tax System; Fiscal Equalizing Power of[4] State Expenditure Programs; Coalition of American Public[6] Employees Equity Ranking

State		(1)	(2)	(3)	(4)	(5)	(6)	(7)	(8)	(9)	(10)	(11)	(12)
Montana	X	9.2	8.8	225.48	96	4.2	117	13	36	4	50	5	20
Nebraska	X	9.0	7.4	88.95	82	1.5	42	4	13	31	29	13	12
Nevada	X	5.5	3.1	134.65	56	3.0	83	32	43	40	25	13	34
New Hampshire	X	8.2	5.1	70.70	62	1.3	36	13	43	26	15	43	30
New Jersey	X	14.4	9.6	147.70	67	2.2	61	20	35	28	20	13	26
New Mexico	X	7.4	7.6	273.21	103	5.7	158	1	9	45	33	20	20
New York	X	10.6	15.0	337.46	142	5.2	144	24	6	26	18	32	19
North Carolina		9.0	8.8	209.94	98	4.3	119	32	17	6	9	34	15
North Dakota	X	7.8	8.5	161.16	109	2.7	75	19	28	8	43	6	18
Ohio	X	7.9	7.1	146.08	89	2.5	69	26	31	8	23	43	28
Oklahoma		6.4	6.8	129.91	106	2.5	69	11	18	45	39	46	37
Oregon	X	8.4	10.6	118.99	126	2.1	58	13	14	4	1	6	1
Pennsylvania		11.5	8.9	248.32	77	4.2	117	40	39	28	23	27	35
Rhode Island	X	10.5	8.8	269.85	84	4.7	131	43	21	31	31	46	45
South Carolina		7.3	8.0	83.45	109	1.8	50	45	24	31	36	27	40
South Dakota	X	8.8	5.2	102.92	59	2.1	58	22	43	35	12	2	23
Tennessee	X	7.2	4.0	142.67	56	3.0	83	50	43	18	42	31	48
Texas	X	6.1	3.5	174.69	57	3.1	86	38	43	47	46	6	47
Utah		8.2	7.4	177.64	90	3.7	103	35	32	1	37	10	25
Vermont	X	10.4	11.0	187.64	106	3.8	64	35	12	24	12	43	14
Virginia	X	7.9	7.5	151.02	95	2.6	72	2	25	19	30	35	32
Washington	X	6.8	3.5	268.21	51	4.0	111	36	43	49	19	2	37
West Virginia		5.6	6.1	169.09	91	3.4	94	46	30	11	38	46	41
Wisconsin	X	14.8	14.6	269.24	99	4.8	133	41	1	19	3	11	3
Wyoming	X	5.8	3.3	135.95	57	2.2	61	23	43	47	49	35	49

NA means not computed by ACIR

SOURCES: Coalition of American Public Employees, *Tax Equity in the 50 States*, Washington, D.C., February 1979; Advisory Commission on Intergovernmental Relations, Staff Calculations.

NOTES:

1. The power of the State/Local tax system to redistribute resources from the rich to the poor through taxes.

2. Classified as Progressive (Prog.), Proportional (Prop.) or Regressive (Reg.) by the ACIR, based on the tax redistribution index: states with an index value of less than 90 are classified regressive, 90–110 proportional, and greater than 110, progressive.

3. The index is defined as the tax burden for a family of four in the $50,000 class as a percent of the burden for a family of four in the $10,000 income class. Median state index is 87.

4. State expenditure programs that reduce interjurisdictional economic and fiscal disparities are listed in John Shannon's testimony before the Senate Committee on Governmental Affairs, June 28, 1978.

5. The index expresses the state's equalization expenditure as a percent of the state median.

6. The ranking shows the ordering of the equity of each tax by state, with the most equitable being 1, and so on.

The clearest expression of the strains in the system have been the pleas for direct federal aid by some cities, and the taxpayers' revolt. More subtle, and more harmful, has been the tendency for high income households to move into homogeneous suburban communities to avoid paying for—and living near—poor and minority groups.

EQUITY

The present system does not ensure either vertical or horizontal equity. Vertical inequity arises because state taxes are often regressive—that is, the higher a household's income, the lower the share of income paid in taxes. Table 7 shows the burden of state and local taxes as a percent of household income for families earning $10,000 and $50,000. New York has the most progressive system, as well as one of the highest rates. A family earning $10,000 would pay 10.6 percent of its income in taxes, one earning $50,000 would pay 15.0 percent. By comparison, the comparable rates in the state of Washington are 6.8 percent and 3.5 percent (this issue is discussed in more detail in Chapter 7). Only New York, Idaho, Oregon and California have progressive systems.

Horizontal inequity arises because households with similar incomes living in different jurisdictions pay different tax rates for similar public services. Those living in jurisdictions with high concentrations of low income households will tend to pay much higher tax rates to finance locally-funded redistributive services. States can reduce horizontal inequity by assuming fuller fiscal responsibility for services for the needy, by targetting expenditures toward poor jurisdictions, by instituting state revenue sharing, or by state tax sharing programs. The inadequacy of present efforts has been recognized in court decisions that call for greater state efforts to equalize education expenditures among jurisdictions.

The urban crisis has brought the question of horizontal equity to the foreground. Many of the distressed cities in the Northeast face appalling tax burdens because of extensive social programs and receive relatively little assistance from their state governments. In many instances, the fact that the city tends to be run by a Democratic government while the statehouse is dominated by Republicans has further contributed to political polarization.

A recent study by the Coalition of American Public Employees ranked states according to the equity of their taxes. Their rankings, shown in Table 7, were based on the extent to which a state's taxes placed burdens on the poor, or gave relief to corporations, and the steps states took to make individual taxes less regressive—such as the exemption of food from sales taxes. Oregon emerges as having the most equitable system, Alabama the least.

The Advisory Commission on Intergovernmental Relations (Shannon, 1978) has ranked states according to the extent to which their expenditure patterns reduce interjurisdictional fiscal disparities. A state payment was classified as equalizing if it involved:

■ Direct or indirect public welfare expenditures;
■ Direct or indirect medicaid expenditures; or
■ State expenditures based on local needs such as schools, urban aid, and revenue sharing.

ACIR found that states scoring highest are those characterized by centralized fiscal systems (Alaska, Delaware, Hawaii, and New Mexico) and those with high welfare obligations (Massachusetts, New York, and Rhode Island). Their index of the fiscal equalizing power of state expenditures is shown in Table 7. States have greatly expanded their redistributive programs, both through grants to local governments and through direct expenditures. Intergovernmental transfers totaled $57 billion in FY1976, but when direct state expenditures for state-local functions are added, the sum climbs to $73 billion. This compares with only $21 billion in FY1965. The comparable figures for federal assistance are $1.2 billion and $21.0 billion (National Governors' Association, 1978a).

($ Billions of State Assistance to Local Governments)

Period	Total	Local Schools	Highways	Public Welfare	Health & Hospitals	General Local Support	Other State Aid to Local Govt.
1964-65	$20.9	8.7	5.7	2.3	2.6	1.1	0.5
1975-76	$72.8	29.6	11.6	12.2	9.7	5.7	4.1

A number of states have undertaken a form of state revenue sharing—grants allocated to jurisdictions in much the same way as federal revenue sharing. Allocation should ideally be from richer jurisdictions to poorer ones. Unfortunately, this rarely occurs. First, like federal revenue sharing, population is used in the allocation formula which spreads funds among all jurisdictions. Second, many of the state taxes earmarked for redistribution are regressive— collecting proportionately more per capita from poor jurisdictions than rich ones. Collection and redistribution according to population makes poor jurisdictions worse off. State revenue sharing programs are summarized in Table 8. Only Florida has an explicitly equalizing factor as an important element in its allocation formula, but the regressivity of the excise tax vitiates its effect (Rafuse, 1974).

Twenty-six states share receipts from one or more taxes with their local governments. In 1973, these payments amounted to less than 13 percent of the total non-categorical aid payments to local governments **45** in those states (ACIR, 1974). This policy offers little opportunity for redistributing funds from rich to poor jurisdictions.

Some states have taken steps to increase aid to localities. North Dakota adopted a statutory sharing of 5 percent of the state's income tax revenue in November 1978. Starting in 1979, Kansas will distribute 3.5 percent of its sales tax revenues among its cities and counties, 65 percent of which will be based on population and 35 percent on the value of local property. This replaces the sharing of cigarette and liquor taxes. Massachusetts has assumed full fiscal responsibility for local court costs ($88 million), and has distributed over $200 million to distressed local communities. Connecticut is compensating local governments for tax losses attributable to incentive tax abatements. Michigan and California have devised aid programs for distressed areas. New York now pays for all SSI costs. California and Maryland have assumed county medicaid costs and Iowa pays the full administrative costs for the food stamp program.

While these are positive steps, there are still many states that are not doing enough to redress local fiscal imbalances. The reluctance of many states to assist the economically disadvantaged has given rise to the view that income redistribution is primarily the responsibility of the federal government, and the role of state and local governments is marginal.

Growing Opposition to Local Property Taxes Recent referenda have provided taxpayers with a means of protesting rising tax levels to all elected officials. While all taxes have been growing, property tax increases have been the most visible. They have risen as a result of inflation, rising property values, and reassessment.[5] The fiscal squeeze during the 1974-75 recession increased the enthusiasm of local assessors for reassessment. Gallup reports that 58 percent of survey respondents felt their property taxes had increased "a great deal," while only 36 percent felt that federal income tax increases fell into this category; 25 percent named state and local income taxes, and 15 percent the sales tax.

As well as through increased rates and assessed valuations, the burden of the property tax has been increased through the dramatic decline in the number of taxpayers itemizing their federal tax returns. In 1969, more than 60 percent of all returns were itemized, allowing households to deduct local taxes when computing taxable income—a savings, on the average, of 30 percent of the cost of local taxes. By 1978, as a result of the increase in the standard deduction, only 25 percent of the nation's households were itemizing. In nine years, the share of households paying the full cost of local taxes has nearly doubled. The group that has felt this additional bite most strongly are middle

Table 8
State Programs of Revenue Sharing with Local Governments, $25 Million or More: Characteristics and Relative Degree of Fiscal Capacity Localization Achieved, 1973

State	Source of Revenue	Allocation Factors	Amount Shared (millions)	Relative Degree of Equal- ization
Arizona	General sales tax	Counties: origin basis Municipalities: population	$83.8	Negligible
California	Motor vehicle licenses	Population	245.0	Negative
	Cigarette taxes	Sales tax collections and (cities) population	74.3	Negative
Florida	Miscellaneous excise taxes	Population, sales tax collections and (inversely) property tax capacity	171.3	Slight
Illinois	Personal and corporate income taxes	Population	95.0	Slight
Louisiana	Tobacco taxes	Population	26.0	Negative
	General funds	Population and number of homesteads	86.0	Negligible
Michigan	General sales tax	Population	116.0	Negligible
	Personal income tax	Population and relative tax effort	82.0	Negligible
	Intangibles tax	Population and relative tax effort	27.5	Slight
Minnesota	General sales tax	Population	100.7	Negligible
New Jersey	General sales tax	Population	25.0	Negligible
New York	Personal income tax	Population, personal income, real property full value	450.8	Slight
North Carolina	Intangible property tax	Population, origin, property tax rates	25.6	Negligible
Ohio	Miscellaneous taxes	Population, municipal valuation, "need)	117.7	Negligible
Tennessee	General sales tax	Population	27.5	Negligible
Wisconsin	Miscellaneous taxes	Population, property tax rates, value of utility property	265.4	Negligible

SOURCE: Advisory Commission on Intergovernmental Relations, *Federal-State-Local Finances: Significant Features of Fiscal Federalism*, Report M-79 (1974), pp. 79-81. Interpretation by Rafuse, 1974.

47

income taxpayers—the same group that has probably tipped the political balance in favor of tax limitations.

Taxpayers, angry about spiralling property taxes, have a hard time knowing who to blame—the assessor, the school board, the city council, or the county board. But much of the blame must be borne by the inequity of the tax itself. Real estate, the only real asset for low- and moderate-income households, is but a small share of the assets of the relatively affluent. Yet property taxes are usually limited to real estate,[6] making the tax relatively regressive. Assessment practices are far from satisfactory in many areas. Because assessments fail to keep up with market trends, housing in growing areas pays a lower rate than housing in declining areas. Property owners are often unaware of what their taxes will be until they receive a notice. Assessors have been accused of political favoritism. Publicity about low taxes paid by prominent local politicians has not endeared the assessment system to taxpayers. And finally, taxes are paid in lump sums, rather than through the more subtle weekly payroll deductions used for income taxes.

Resistance to Income Redistribution at the Local Level Many of those objecting to taxes are especially incensed by the cost of welfare and other social services that are essentially redistributive.[7] There are two somewhat differing themes running through this protest. First, some object to what they feel is waste—"welfare cheats." Others object to the unequal sharing of the burden of providing services to the poor.

Expenditures on transfer payments and social services for the needy have risen dramatically, and federal grants have only partly offset the cost. Transfer payments now constitute 13 percent of national income, compared with 10 per cent a decade ago. In spite of a spate of welfare reform rhetoric during the last two presidential election campaigns, little has been done to make the delivery of services and income transfers to the poor more efficient. The recession of 1974-75 served to swell the welfare rolls and increase medicaid payments.

More troublesome than the overall level of the costs of these redistributive services is the unevenness of the burden among states and counties. Residents of Northern states and of the large metropolitan areas in those states face a much heavier burden than those elsewhere. New York City government spent $338 per capita on welfare in FY 1974, of which 75 per cent was covered by state and federal grants. Detroit only spent $2.63 per capita in the same year. A move across county or state lines may bring about a significant reduction in taxes levied to pay for welfare. This inequity—the feeling that neighbors may not be paying their share—has led to a desire to restrict local

Table 9
Percent of State Personal Income Collected As State Income Tax and Disbursed as State-Local Welfare Expenditures, FY 1975
(States Above Median Welfare Spending)

State	Percentage of State Personal Income:	
	Collected as State Income Tax	Disbursed as State-Local Welfare Payments From Own Funds
District of Columbia	3.35	2.66
Massachusetts	3.75	2.16
Michigan	2.00	1.61
California	2.94	1.59
Rhode Island	2.32	1.58
New York	4.08	1.53
Hawaii	3.91	1.41
Pennsylvania	2.47	1.34
Wisconsin	4.29	1.29
Minnesota	4.72	1.25
Vermont	3.05	1.19
New Hampshire	0.87	1.13
Maine	1.35	1.12
New Jersey	0.54	1.09
Illinois	2.08	1.08
Ohio	2.06	1.02
Oregon	4.33	1.02
Iowa	2.81	0.92
Kentucky	2.45	0.90
Delaware	4.29	0.90
Maryland	3.11	0.88
Connecticut	0.77	0.82
Washington	0.00	0.81
Alaska	4.38	0.77
Colorado	2.45	0.77
Median for 50 states	2.50	0.75

SOURCE: John Shannon, Testimony before House Committee on Banking, Currency and Housing, September 28, 1976, reprinted by the Committee in *The Rebirth of the American City*, U.S. House of Representatives, Washington, D.C., 1976, and U.S. Bureau of the Census, *Governmental Finances, 1974-75, Washington, D.C. 1976.*

taxes so that the burden is passed on to a higher level of government. Ultimately, many taxpayers would like to see federal assumption of welfare responsibility, following the example of the Supplemental Security Income program (SSI).

Table 9 shows the percentage of state personal income collected through state income taxes and the percentage disbursed in state and local welfare payments for selected states with high personal income tax rates. High income tax payments are associated with a high level of locally financed welfare payments.

The Prospect for Future Federal Aid

The rapid expansion of federal aid to cities and states in response to the sharp 1974-75 national recession enabled most areas to escape relatively unscathed.

This cornucopia is unlikely to continue. In fact, Richard Nathan of the Brookings Institution has pointed out that the most generous period for fiscally distressed areas is likely to have been the period immediately preceding the announcement of President Carter's urban program. Among the several casualties of a conservative Congress, Antirecessionary Revenue Sharing was not renewed before Congress adjourned in December 1978. Local Public Works will not be extended, and the soft public works program has been abandoned.

Tax Exempt Property

Between one-third and one-half of all real property is exempt from property taxes— worth between $800 and $1000 billion (Hellman and Sifniotis, 1977; and Netzer, 1973). Seventy percent of the exempt property belongs to the federal, state or local governments, 15 percent is owned by religious groups, and the remainder belongs to schools, cemeteries, museums, and various charitable organizations. Central cities typically have the greatest concentration of exempt property. Yet exempt property requires fire and police protection, and its occupants must use roads, sewers, and water supplies. Owners of non-exempt property must pay extra. Compensation by higher levels of government has been less than adequate in most states.

State Mandated Programs

One final problem with state/local relations is the issue of state mandated programs whose cost must be borne, in whole or in part, by local governments. Many of these mandates involve programs that local governments wish to carry out anyway, and provide strictly local benefits. The most commonly mandated functions are: solid waste disposal standards; special education programs; workmen's compensation for local personnel; and local public sector pension provisions (ACIR, 1978c).

Mandates that may seriously affect local fiscal conditions include those that set quality standards for local public service delivery, those that set tax assessment and collection procedures, those that influence the definition of the local tax base (excluding certain property from the property tax base, for example) and those that set local public employee salary or benefit levels.

There are no estimates of the cost of mandates to local governments by state. A survey by the Advisory Commission on Intergovernmental Relations found that New York, California, Minnesota and Wisconsin had the most state mandates, while the least were in Southern states, particularly Alabama. Opponents of mandates claim that they represent a loss of local autonomy, allow state legislators to introduce programs without any idea of their true cost, and create local fiscal distress. Proponents argue that mandates are necessitated by poor local administration, and ensure that services are coordinated and uniform throughout the state. Three states have constitutionally limited the state's mandating powers (Alaska, Louisiana, and Pennsylvania), ten have provisions for state reimbursement to local areas for the costs of mandated programs, and 25 states require mandates to be accompanied by notes indicating their fiscal impact.

WHAT CAN BE DONE TO IMPROVE THE STATE/LOCAL FISCAL SYSTEM?

Improving the horizontal and vertical equity of the present system and providing local fiscal relief in the face of federal cutbacks will require extensive reforms. The most important steps that state governments can take are:

■ Facilitate metropolitan revenue and tax base sharing.
■ Target the allocation of state aid and expenditures much more effectively.
■ Develop state-financed property tax circuit breakers.
■ Increase the progressivity (or reduce the regressivity) of the state tax structure.
■ Reimburse local governments for the cost of state mandated programs.
■ Lobby for increased federal funding of programs aimed at the poor.

Metropolitan Revenue and Tax Base Sharing

The sharp disparity between the economic characteristics of suburban and central city residents has contributed to urban fiscal problems. The incidence of poverty in suburbs is below 8 percent, but over 15 percent in central cities. Per capita suburban incomes are more than 10 percent above central city incomes. As we shall see in Chapter 7, this outcome is not accidental; it has been *51* caused, in part, by the heavy redistributive tax burden in central cities. Yet many suburban dwellers commute downtown, implicitly taking advantage of the public services provided by the central jurisdiction.

This has led several observers to recommend policies that would, in Peterson's (1976) words, "reunite the city with its market area." These policies range from sharing part of the proceeds of taxes within a metropolitan area to allowing cities to tax commuters or annex their suburban communities.

Progress in each of these areas has been slow and the prospects for swift action are not bright.[8] But the situation is not hopeless. In 1978, a voter-elected regional council was approved in Portland, Oregon. The body will coordinate programs throughout the metropolitan area, and may assume responsibility for the provision of public services. The metropolitan area of Portland, however, is not as racially or economically segregated as those of more fiscally distressed areas where tax sharing and regional government are even more necessary. Most state governments have shown reluctance to take the necessary steps in the face of strong suburban opposition. Retargeting state grants, while politically more expedient, does not remove the underlying incentives that perpetuate interjurisdictional segmentation. Peterson (1978) observes that "only tax changes that go beyond the city's borders and produce tax-base sharing at the metropolitan or state-wide level promise significant reduction in the magnitude of the overall city tax burden." Revenue sharing is a much less equitable and effective method of reform, for it fails to equalize fiscal effort across jurisdictions (Fischel, 1976).

The federal government can assist states in the difficult task of implementing tax base sharing. As Barro (1978) argues, "there are many ways in which incentives for structural change could be built into the various federal grant programs." The Comprehensive Employment and Training Act was the first to take steps in this direction by providing a small bonus to jurisdictions that formed consortia.

Although unpopular in suburban areas, tax base sharing is a necessary step in placing state/local fiscal relations on a more equitable basis.

Targeting State Expenditures The basic principle in attempting to improve interjurisdictional horizontal equity is that the state must take from rich jurisdictions and give to poor ones, or from rich households and give to poor ones. That is, targeting must be improved both in grants to local jurisdictions and in grants to individuals.

Any allocation formula for a jurisdictional grant that includes population as an argument is bound to be almost useless. Similarly, 52 any matching fund system will probably fail because poorer jurisdictions are frequently unable to come up with the necessary match. Unfortunately, state politics makes effective targeting difficult. A narrowly targeted program tends to be spread further and further over time as political pressure broadens jurisdictional eligibility.[9]

The circuit breakers discussed below are one example of a program that does target effectively and automatically. Perhaps the most important reform will have to be in the area of state education and assistance. At present, in some states, rich school districts actually receive more per pupil than poor districts because of matching fund requirements.

Even if there were no political constraints on how to distribute state assistance, there would still be many technical problems in designing an efficient and equitable allocation formula. Consider the problem of education aid. How are we to take account of the following issues:

■ The number of pupils per capita differs among school districts.
■ The share of students requiring special training and facilities differs among districts.
■ Some districts have a high per capita amount of commercial and industrial property to provide revenue.
■ Per pupil income and wealth differ among districts.
■ The amount of necessary maintenance and repair on facilities differs among districts.

This is not the place to solve such vexing grant allocation questions. But it is the place to make the point that state involvement in redistributive programs will increase in the future, and the combination of political and judicial pressures will necessitate the development of effective allocation formulas.

State-Financed   The circuit breaker is a form of property
Circuit Breakers[10]   tax relief in which benefits depend on
                          both household income and on the
amount of property taxes paid. The circuit breaker may take two forms (ACIR, 1975):

> Under the threshold approach, an "acceptable" tax burden is defined as some fixed percentage of household income (different percentages may be set for different income levels), and any tax above this portion of income is "excessive" and qualified for relief. Under the sliding scale approach, no threshold is defined. Rather, a fixed percentage of property tax . . . is rebated for each eligible taxpayer within a given income class; the rebate percentage declines as income rises.

Wisconsin (1964) was the first state to provide property tax relief this way. By 1970, six states had circuit breakers, and by 1978, 29 states *53*

Table 10
Summary of State
Revenue Sharing Receipts and Circuit Breakers

State	Residential Property Tax Per Capita 1975	State Revenue Sharing Receipts FY 1977 Per Capita	State Revenue Sharing Receipts FY 1977 $ Millions	Circuit Breaker, 1977 Total Program Cost ($ Millions)	Circuit Breaker, 1977 Number of Beneficiaries	Circuit Breaker, 1977 Cost Per Beneficiary
Alabama	22	9.67	35.7	—	—	—
Alaska	79	10.89	4.4	—	—	—
Arizona	106	11.25	25.9	NA	NA	NA
Arkansas	35	10.85	23.3	0.7	8,916	75.76
California	202	10.61	232.4	85.0	440,000	193.18
Colorado	97	9.22	24.2	11.0	58,875	187.00
Connecticut	199	9.09	28.3	24.7	101,574	243.70
Delaware	53	11.95	7.0	—	—	—
D.C.	102	—	—	0.6	6,000	100.00
Florida	82	7.94	67.1	—	—	—
Georgia	72	9.16	46.3	—	—	—
Hawaii	86	11.25	10.1	4.2	NA	NA
Idaho	51	9.55	8.2	4.0	17,323	231.00
Illinois	117	9.96	112.0	100.0	405,000	250.00
Indiana	88	8.62	46.0	0.8	28,665	29.45
Iowa	87	9.48	27.3	9.6	83,200	114.56
Kansas	83	8.49	19.7	8.8	62,955	140.17
Kentucky	37	10.81	37.4	—	—	—
Louisiana	32	11.96	46.9	—	—	—
Maine	104	12.63	13.6	4.3	20,786	209.10
Maryland	126	11.82	48.9	20.8	83,863	248.12
Massachusetts	229	11.78	68.1	—	—	—
Michigan	130	10.00	91.3	275.6	1,234,800	223.18
Minnesota	103	11.85	47.1	134.2	857,277	156.54
Mississippi	38	14.02	33.5	—	—	—
Missouri	76	8.64	41.5	7.0	56,260	124.57
Montana	95	10.65	8.1	—	—	—
Nebraska	91	8.95	14.0	—	—	—
Nevada	133	8.43	5.3	1.4	10,560	127.84
New Hampshire	163	8.54	7.3	—	—	—
New Jersey	216	9.37	68.7	—	—	—
New Mexico	34	12.09	14.4	1.5	40,000	37.50
New York	181	16.38	293.7	NA	NA	NA
North Carolina	48	10.92	60.3	—	—	—
North Dakota	54	9.38	6.1	1.2	9,964	120.20
Ohio	86	8.28	88.6	44.6	329,462	135.42
Oklahoma	41	8.58	24.1	0.4	4,159	85.93
Oregon	128	9.99	23.8	74.1	502,575	147.52
Pennsylvania	62	9.81	115.6	58.9	413,974	142.32
Rhode Island	150	13.12	12.3	0.01	249	51.92
South Carolina	42	11.81	34.0	—	—	—
South Dakota	80	10.78	7.4	1.5	15,095	98.51
Tennessee	52	9.47	40.7	—	—	—
Texas	68	8.61	110.6	—	—	—
Utah	65	9.80	12.4	0.9	10,000	95.00
Vermont	137	12.87	6.2	7.7	36,516	210.05
Virginia	83	8.63	44.3	—	—	—
Washington	123	11.22	41.1	—	—	—
West Virginia	39	12.54	23.3	0.02	1.265	13.94
Wisconsin	115	11.55	53.7	48.1	234,201	205.55
Wyoming	66	8.70	3.5	—	—	—

NA means not available.

SOURCE: ACIR, *Family Tax Burdens Compared Among States and Cities,* Washington, D.C., 1978; John Shannon, "After Jarvis: Tough Questions for Fiscal Policy Makers," *Intergovernmental Perspective,* Summer, 1978; U.S. Bureau of the Census, *Governmental Finances 1976-77,* Washington, D.C., 1978; "Tax Wealth on Fifty States," *State Government News,* July 1978.

and the District of Columbia had adopted some form of circuit breaker. Most states without circuit breakers have below average property tax rates.[11]

In 1977, more than 5 million households received circuit breaker benefits totalling nearly $1 billion—an average of nearly $184 per household (Table 10). Both homeowners and renters are covered in 24 of the states.[12] Benefits vary among states, from $250 per beneficiary in Illinois to $14 in West Virginia.

Since the purpose of a circuit breaker is redistributive, its design must ensure that the greater benefits flow to those in greatest need, and that no benefits are received by those not in need. To ensure that the program operates effectively, one must resolve such issues as *eligibility* and the *distribution of benefits* among the eligible.

Three of the most common characteristics used to define eligibility are income (in all but four states), age and occupation. Upper income limits range from $3,750 for single homeowners in New Mexico to no limit for elderly homeowners in the District of Columbia. Some upper limit seems essential. Some programs are limited to the elderly because many elderly are poor, tend to be relatively immobile, live on fixed incomes, and cannot easily adapt to soaring local property taxes. However, this may make the program relatively regressive since there are also many relatively affluent elderly. An upper limit of about $12,500 seems reasonable.

Treatment of renters is a difficult problem. Most programs include renters, but homeowners receive more generous benefits (ACIR 1973a). Programs that extend benefits to renters assume that an average of 20 percent of the rent reflects local property taxes, but the range is from only 6 percent in New Mexico to 30 percent in Illinois. There is also a problem in that incomes in the two groups are not directly comparable. A homeowner is "better off" in some sense than a household with a comparable money income that rents because of the tax advantages. Whether this should be taken into account depends upon whether the circuit breaker is used primarily as property tax relief or as an income supplement. As an income supplement, a circuit breaker can never perform as well as a cash transfer, but may be more politically expedient and administratively simple. Overall, the circuit breaker works well in targeting benefits to those who need them.

To reduce interjurisdictional movement by households seeking maximum benefits, responsibility for financing a circuit breaker should rest with the state government, not with local jurisdictions. The program would, in effect, redistribute resources toward jurisdictions with relatively high concentrations of low income households.

The cost of a circuit breaker depends on the percent of the "excess" property tax a household receives in a rebate. This is defined by two factors: the percent of income that tax payments cannot exceed for 55 threshold type programs, and the design of the sliding scale. In 1970, ACIR (1973a) estimated that if 7 percent of income were the threshold level, a nationwide program would cost $2 billion and reach 13.5 million households. A 5 percent threshold would cost $4.3 billion, reaching 21 million households; and a 4 percent threshold $6.1 billion, reaching half of all households. If costs have risen proportionately with property tax payments—surely a conservative estimate—costs today would be more than double. Within states, net benefits would be greatest in those jurisdictions with a high incidence of poverty and high property tax rates.

While central cities have greater concentrations of the poor, they have lower valued housing and, often, lower property tax rates. In general, a circuit breaker would tend to provide greater per capita benefits for cities than suburbs, depending upon the fraction of rent ascribed to property taxes—the higher the proportion of rent, the greater the "urban" benefit of the program. The benefits would be effectively targeted toward poorer jurisdictions, allowing them to raise local taxes without imposing extreme hardship upon the local poor and lower middle income groups. It would, therefore, strengthen the fiscal position of those jurisdictions with a relatively weak fiscal base. It would also weaken property tax limitation movements, and, perhaps, avoid too many repetitions of the clumsy efforts made in California.

The program does target effectively on distressed cities. Table 11 shows 15 cities grouped according to their urban conditions index, showing the per capita residential property tax and the percent of the population below the poverty level—the two main determinants of the relative benefits under a circuit breaker program. The final column shows a crude index of the likely relative benefits under a circuit breaker—calculated as the product of their tax payments and poverty rates indexed to the average of all 15 cities. Among the severely distressed cities, only Buffalo scores significantly below 100, because of its relatively low poverty rate.

The state-financed circuit breaker may encourage increased activism by the poor, since they would not have to bear the cost of increased local services. It might also encourage their concentration in the central city. This seems unlikely since a considerable fraction of the poor already receive some form of housing assistance, and they are concentrated in central cities already.

A more important problem is that the burden of assisting the poor through a state-financed circuit breaker will be much heavier in high-taxing states with high concentrations of the poor. Given the generally accepted proposition that the poor are a federal rather than a local responsibility, a strong argument could be made for federal help. However, increased federal expenditures for local tax relief seems

56

Table 11
Urban Conditions Index,
Per Capita Residential Property Tax,
Percent Poverty, and Benefit Index
(Selected Cities)

City	Urban Conditions Index[a]	Per Capita Residential Property Tax, 1976	Percent Poverty 1970	Index of Per Capita Benefit from Circuit Breaker (15 City Average = 100)[b]
St. Louis	351	228	33.6	148
Newark	321	493	22.1	211
Buffalo	292	307	14.8	88
Cleveland	291	286	17.0	94
Boston	257	483	15.3	143
Unweighted Average	302	359	20.6	137
Baltimore	226	196	18.0	68
Philadelphia	216	237	20.8	95
Detroit	201	352	14.7	96
Chicago	201	319	14.3	88
Atlanta	118	256	19.8	98
Unweighted Average	192	272	17.5	89
Denver	106	284	11.5	63
Los Angeles	74	419	11.2	91
Dallas	39	247	13.3	64
Houston	37	286	13.9	77
Phoenix	20	218	11.6	49
Unweighted Average	55	290	12.3	69
All 15 Cities	183	307	16.8	100

SOURCES: Paul R. Dommel et al., *Decentralizing Community Development,* The Brookings Institution, Washington, D.C., January 1978; *Monthly Tax Features,* The Tax Foundation, August 1978.

[a] For definition see Dommel et al., 1978.

[b] Calculated as:

$$\frac{\text{Per Capita Residential Property Tax}}{\text{Mean for all 15 Cities (= \$307)}} \quad X \quad \frac{\text{Percent Poverty}}{\text{Mean for all 15 cities (= 16.8)}}$$

unlikely at the moment. One possible source of funds for circuit breaker assistance is the state portion of revenue sharing funds.

The fraction of revenue sharing grants going to states could be used to help pay for state initiated property tax relief, with some increased federal grants used to reward states that have already introduced equitable circuit breaker programs. Table 10 shows state revenue sharing receipts in both total volume and per capita terms in FY 1977. States could use their $2.5 billion in revenue sharing grants to help pay for circuit breaker. States would not be compelled to participate. Circuit breakers would also deflate local "Proposition 13-type" movements.

Increased Tax Progressivity The redistribution from rich to poor jurisdictions can be influenced not only through state expenditure patterns but also through state revenue practices. There are several ways that states with regressive tax collection systems could do this:

■ Those poor states with rich endowments of natural resources can raise severance taxes to export their tax load.
■ Sales taxes can be modified to include special allowances for clothes, food and utility payments (Chapter 7).
■ Circuit breakers can be provided for the poor.
■ States without personal income taxes can switch from regressive sales taxes to progressive income taxes.
■ States with flat rate income taxes, which are regressive because of the offset against federal income taxes, could consider introducing a graduated income tax.

Some states[13] have flat rate rather than graduated taxes. There are four arguments in favor of switching to a graduated income tax (Moscovitch, 1972):

1. Graduated taxes are more equitable since they require the well-to-do to pay a higher share of their income than the poor. In fact, since higher income taxpayers tend to submit itemized federal tax forms, a flat rate state tax results in the poor, who do not itemize, paying a higher share of their income in state taxes than the rich.
2. A graduated tax allows the state to shift a large part of the local tax burden onto the federal government.
3. The graduated tax is more responsive to changes in income—such income taxes rise more than proportionately.
4. State tax revenues can be increased without increasing the tax
58 burden on the poor.

For example, for FY 1973, for the state of Massachusetts, it was calculated that a move to a graduated structure from the actual flat rate with no change in total revenue could have yielded the following range in incidence (Moscovitch, 1972):

	1973 Tax Structure		Shift to Progressive Tax*	
Tax Bracket in 1973	Actual Tax Paid	Net Cost After Federal Tax Deduction	Actual Tax Paid	Net Cost After Federal Tax Deduction
$ 5,300 - $ 6,600	153	153	38	38
$ 9,300 - $10,600	292	292	111	111
$13,000 - $20,000	588	459	390	304
$26,000 - $33,000	1367	930	1705	1159
$100,000	5451	2453	11,723	5275

*Based upon the New York State graduated tax structure modified to yield unchanged total revenue for Massachusetts.

Such a change would have reduced taxes for 1.3 million households, raised them for 95,000, and reduced the federal tax liabilities of Massachusetts residents by $100 million.

It has long been believed that a progressive tax is more stabilizing. The theory is that as incomes fall during a recession, progressive taxes fall more than proportionately, softening the blow, leading expenditures to fall less than they would otherwise. Some evidence suggests that, since the burden of a recession does not fall equally on all groups, the shift from a graduated to a progressive tax would have little stabilizing impact (Cassidy, 1970).

However, as we argue in Chapter 7, states that try to increase the progressivity of their income taxes in absence of similar changes in neighboring states may find their affluent households leaving, thus raising the burden on the less well-to-do who remain. A federal grant system that rewarded states with progressive forms of taxation would help to soften this blow.

State Reimbursement of Mandated Program Costs   There are several options for states that wish to reduce the inequities arising from state mandated programs. First, states may be required to pay, in full, for mandated program costs. Florida now requires full state reimbursement for any state general law that requires local jurisdictions to spend additional funds or that changes local tax assessments or authoriza- *59* tions. Tennessee, Hawaii, and Michigan enacted state reimbursement measures on proposed new mandates as part of their constitutional amendments for spending limits in 1978. This may not necessarily contribute to fiscal equalization. It depends on the distribution of the benefits of the mandated program. An alternative is to place constitutional limits on the types of programs that can be state mandated. This is a relatively clumsy recourse. Finally, states may require that each mandate be accompanied with detailed estimates of its fiscal impact. This will ensure that program costs are an integral part of the mandate debate.

The principle of reimbursement can be extended to cover compensation to local authorities for tax exempt state facilities. Over 50 percent of Boston's real property tax base is tax exempt, representing an annual revenue loss of $100 million. In 1978, New Jersey enacted a law requiring state reimbursement for tax losses due to state-held properties. Connecticut has a law requiring state compensation for losses due to the tax exempt status of hospitals and universities. Not only should other states follow these leads, they should also lobby the federal government for an effective compensation program for federal property.

***Increased Federal Assistance*[14]** In may seem futile to call for increased federal assistance at a time when federal programs are being cut back. However, the emphasis should be on improved targeting of assistance rather than on increasing the level. One way to reduce the interstate inequities that arise as a result of the concentration of the poor in certain areas would be through federal assumption of the responsibility for programs currently financed, in part, at the local level. The clearest candidates are welfare and health programs.

Federalization of Welfare. In 1974, the Supplemental Security Income program (SSI), encompassing state-run programs for the disabled, blind, and aged, was federalized. However, this was not a pure case of federal assumption, since states must supplement federal benefits so that no one who received assistance under the superceded programs suffers a reduction in benefits. States may also voluntarily supplement federal benefits, and most have chosen to do so.

Welfare federalization proposals focus primarily on the AFDC program, which is the largest welfare program, spending $9.2 billion in 1975, of which 56 percent was financed by the federal government, 37 percent by the states, and 7 percent by local governments (Hamilton and Rabinowitz, forthcoming). But federalization would not save states their $4 billion. Most proposals call for a nationally uniform schedule and eligibility standards, with provision for state supplementation, very much on the model of SSI. No proposal would main-

60

tain the present differences in benefits, for that would imply a massive federal subsidy flowing North from the low-benefit Southern states. With high federal benefit levels, the incentive for high-benefit states to supplement would be small, and they would therefore gain substantial fiscal relief. With low federal levels, these states would receive little additional assistance from federalization. A relatively low level seems the most likely outcome from any successful reform.

Local fiscal relief would depend on state decisions about the division of the total fiscal relief between states and local jurisdictions. Full federal assumption would provide substantial relief to only six major cities—Baltimore, Denver, New York, Philadelphia, San Francisco, and Washington, D.C.—to a few smaller cities, and to a few urban counties in New York and California (Hamilton and Rabinovitz, forthcoming). However, these gains would be diluted if state governments cut back aid to localities, imposed the supplementation costs on the cities, or reduced the taxing authority of the city to a degree commensurate with the reduction in welfare costs.

Rather than complete federal assumption, John Shannon (1976 b) has suggested a "welfare payments circuit breaker." Under this program, the federal government would provide grants to those states in which state and locally-financed welfare payments claimed a share of state personal income that was above the national average. Thus, in 1975, the average state spent 0.75 percent of total personal income on state and locally-financed welfare (Chapter 7). In Massachusetts, the fraction was 2.16 percent. Those overburdened states would receive a federal grant equal to some percentage of their overburden— perhaps 50 percent, or $240 million in the case of Massachusetts. The program has the advantage of helping heavily burdened states without some of the problems of full federal assumption.

Federalization of Health Care Programs. National health care financing may provide as much state and local fiscal relief as welfare federalization. Table 12 shows that state and local governments spend more for health and hospitals (when medicaid is counted as a public welfare program), net of federal assistance, than they do on welfare. If a comprehensive health care system could assume medicaid costs and medicaid is included in the health category, then state and local spending for welfare (excluding medicaid), net of federal aid, was slightly over $7 billion in 1975, compared with over $22 billion for health (including medicaid). A broad national health program has considerable potential for local fiscal relief.

States differ in their per capita outlays for health services, ranging from less than $2 per capita in Arizona, Indiana, Maine, Maryland, Nevada, North Dakota, Oregon, and Wyoming, to $97 per capita in New York, $52 in California, and $50 in Pennsylvania (1975 data reported in Hamilton and Rabinovitz). The fiscal relief from federal- *61*

Table 12
State and Local Spending and Federal Aid for Public Welfare
and Health and Hospitals, 1974-75
($ Billions)

Function	State and Local General Expenditure	Federal Aid to State and Local Governments	State and Local Expenditure Net of Federal Aid
Public Welfare (including Medicaid)	27.2	14.4	12.8
Health and Hospitals	18.8	2.1	16.7
Medicaid	12.6	6.9	5.7
Public Welfare (less Medicaid)	14.6	7.5	7.1
Health and Hospitals (including Medicaid)	31.4	9.0	22.4

SOURCE: All data except Medicaid from U.S. Bureau of the Census, *Governmental Finances in 1974-75*, GF75, No. 5, Washington, D.C., September 1976, Table 6. Medicaid data from Hamilton and Rabinovitz (forthcoming).

ization would be enjoyed primarily by a few large urbanized states.

Other Possibilities for Federal Assumption. There are other functional areas in which the federal financial role could become substantially larger. Education is the most obvious candidate. The federal government could take on a much larger fraction of the burden of financing elementary and secondary education. State-local spending for public schools is currently so large that a federal assumption of even a small fraction of this burden (special education, for example) would have a significant effect on the finances of the whole state-local sector. Higher education also offers the opportunity of either an expanded federal program of tuition aid or an expansion of institutional grants to colleges and universities—both of which would reduce state costs. Other possibilities include expanded federal support for both the construction and operation of mass transit or for capital construction projects. Federal involvement would take the form of larger grants.

FOOTNOTES TO CHAPTER 4

1. Details of state business and household taxes are given in Chapter 5 and 7 respectively.

2. These taxes are authorized in five states: Alabama, Kentucky, Missouri, Ohio, and Pennsylvania.

3. Authorized by the state of Michigan, 1964. The enabling legislation mandates a one percent tax on residents and 0.5 percent tax on non-residents. No other state has yet followed Michigan's lead.

4. In Maryland, every county, and Baltimore city, is required a levy a supplement of at least 20 percent of the state liability, and may adopt a rate as high as 50 percent. Indiana authorized local supplements in 1973 and one-third of all counties and 315 small municipalities have enacted supplements.

5. The *Wall Street Journal* reported annual tax increases as high as 200 percent in parts of Southern California, 300 percent in Cook County, Illinois, and 126 percent in Bucks County, Pennsylvania ("Soaring Property Taxes Infuriate Homeowners," *Wall Street Journal,* 9/7/77.)

6. In some states, such as Virginia, there are taxes on the value of other assets, including automobiles, boats and furniture. However, this is unusual.

7. Asked in a Gallup Poll whether their community spent too much or too little on a number of local services, 42 percent of the respondents felt too much was spent on social services, and only 19 percent felt too little was spent. For all other services, more respondents felt too little was spent than too much ("The Big Tax Revolt," *Newsweek,* 6/18/78).

8. See ACIR, 1973b; Bahl and Puryear, 1976; Bahl and Vogt, 1975; and Peterson, 1976. See also the discussion of the issue in *Rebirth of the American City,* Volume 2, Committee on Banking, Currency and Housing, U.S. House of Representatives, Washington, D.C., 1976, p. 727ff.

9. A good example of the way that a program can be spread further and more thinly over time is the Community Development Block Grant program. Originally concentrated in a relatively few, poor communities, funds have been gradually extended to more and more urban communities by city governments.

10. This discussion has benefited from a manuscript by Steven Gold, *Property Tax Relief,* forthcoming.

11. The four major exceptions are Massachusetts, New Jersey, Nebraska, and New Hampshire.

12. Robert Reinhold, "Carter Weighs Pushing States to Assist Cities," *New York Times, 2/12/78.*

13. Illinois, Indiana, Michigan, Massachusetts, and Pennsylvania.

14. This discussion rests heavily on the excellent exposition by Barro, 1978, p. 94ff.

5

WHAT SHOULD STATES DO ABOUT BUSINESS TAXES?

Few policy discussions are fueled by as much passion, encompass as many conflicting parties, and are based on as little evidence, as the debate on what to do about business taxes. Households and consumers, who have borne the brunt of spiralling taxes, demand that the burden be shifted to businesses. Businesses, facing rising competition from the "New South" and the Far East, demand tax breaks. The unemployed demand jobs. And state governments need revenues. This chapter examines business taxes. The following chapter reviews the use of specific tax incentives to achieve state development goals.

There are several types of business taxes, and their use varies among states. The most important are:

■ *Business income taxes.* These include corporate, financial, and unincorporated business income taxes. Several states have no business income taxes,[1] but tax the value of output[2] or gross sales.[3] Revenues were $7.2 billion in FY 1976.

■ *Property Taxes.* These include taxes on the value of land and structures owned (or even leased) by the company. Some states and localities include the value of equipment and inventories when estimating property values. States collected $2.1 billion in property taxes in FY 1976, localities $32.9 billion.

■ *Payroll Taxes.* Companies must contribute toward unemployment insurance and workmens' compensation. These are not regarded as business taxes, nor are they regarded as being within the scope of state tax policy. They are computed on an actuarial basis and paid into a trust fund. Although they are not traditionally considered part of general state revenue, they vary among states and have an influence on development. Unemployment insurance premiums totalled $5.1 billion in FY 1976.

■ *Severance Taxes.* States with rich endowments of natural resources charge for each unit of raw materials extracted. For example, in 1978, half of Alaska's revenue from its own sources came from severance payments on oil production. In FY 1976, three quarters of all state severance taxes were accounted for by Texas ($800 million), Louisiana ($558 million), and Oklahoma ($151 million).

■ *Sales Taxes.* In some states, all sales, including interindustry purchases, are taxed; in most, only retail sales. General and selective sales tax revenues account for nearly half of all state tax receipts.

■ *Excise Taxes.* Taxes on gasoline and fuel oil may be important to some companies. Rates exceed 10 cents a gallon in Connecticut, Hawaii, Michigan, New Hampshire, Rhode Island, Washington, West Virginia, and D.C. Recently, they were only 5 cents in Texas.

■ *License Fees.* States charge license fees to set up and operate businesses. Nationwide, these fees comprise 7.7 percent of state tax revenues, but they top 31 percent in Delaware, 16 percent in New Hampshire, and 15 percent in Nevada. General corporation license fees are collected in all 50 states, but Texas ($213 million), Pennsylvania ($200 million), and Michigan ($158 million) accounted for 50 percent of all such revenues in FY 1976.

This list is by no means exhaustive. States also have fees for motor vehicle registration, hotel room occupancy taxes, user fees for state services and facilities, water and sewer link-up charges . . . the list is limited only by the imagination of state finance departments over the last 200 years and the United States Constitution. The listed taxes do represent the major sources of revenue to state and local governments. Table 13 shows state revenue from the most important of these taxes.

Table 14 shows the characteristics of business taxes in each of the fifty states and the District of Columbia. Comparing business tax rates is extremely difficult. For example, although there is a wide range in corporate income tax rates, the actual differences in the burden may be very different from the data in the table. States differ in how they define the taxable income base upon which the rates are levied. For example, although the Colorado rate is half that of New York, the fact that New York reduces taxable income by an amount that is related to the amount of out-of-state sales, while Colorado does not necessarily do so (see below), reduces the differential. It is further reduced by the fact that New York does not include inventories in the property tax base, while Colorado does. Six states—Alabama, Arizona, Iowa, Missouri, North Dakota, and Utah—allow federal income tax payments to be deducted when calculating the local tax base. There are also great differences in special tax incentives (see following chapter).

A second point is that taxes influence business behavior not only through what is collected, but also through what is not collected. Through special tax treatment of certain types of activities—for example, accelerated depreciation of certain types of business equipment purchases—resources are diverted from other activities into the activity receiving special treatment. These "tax expenditures" are important. At the federal level, it has been estimated that tax expenditures—tax receipts foregone through special provisions—total over *65*

Table 13
State Revenue from Selected Business Taxes
FY 1977

Tax	Revenue ($ Millions)
Business property taxes (state & local)	32916.0
Corporate net income	7259.7
Licenses	6897.0
Severance	2028.7
Unemployment insurance (FY 1975)	5135.0
Motor vehicle fuel sales	8660.0

SOURCE: U.S. Bureau of the Census, *Governmental Finances 1976-77,* Washington, D.C., 1978, and data presented in Tables 14 and 22.

$100 billion. Yet there are no Congressional committees overseeing these large "programs." At the state level, even less is known. The only states which systematically prepare a thorough annual review of state and local tax expenditures are California, Wisconsin, and Maryland. Other states should follow suit.

With these caveats, we can still make some general observations (Table 14). There are large differences among states in unemployment compensation payments, expressed as a percent of total wages. These differences arise because of differences in local wage rates, benefit levels, turnover rates, and unemployment rates and duration. In Colorado and Texas, employer contributions average less than 0.2 percent of the total wage bill, but top 2 percent in Alaska and Rhode Island. Since wages are about one-third of total costs in manufacturing (two-thirds of value added), these variations will be much more important than the difference between corporate tax rates of 4 and 8 percent since corporate income rarely tops 10 percent of gross sales.

The discussion in this chapter yields several conclusions concerning the impact of business taxes:

■ First, contrary to popular belief, interstate variations in business income taxes have had little impact on the location and relocation of businesses. Firms have not fled South to escape from high corporate tax rates in the North. High rates may deter new investment—but not *66* by a great deal.

■ Second, more important than *interstate* variations in business income taxes are *intrastate* variations in business property taxes. Business has expanded more rapidly in suburban or even exurban areas in part because of high taxes in central cities. Those same high taxes may have deterred investment and development. Some areas may benefit from shifting some of the tax burden onto land and off improvements.

■ Third, payroll taxes have exacerbated the problem of unemployment, and have probably affected low income employment.

■ Fourth, the corporate income tax is equitable inasmuch as it is related to ability to pay. However, it is not necessarily related to the value of services received, nor is it a predictable or stable revenue source. Some states may benefit by shifting toward a tax related to value added.

■ Fifth, the allocation of business income among states for multistate firms is inequitable. Some states have taken steps to reduce this inequity. Others should follow.

■ Finally, there is no reason for states to strive to cut business tax levels. In fact, households rather than business have paid for most of the increase in state expenditures since World War II. States with excessively high taxes may gain from reducing their disparities, and perhaps from simplifying their tax structure. But if taxes are to be cut, states should focus on personal rather than business taxes.

EFFICIENCY

Proponents of business tax cuts raise three efficiency arguments against the present level and structure of business taxes. First, they argue that high tax levels in some states deter business activities leading to reduced unemployment and lower investment. Second, interjurisdictional differences in tax rates have contributed to the movement of firms away from high taxing locales—particularly large central cities in the Northeast. Third, it is argued that business taxes fall on capital and therefore discourage new investment.

These beliefs are widely held. Their persuasive presentation by the business community has led to a general shifting of tax revenues from business to personal taxes, and to a general pressure on states to offer special tax incentives to stimulate investment and attract business. We shall see that there is no evidence to substantiate the first two claims, and that the third effect is relatively weak. However, in an area which has received little attention—payroll taxes—tax policy is contributing to unemployment among the unskilled.

Overall Tax Levels

Do high state taxes deter economic development? Few topics have been debated as heatedly and with less empirical foundation. Many state 67

Table 14
Characteristics of State/Local Business Taxes, 1977

State	Corporate Income Tax — Rate (%)[2]	Per Capita Revenue	UDI[6]	MSTC[7]	Business Property Taxes — Inventories Exempt or Not Taxed	P.C. Business Property Taxes 1975	Unemployment Compensation as Percent of Total Wages (1976)	Other Taxes — Licenses Per Capita	Severance Taxes Per Capita
Alabama	5.0	16.3	X	X		30.9	.53	24.5	3.1
Alaska	5.4 (+4.0*)	77.8	X	X		136.3	2.34	53.3	70.0
Arizona	2.5 - 10.5	20.2			X	127.3	.52	26.7	—
Arkansas	1 - 6	26.8	X	X		54.6	.85	29.4	4.2
California	9	58.6	X	X	X	171.3	1.34	23.6	0.1
Colorado	5	26.8		X		117.0	.19	25.9	1.7
Connecticut	10	46.4			X	152.6	1.35	29.1	—
Delaware	8.7	38.2			X	74.8	.87	186.8	—
D.C.	9.0[2]	—	X		X	94.8	—	—	—
Florida	5.0	21.3				80.6	.49	34.3	5.6
Georgia	6.0	26.5				90.4	.42	13.7	—
Hawaii	5.85 - 6.44	39.3	X	X	X	64.4	1.74	5.7	—
Idaho	6.5	35.3	X	X	X	109.2	1.14	46.3	0.4
Illinois	4.0	28.2	X			156.5	.42	35.7	—
Indiana	3.0[3]	16.1	X			143.5	.49	20.5	0.1
Iowa	6.0 - 10.0	26.8				175.9	.47	47.9	—
Kansas	4.5	40.3	X	X		170.0	1.01	30.2	0.3
Kentucky	4.0 - 5.8	38.5	X			57.9	.75	20.6	26.1
Louisiana	4.0 - 8.0	22.5				53.1	1.19	29.3	143.2
Maine	4.95 - 6.93	29.6	X		X	127.0	1.50	33.3	—
Maryland	7.0	26.7				86.6	.65	23.4	—
Massachusetts	8.33	56.1			X	201.5	1.69	14.0	—
Michigan	2.35	36.8	X	X	X	161.7	1.06	41.5	0.8
Minnesota	12.0	49.1			X	128.2	.80	34.5	14.6
Mississippi	3.0 - 4.0	17.1			X	59.2	.43	24.7	9.8
Missouri	5.0	14.0	X	X		107.9	.69	30.6	—
Montana	6.75	28.8	X	X		208.7	.95	32.1	39.1
Nebraska	4.0 - 4.4	17.8	X	X	X	189.8	.50	30.5	0.7

State	Rate							
Nevada	—				120.4	1.60	74.3	0.2
New Hampshire	8.0			X	152.0	.93	36.9	0.1
New Jersey	7.5			X	196.6	1.48	41.9	—
New Mexico	5.0	X	X	X	61.5	.95	31.8	72.9
New York	10.0	X		X	187.7	1.17	23.1	—
North Carolina	6.0	X			69.7	.60	32.5	—
North Dakota	3.0 - 8.5	X	X		137.7	1.03	43.7	18.0
Ohio	.4				116.2	.55	39.3	0.4
Oklahoma	4.0	X			76.0	.55	43.5	54.0
Oregon	7.5	X	X	X	149.0	1.02	47.0	1.5
Pennsylvania	10.5[5]	X			101.3	1.16	50.3	—
Rhode Island	8.0				120.0	2.08	24.6	—
South Carolina	6.0	X		X	58.6	.53	17.1	0.4
South Dakota	—	X		X	186.6	.39	31.1	0.4
Tennessee	6.0	X		X	64.8	.72	40.8	62.6
Texas	—				123.5	.17	39.2	62.6
Utah	4.0	X	X	X	86.8	.83	18.6	9.0
Vermont	5.0 - 7.5			X	162.4	1.14	43.8	
Virginia	6.0	X	X		74.5	.13	24.3	0.1
Washington	—				106.9	1.74	31.1	10.1
West Virginia	6.0	X			61.8	.51	25.5	
Wisconsin	2.3 - 7.9	X		X	156.1	.87	28.1	0.1
Wyoming	—			X	217.2	.80	78.0	102.5

*Surcharge

SOURCE: Commerce Clearing House. *State Tax Guide 1978.* Chicago, Ill., 1978; Tax Foundation, *Facts and Figures on Government Finance,* Washington, D.C., 1977; U.S. Bureau of the Census, Governmental Finances, various years; estiamtes for the business property tax were made by subtracting per capita residential property taxes ("Tax Wealth in Fifty States," *State Government News,* July 1978), from total property tax revenues, per capita.

NOTES:
1. Where a range is given the state has a progressive corporate income tax. Highest and lowest rates are shown. Federal taxable income is used as a base except in Alabama, Arkansas, California, D.C., Louisiana, Minnesota, Mississippi, Oregon, South Carolina, Utah, and Wisconsin. Federal income tax paid is not deductible except in Alabama, Arizona, Iowa, Louisiana, Missouri and North Dakota.
2. A 10 percent surcharge is also imposed.
3. Domestic and interstate corporations pay a tax of 3 percent on adjusted gross income from sources in Indiana.
4. The greater of 4 percent of the first $25,000 of the value of stock plus 8 percent of the value over $25,000 or 5 mills times the value of each stock.
5. Do not allow the federal accelerated depreciation allowance in computing state taxable income.
6. Uniform Division of Income for Tax Purposes Act adoption is indicated by a check.
7. Multi-State Tax Compact membership is indicated by a check.

SOURCE: Will Meyers of ACIR.

NOTES:
a Membership subject to congressional approval (which hasn't come so far).
b UDI Act adopted only for allocation of nonbusiness income.

officials believe so, and have been persuaded by the demands from business that the tax burden be reduced.

The theory behind these demands is simple. If local taxes are lowered, then the local cost of doing business is reduced, existing firms become more competitive with firms elsewhere, and new firms may be induced to move in. The result is more jobs. This theory has achieved popular conceptualization in the "Laffer curve." Arthur Laffer, an economics professor at the University of Southern California, argues that if tax rates are increased beyond a certain point revenues decline because economic activity is reduced—labor force participation falls, investment is choked, and some businesses move to more favorable tax climes. There is no empirical evidence for the Laffer curve, although studies have found that rising personal income tax rates reduce male labor force participation, and rising business tax rates increase investment abroad.[4]

There is little evidence that overall tax levels are too high. A recent study by the Federal Reserve Bank of Boston found that the average U.S. business paid 4.4 percent of its income to state and local governments. In 1973, this broke down to 0.9 percent in corporate income taxes, 1.9 percent in property taxes, 0.8 percent in unemployment compensation contributions and 0.8 percent in "other business taxes."

The role of the corporate income tax and business property taxes on investment decisions has been small. Payroll taxes, which have recei ed much less analytical and political attention, do appear to have raised the rate of unemployment and may have influenced industrial location decisions. Unemployment insurance premiums, workmen's compensation, and social security have raised the cost of labor, especially low wage labor, creating unemployment. They have raised the rate of layoffs and increased the duration of unemployment.

The level of unemployment insurance premiums has two effects in economic development. First, insurance checks allow workers to spend longer periods hunting for an attractive job before accepting a position (Ehrenberg and Oaxaca, 1976). The result has been an increase in the average duration of unemployment, and a tendency for the unemployed to seek higher paying employment. This is not necessarily bad, for the match between a worker's skills and preferences and his or her job will be improved, but it also means that the local *rate* of unemployment will be higher. In fact, the secular increase in unemployment—with strong cyclical variations—is due, in part, to the extension of unemployment insurance coverage to more sectors, the increase in the duration of assistance (through federal supplements to local programs), and increases in the level of assistance.

The second effect is upon the frequency of lay-offs. The amount that firms must pay in insurance premiums is meant to be linked to the *70* frequency with which employees (or ex-employees) claim benefits.

However, there is an upper limit on the premium rate which is well below the "actuarial" rate, so that firms with a high labor turn-over are subsidized by less volatile companies. Feldstein (1976, p. 956) concludes that this subsidy "has a potentially very large impact on the rate of unemployment, causing layoffs when they would not otherwise happen and substantially magnifying the size of layoffs that do occur."

The states with a high concentration of their labor force in the volatile consumer durable industry will experience higher unemployment rates during recession as a result of the way the program is designed.

Interstate and Intrastate Tax Differences While the impact of tax levels has received little attention, the influence of interarea variations in the tax rates on growth and industry location has been studied extensively (albeit not satisfactorily). Do interstate differences in business tax levels affect industrial location decisions and spatial differences in economic growth? The answer, it seems, is very little. Counter to many myths, tax differences can be blamed for very few of the regional shifts in employment and for relatively few of the shifts from central cities to suburbs. *In fact, the major influence of taxes on economic development may not be through business taxes, but indirectly through personal taxes that influence the migration pattern of households and thus the growth of employment (see Chapter 7).*

There are several reasons for a conclusion that seems to contradict the conventional wisdom:

■ First, state and local tax payments are deductible for federal income tax purposes, and since corporate income is subject to a marginal federal tax rate of 48 percent, both the net burden and the amount of any differential are essentially cut in half.

■ Second, differences in tax rates are often compensated for by differences in the level and quality of local public services, which also affect business location decisions.

■ Third, the costs of many other factors vary among locations and may be much more important in location decisions. For most firms, labor costs are 20 times as large as state and local tax payments. A 2 percent wage differential is as important, therefore, as a 40 percent tax differential.

■ Fourth, local tax rate differentials are capitalized, at least in part, in property values. Land in a high taxing locale is depresed in value, while a low tax area will have higher land values.

■ Finally, there are relatively few footloose firms whose location decisions might be influenced by tax differentials.

One of the few studies that did find that taxes have a significant effect was conducted for the Budget Bureau of New York City (Grieson et al., 1977). New York is in a somewhat unique position, since its commuters and businesses can move to either New Jersey or Connecticut and maintain close contact with the city. Both states have maintained a quite distinct tax structure—in part, one assumes, to try to syphon off some of the city's business. The study, which examined the shift from a gross sales tax to a corporate profits tax in 1966, concluded that manufacturing activity had left New York City in response to high taxes. In fact, a 10 percent increase in local taxes would reduce employment by about 3.5 percent. Unfortunately, it is difficult to identify what part of the ensuing exodus of manufacturing from the city is attributable to the tax change.

One reason why tax rate differentials within a metropolitan area have not contributed more to the suburbanization process is that part of the tax rate differential will be reflected in land prices. Land prices in a low taxing jurisdiction will, all other things being equal, be bid up when firms try to move in, while land in high taxing locales will decline in value. A firm must compare the tax savings with the higher purchase price of the site.

There is ample evidence of the capitalization of property tax differentials. There is also evidence that central city/suburban differences have not been very important. (Fuller and Towles, 1978; and Levin, 1976). However, as Cornia, Testa, and Stocker (1978) point out: "States do resort to fiscal and other incentives . . . These actions therefore suggest that these differences are not always fully capitalized in land prices. The capitalization process is limited by imperfections in the land market. Among these are a paucity of available sites or potential bidders, unique qualities of individual sites, and requirements of individual businesses, zoning and other land use restrictions, or limited knowledge of both sides of the market."

Thus the burden of high local taxes may be greater for firms with unique site requirements, which would tend to be large manufacturing concerns for whom rail spurs, harbor facilities and other features are important. Firms that are less mobile may, therefore, be induced to pay a higher tax rate than more mobile sectors. However, the few firms that fall into this category manage to gain a degree of political power that in the long run appears to minimize the extent to which local governments can capture any location rents.

The overwhelming evidence from many studies of industrial location decisions suggests that firms select their region on the basis of broad criteria, such as anticipated market growth, availability of raw materials, transportation, energy prices, and the quality of the labor force. The last factor includes the education and skills of the labor force, but also its wage rate and degree of unionization. Compared
72 with these factors, state and local taxes shrink in importance.

Of course, irrefutable evidence is hard to find. It is difficult to determine why a company chooses a particular location. Rigorous econometric models rarely have appropriate or accurate data to work with, and questionnaires are only as reliable as their often biased respondents.

The near unanimity of findings from all sources gives some credibility to the basic proposition that tax rates have not been important. Schmenner (unpublished) concludes that "cities and towns need neither fear that high tax rates alone will drive out all industry nor rejoice that low tax rates guarantee rapid industrial development.' Schmenner also points out that analyzing the relationship between taxes and location is confounded because the causation runs two ways. While industry may be marginally attracted by low tax rates, a heavy local concentration of industry can lead to a low tax rate because of the size of the base.

There are other aspects of the business tax structure that may also influence location decisions. From the point of view of computing taxable income, land cannot be treated as a depreciable asset. This encourages firms to avoid areas where land prices are high and may decline. The bias is toward suburban areas where prices are low and expected to rise. This bias is reinforced by the fact that capital gains are taxed at a lower rate than corporate income. This shelters rapid appreciation from taxes, encouraging location at the urban fringe. Fulton (1971, p. 10) illustrates this process with the case of a company that:

> 10 years ago acquired a very large site on Route 128 near Boston. Before the company could complete its plans for construction on the new site, it received—and accepted—an offer for a small portion of the property at what constituted a substantial profit. This was the first of many such transactions, all with increasing profitability, to the point where the company was realizing greater profits in land sales than in manufacturing. As a result, when another division of the same company planned expansion in the Chicago area, the company insisted on the acquisition of 100 acres, even though the utmost requirement for the proposed facility was only 10 acres.

Business Taxes and New Investment The fact that the corporate income tax falls upon the net income from capital makes it quite progressive (see below) but also encourages the substitution of labor for capital, and discourages new investment. We do not know how powerful these tendencies are. Labor is also heavily taxed through such payroll taxes as unemployment insurance and social security. And capital receives a multitude of special allowances such as investment tax credits and depreciation allowances above the true depreciation rate.   *73*

Hodge (1979) studied the impacts of corporate income and business property taxes on investment across a sample of metropolitan areas. Although he found no significant influence as a result of the corporate income tax, investment was reduced in some industries by high property taxes. Comparing his results with others that found no influence on location, he hypothesized that "while the total profitability of location in one area versus another is not significantly affected by the presence of high property taxes, these taxes do affect the most profitable combination of inputs to be employed." This effect has not been strong.

Another inefficiency arises because the effective tax rate in manufacturing and commercial property is above that on residential property. This, coupled with more generous federal income tax allowances for residential investments (Peterson, 1978), has favored the residential sector. This has likely contributed to the suburbanization of the relatively affluent, and, therefore, to the social and fiscal problems of central cities.

EQUITY

Judging the equity of the business tax structure involves knowing the incidence of the taxes, and here there are many unanswered questions. Observers of state/local business taxes have alleged that the structure lacks both horizontal and vertical equity, and has been regressive inasmuch as households have borne an "excessive" share of the tax burden.

Horizontal Equity

The statewide corporation income tax ensures that it is relatively equitable, at least spatially. The wide variation in the business property tax is much less equitable, as we have seen. However, the way in which the net income tax base is defined—the inclusion of special allowances—does not guarantee intersectoral horizontal equity. The tax structure has not developed by chance. Rather, it reflects the needs of the most powerful local business sectors. For example, those industries that are relatively concentrated[5] in New York City—apparel, textiles, printing, leather, and miscellaneous manufacturing—are labor intensive and low profit. Yet taxes in New York City fall most heavily on high-profit, capital intensive firms (Gerard, 1974). This tendency for the tax structure to favor established local industries is fine while those industries are growing. But when these industries fall into decline, it could provide a barrier to local redevelopment by deterring expansion in less fiscally-favored but potentially growing industries. The long-established client relationship between older sectors and local politicians makes it difficult to adjust to new economic realities. In this case, the state, whose legislative process may be less centered around specialized economic activities than that of the city government, could play an important function in neutralizing the local tax bias. Again, New York provides a good illustration. The state investment tax credit reduces New York City's anti-capital intensive bias, and thus encourages growth in non-traditional sectors.

Relation to
Public Services
There is no relation between the value of public services used and the amount of corporate income tax due. The property tax is in some way related, since the more valuable the menu of public services offered to a particular site, the greater the amount of property taxes paid. But shifting across jurisdictional boundaries destroys this simple relationship, and a firm in one jurisdiction may enjoy greater services than a similar firm in another jurisdiction at a lower tax "price."

Exporting Tax
Burdens Across
State Boundaries
Not all business tax revenues are paid by state residents, either directly or indirectly. For a company with a nation-wide market, consumers across the nation pay part of the business taxes—the exact amount is determined by the competitiveness of the industry and the particular advantages the state offers for the industry in question. Basically, the more competitive the industry, the less the ability of the individual firm to pass on local tax increases in the form of price increases. For example, Alaska's taxes on oil extraction do nothing to influence the price that is determined for oil in the world market. Louisiana and Texas can influence the price and availability of natural gas elsewhere because the price of domestically produced gas is below the world price. New York can export some of its tax burden by taxing tourist-related activities such as hotel occupancy—and Colorado can tax skiing—and these taxes will be paid by the residents of other states.

The equity of tax exporting depends upon two vital factors: 1) Who benefits from the local services paid for by the exported tax; and 2) who, in other states, pays the tax. Thus one could argue that New York City manages to export a tax burden on out-of-staters through its 4 percent sales tax surcharge on the state 4 percent rate because only the rich will travel from out of state to take advantage of the city's unique and high priced retail outlets. But the issue is less clear-cut. The sales tax is, overall, regressive (see the following chapters). Taxing recreation and tourism may be progressive because high income households tend to travel more extensively. But taxing raw material extraction may not be—for example, low income households spend a higher proportion of their income on utility bills than do high income households. Politically, it is expedient to try to export a portion of the local 75 tax burden. But there is no guarantee that this will improve equity.

One of the most difficult equity problems in developing state business tax policy rests with the computation of the taxable income of companies that operate in more than one state. Typically, the total taxable income of a company is "allocated" among the states in which the company operates according to three factors: the share of the company's sales, employment (or payroll), and plant and equipment within the state in question.[6] Each factor is weighted equally. Thus a company which has 75 percent of its employees and plant and 10 percent of its sales in a given state will pay taxes to that state on 52.8 percent of its taxable income.

The diversity of tax structures and tax base definitions has created an equity and administrative nightmare for multi-state firms. This leads to considerable inequity. From the viewpoint of the relationship between public services received and taxes paid, the share of employment and plant should be weighted much more heavily than sales, since the level of economic activity a much better measure of the use of local services (roads, transit use, fire protection, etc.). Horizontal equity is also impaired, because of two equally profitable and equal size companies, the one with the largest share of its sales out-of-state will pay the lowest tax.

In fact, the inclusion of sales in the formula creates an incentive for firms to move out of the state in which they make the majority of their sales. Consider a company that sells all of its output in state A, and that is able to move to state B, which has similar taxes and factor prices. It will reduce its tax burden by 33 percent by moving. Transportation costs will increase, and other factor prices may not be identical. But for a multibranch firm, there is a "tax incentive" to concentrate its employment expansion in branches in states where the firm's sales are relatively low.

Aware that firms in national markets can—quite inequitably—escape paying taxes in states where they only have sales, many states have either joined the Multi-State Tax Commission or adopted the Uniform Division of Income for Tax Purposes Act, which includes throwback provisions.[7] Under the throwback provision, sales by a company in other states in which the company pays no taxes (because it has no property or employees there) are counted as sales within the originating state. Membership is indicated in Table 14. Many of the non-members are located in the Northeast, where, as we shall see in the following chapter, the wasteful competition to offer tax incentives is most acute. If all states were members of these compacts, and if all states allocated income in the same way, then all companies would pay taxes on 100 percent of their taxable income, albeit at different rates, reflecting the different tax rates in different states. At present,
out-of-state sales by companies in non-compact states with neither

employees nor property out-of-state represent a major tax exemption. Non-membership in a tax compact should properly be regarded as a tax incentive.

The allocation system is inequitable not only because it includes sales, but also because of the way that the treatment of each of the factors differs among states. New York, Florida, and Massachusetts double-weight sales, reducing the portion of taxable income on which state taxes are paid by the hypothetical company cited above from 52.8 percent to 42.5 percent. Minnesota allows companies the option of weighting sales by 70 percent, and payroll and property by 15 percent each. Wisconsin allows either double weighting of sales, or two-thirds to sales and one-third to either property or payrolls. In addition, New York does not count executive personnel payrolls in the state as part of the state's share of the payroll, thus favoring headquarters establishments over production facilities. The Tax Compact has failed to bring uniformity to state tax codes principally because states fear the loss of tax revenues or the loss of a tax incentive (Cahoon and Brown, 1973).

An even more complex allocation issue is how to treat multinational corporations and their affiliates (ACIR, 1975; Ebel, 1978; and Hellerstein, 1976). Businesses argue that U.S.-based affiliates should be treated as separate entities with transactions with other units of the firm treated on an "arms length" basis, with each affiliate computing its own profits. However, this is expensive administratively—it is difficult to compute prices of goods sold between affiliates—and it ignores the inherent economic advantages of multinationals, which are, after all, formed to take advantage of the fact that they can cooperate more cheaply than if they were separate entities. California, Oregon, and Alaska attempt to treat corporations as unitary wholes. This issue must be addressed in the near future.

Shift Between Business and Households

Due (1961) has argued that more harmful than high taxes themselves is the *belief* that taxes are influential (p. 171).

The endless propaganda on the subject and strategy-inspired announcements of business firms when tax changes are being considered lead many legislators to exaggerate the influence of the taxes beyond any effect which they may have. The result is a potential danger of state cut-throat competition . . . In terror of "driving business out," legislatures become unwilling to adjust taxes to levels necessary to meet the desires of the community for services, and to bring their tax structures in line with popularly accepted ideas of equity in taxation.

These words sound depressingly prophetic. Cut-throat competition has become what Harrison and Kanter (1976) have called "The Great 77

State Robbery" (see following chapter), and an aversion to taxing businesses has led to residential taxes high enough to provoke the 2 to 1 passage of Proposition 13, and thriving fiscal limitations movements in most states (see Chapter 8).

Tax competition among states for business has shifted the tax burden from businesses to individuals. In 1948, personal income taxes provided 7.4 percent of states revenues, and corporate income taxes 8.7 percent. By 1977, while personal income taxes had swollen to 21.0 percent of states revenues, corporate income taxes had actually fallen to 7.6 percent.

Of course, all taxes are ultimately paid by households. The important question is what household activities and characteristics determine the amount of taxes paid. The corporate income tax is paid, at least in the "first round," by the owners of capital (stockholders) and the consumers of the product of the corporation. The personal income tax is paid by those working, and thus tends to discourage labor force participation. The personal income tax may be less progressive than the corporate income tax inasmuch as the ownership of capital tends to be concentrated among the relatively well-off. The net effect of the shift from the corporate income tax to the personal income tax has been to increase the regressivity of the tax system.

ADMINISTRATIVE COST   Administratively, the most convenient taxes are those that are simple add-ons to federal taxes, such as personal and business income taxes and the motor fuel tax, providing that the state employs the same tax base definition as the federal government. The property tax and sales tax involve much greater local efforts. Table 15 shows the ranking of major taxes with respect to their revenue predictability, stabilizing influence, and growth rate, averaged across all states. In terms of revenue growth, the local property tax out performs all state taxes during periods of inflation (Greytak and Jump, 1975). However, its salad days have been numbered by the taxpayer revolt. As might be expected, predictable taxes tend not to exert a strong stabilizing influence. States tend to select a tax package that balances these characteristics.

Companies operating in more than one state face special administrative problems due to the different taxing practices of the states. As Senator Abraham Ribicoff has argued: "The present system of state taxation is so unwieldly, so cumbersome, that many companies, particularly smaller ones, simply do not have the ability to meet the taxing requirements of all the jurisdictions in whch their goods are sold" (*Congressional Record,* S. 4850, March 15, 1973). This legal nightmare requires simplification.

Table 15
Stability, Growth, and Stabilizing Influence
of Selected State Tax Revenues

Tax	Stability of Revenues: Rank	Annual Growth Rate (per cent)	Stabilization Effect: Rank
Motor Fuel	1	5.9	3
Vehicle License	2	5.9	7
Sales	3	7.6	2
Alcoholic Beverage	4	6.0	6
Tobacco	5	8.4	5
Individual Income	6	11.8	4
Corporate Income	7	7.2	1

SOURCE: Adapted from William V. Williams et al., "The Stability, Growth and Stabilizing Influence of State Taxes," *National Tax Journal,* Vol. XXVI, No. 2 1973, p. 271.

WHAT SHOULD STATES DO?

The preceding discussion has revealed a number of problems with the present structure of business taxes. Taking steps to improve the system necessarily involves a leap of judgment, for we really do not understand the operation of the tax system. Improvement appears possible in a number of areas:

■ First, states should resist the tendency to cut business taxes to further economic development. In fact, a strong argument can be made to shift some of the state tax burden from individuals onto businesses.
■ Second, states should take steps to reduce interjurisdictional differences in business tax rates.
■ Third, states should review their allocation formulas for firms operating in more than one state.
■ Fourth, states should consider a Value Added Tax to replace complex business taxes.
■ Fifth, states should consider encouraging local jurisdictions to increase the tax rate on land relative to property improvements.

These issues are discussed in turn below.

Overall Tax Levels   We have argued that overall business tax levels have little impact on regional economic growth, although intrastate differences may lead to the migration of some companies out of high taxing central cities to suburban or exurban areas. States should review their state/local tax structure to ensure that it does not discriminate heavily against certain types of industry, and adjust it so that it is not significantly out-of-line with neighboring states. George Roniger (1978) of Citibank has argued, "because of technical progress, business, economic activity and jobs are no longer captive of any particular area. The ability of any government to extract an economic rent becomes daily less." States should lower taxes that are competitively out-of-line and let the market determine which industries will thrive, rather than tampering with the tax system to save a particular industry. Perhaps the most important guide should be the administrative savings of bringing taxes in line or simplifying the tax structure.

However, they should resist pressure to reduce business taxes to stimulate development, and should consider increasing the burden on industry relative to households. In large part, this could be done by closing many of the special tax loopholes that not only reduce the average tax burden on business but also create considerable inequity among businesses by favoring a relatively few large businesses which are not the main source of local job creation. After all, businesses enjoy only about half of the advantage of low local taxes—the rest goes to the federal government in the form of increased federal taxes.

Interstate Tax   There seems little chance that states
Allocation   acting individually, or through the Tax Compact, will make much progress in simplifying the taxation of multi-state businesses. A fear of revenue loss prevents the necessary steps from being taken. Federal legislation is needed to resolve the complex jurisdictional questions, particularly in the sales and use tax area, that have led to the present inequitable and inefficient system (Cahoon and Brown, 1973).

Interjurisdictional   More important than aggregate state tax
Tax Differences   levels are the wide tax variations—particularly in business property tax rates— among jurisdictions. Firms have moved away from high taxing central city locations toward suburban and even exurban areas. Much of this tax-induced movement does not reflect an efficiency gain but a response to the internal biases of the tax structure, and has tended to exacerbate the problems of fiscally troubled jurisdictions and multiply the benefits of growing areas.

80   In the previous chapter we outlined a number of steps that state governments could take to reduce fiscal inequities, steps that would help reduce the kind of disparities that have contributed to local economic problems.

The redistribution of fiscal burdens among jurisdictions should aim at complete equalization of tax burdens and services. It should be concerned with reducing the disparity of resources so that local areas can choose the quality and quantity of public services they wish. One major advantage of the state/local fiscal structure is that it allows local differentiation on the basis of local preferences. Redistribution can help to ensure that poor areas are not as constrained in their choices as they would be without aid.

Value Added Tax[8]   One alternative to the complex array of business taxes that many states and localities employ is a tax on value-added, patterned on the Michigan single business tax. The corporate income tax has several disadvantages. It is highly volatile. During recessions many firms earn no taxable income—and investment decisions by large firms may also sharply reduce taxable income. Revenues are, therefore, very difficult to predict. It is also complex to administer, and may discourage investment.

The value added tax, as applied in Michigan, is basically a tax on gross sales minus purchases of inputs from other companies. The computation of the tax base is:

> *Add*   Federal taxable income
> + total compensation paid
> + interest paid
> + dividends paid
> + depreciation[9]
> + lease rent payments
>
> *Subtract*   Interest received
> – dividends received
> – capital purchases[9]

There are several modifications that are used in the Michigan structure introduced in 1976. Some of the more important are:

■ A standard deduction of $34,000 prevents a proliferation of small tax returns.
■ Gross receipts limitation. The VAT base cannot exceed 50 percent of gross receipts.
■ Total compensation is limited to 65 percent of the tax base (35 percent for food retailers and private security guards).   *81*

■ Rental real estate. Taxpayers whose interest and depreciation exceed 70 percent of base are allowed to limit their base to 35 percent of gross receipts.

■ For financial institutions, interest received is *added* to the base and interest paid is *deducted.*

Who would benefit and who would lose from the introduction of a Michigan-type single business tax would depend on the taxes replaced and the specific provisions of the new tax. Some impression of the intersectoral shifts that may occur can be gained from some calculations performed by Cropper for a similar (but not identical) tax in New York City (Table 16, col. 2). The studies agree in the following general conclusions: Sectors experiencing a large *increase* in tax liabilities include construction, some manufacturing, and wholesale; those experiencing the most dramatic declines would be finance and some manufacturing. Among manufacturing industries, both studies agree that apparel, furniture, and leather would experience increased liabilities, while chemicals, instruments, and non-electrical machinery would face reduced liabilities. We cannot predict the employment change that would result from these hypothesized changes in tax liability. However, we can make the following qualitative observations:

■ In the manufacturing sector, taxes are reduced on industries that tend to be growing more rapidly nationally, while taxes are raised on declining industries. For growth industries, this may allow an area to capture a greater share of firm births and relocations, and encourage existing companies to grow more rapidly.

■ The high rate paid by services and retail will raise local prices, although some of the service burden will be exported. Some compensating reduction in the retail sales tax may be necessary. The in creased burden on medical and legal services may have a negative effect on city development.

Administratively, the Michigan experience favors the VAT. An ACIR (1977) study cites the Michigan Department of Treasury as concluding that, after a transition period, the administrative costs of the VAT will be less than those of the old tax system, and litigation costs will decline. Although its introduction was opposed by business, there has been no move to repeal it.

The corporate income tax is based on a firm's ability to pay. The VAT tax is more closely related to the value of public services received. The VAT base is a measure of the level of business activity—such as payroll—which, it is agreed, is proportional to the value of
82 local public services received—such as roads, police, and fire

Table 16
Two Estimates of the Percentage Change in Tax Liability by Sector as a Result of Replacing the Corporate Income Tax with a Value Added Tax

Sector	Change in Liability as Percent of Initial Liability	
	Cropper	Aaron
Agriculture	NA	+1524
Transport	+29*	+135
Oil and Gas	NA	+222
Services	-25	+330
Construction	+90	+346
Lumber	NA	+97
Amusements	NA	+80
Trade	NA	+75
Wholesale	+100	NA
Retail	-2	NA
Auto Repair	NA	+395
Food	+22	-15
Leather	+200	+26
Furniture	+150	+9
Textiles	0	+8
Metal Products	+38	+3
Metal Mining	NA	+8
Coal	NA	-5
Coal	NA	-5
Metals	NA	-11
Rubber	+50	-3
Misc. Manufacturing	-22	-19
Home Appliances	+8	-18
Printing	+45	-13
Machinery	-38	-36
Paper	+17	-41
Instruments	-10	-44
Finance	-35	-47
Ordnance	NA	-51
Tobacco	NA	-58
Radio and TV	NA	-57
Chemical	-35	-60
Automobiles	NA	-65
Communications	NA*	-59
Utilities	NA*	-72

SOURCE: Henry Aaron, "Differential Price Effects of a Value Added Tax," *National Tax Journal*, Vol. 21, No. 2, 1968, pp. 162-175; Maureen Cropper, "The Value Added Tax as Alternative to the General Corporation and Unincorporated Business Tax," New York City Finance Administration, August 1970.
NA means not available.
*Transport includes communications and utilities

protection.

The *advantages* of the VAT are:

■ It reduces taxes on relatively footloose growth industries in manufacturing, and on the rapidly growing financial sector, and increases it on captive firms.
■ It is easier to forecast revenues and is a stable source of revenues.
■ It reduces the tax disincentive on capital investment by distributing the burden across all factors of production.
■ It is administratively more simple than the combination taxes it replaces.

The *disadvantages* are:

■ Transition could be disruptive.
■ The retail, wholesale and special services sectors would experience a sharp increase in taxes. Special services (medical, legal, etc.) are a major source of urban employment growth.

Table 17 summarizes the difference between the Michigan Value Added Tax and more traditional business taxes.

Site Value Taxation   An alternative to property taxation that is receiving growing attention is land value taxation—a tax on the value of land exclusive of any building improvement.[10] The present property tax is a combination of two taxes, one on land—the value of location—and the second is a tax on the value of improvements. The tax on improvements discourages new property investment, while the tax on vacant land is so small that speculators leave many vacant lots unimproved.[11]

Land value taxation is politically feasible. Municipalities in Australia and New Zealand use land value taxation. In Pennsylvania, several cities have used their authority for land value taxation for municipal levies, but are limited to taxing land values at twice the rate levied on buildings. School and county levies are excluded. Moreover, state legislative proposals have been introduced to extend the use of land value taxes.

A case study of the impact of the land value taxation in Sydney, Australia endorses its effectiveness (Archer, 1972). The study concluded that the most important aspect of the tax was that it put pressure "on owners to sell their property for redevelopment if they cannot or will not develop it themselves." This is accomplished by the cash outflow required by the site value system (p. 38). This also:

84 ■ Promotes a more active and informed market in redevelopment

Table 17
Comparison of the Michigan Value Added Tax to the Typical State Business Tax Structure

Issues	Typical State Structure	Michigan Value Added Tax
Composition	Complex—relies on many tax bases such as corporate, partnership, and sole proprietorship income, capital value, business inventory.	Simpler—replaces income, capital value, and franchise bases with the value added.[1]
Philosophy	Emphasis on net profits of business firm, therefore related to *ability* to pay.	Emphasis on business activity (use of capital and labor), therefore more closely related to *benefits received.*
Uniformity of Treatment of Business Firms	Scores poorly because the tax liability of the firm often depends on the form of business organization, i.e., whether or not the firm is incorporated.	Scores well on uniformity—businesses are taxed on basis of economic size rather than form of business organization.
Uniformity of Treatment of Capital and Labor	Taxes fall more heavily on capital than on labor—net profits, inventories, and net worth taxes in particular. Income of corporation is taxed not only when earned but also when distributed to shareholders.	No bias against capital because the impact of the tax is on capital and labor in proportion to their contribution to the value added to the product.
Incentive for Increased Capital Investment	Not available unless provided by special treatment such as accelerated depreciation or investment credit.	No inherent discrimination against capital. One benefit-may reduce pressure to grant special concessions.
Stability of Revenue	Heavy reliance on income tax base results in sensitivity of collections to changes in the economy. To taxpayers this appears as an advantage, because lower profits result in lower tax liability.	Inclusion in the tax base of compensation to labor results in more stability in tax liability. To taxpayers this appears as a disadvantage, because taxes must be paid even if no profits are earned.

[1]Local real estate and personal property taxes on machinery and equpment are still paid by Michigan businesses.

SOURCE: Compiled by ACIR staff, and reproduced in the Advisory Commission for Intergovernmental Relations, *The Michigan Single Business Tax,* Washington, D.C. March 1978.

properties.
■ Facilitates the consolidation of smaller sites.
■ Allows developers to expand their role in the redevelopment building market at the expense of single project redevelopment by property owners.

Transition to a site value tax system involves considerable disruption. It should, therefore, be carried out slowly. In fact, the site value tax need not be regarded as an alternative to the property tax, but as merely a modification. The rate on land could be raised relative to that on buildings; the tax on improvements need not be reduced to zero. In many areas, this may only bring into line a property tax which frequently taxes land at a lower rate than improvements. However, Hawaii, which introduced a modified site value tax in 1963, intending to slowly raise the rate on land relative to buildings, found the process too cumbersome and repealed the differential tax in July 1978. Although the Tax Foundation of Hawaii argued the differential was ineffective, another recent study estimated that had a significant differential been tried, it would have reduced sprawl (Pollock and Shoup, 1977). The tax was recommended for New York (Finkelstein, 1975), but rejected for the District of Columbia (Peterson, 1978). Opponents argue that zoning, removal of red tape, and land assembly grants are more effective incentives than a differential rate on land and improvements. Many jurisdictions already assess land and improvements separately. The rate on land could be steadily increased while that on improvements is reduced. A temporary circuit breaker could be used to ensure that no one experienced radical annual changes in tax payments.
    The problem with implementing a land value tax is that there are relatively few unimproved land sites that change hands in any year from which estimates of surrounding land values could be assessed. However, it is possible, by regression analysis of full property values (land plus buildings), to estimate the contribution of site value to total value. This change, therefore, requires relatively sophisticated assessment techniques, a practice that few jurisdictions have adopted. However, Oldman and Teachout (1977) conclude that even the most sophisticated assessment technique "could not withstand court appeal by an aggrieved taxpayer, because none adequately establishes (according to the criteria employed by courts) the market value of the land underlying individual properties" (Ebel, 1978, p. 7). But, they argue, legal and administrative remedies are potentially available to make the tax operational.
    In addition, there is some dispute concerning the equity of the change. Landowners of property with a high ratio of improvements
86 to land value—owners of office buildings, hotels, theaters, and some

manufacturing—would receive a tax reduction, while single family homes and the owners of vacant land would experience a tax increase. The site value tax, or an increase in the tax on land, may not be efficient in all places. Rapidly growing areas are most likely to benefit, since they experience the greatest problem with land speculation. For example, areas that already effectively assess land will benefit less than those that under-assess land. Also, those jurisdictions that have introduced tax abatement or exemption on any increases in property values have removed much of the disincentive impact of the property tax. Peterson (1978) estimates this is equivalent to a 25 percent reduction in the cost of capital, but concludes that this has not been a major incentive and that cash grants on improvements have been more effective. Also, in many jurisdictions, vacant land is effectively taxed at rates well below the rate on improvements due to poor assessment techniques. Simply enforcing a uniform rate, as is mandated in almost all jurisdictions, would improve the equity and efficiency of the tax. While there are potential problems with a site value tax, or an increase in the tax on land relative to improvements, it is an option that merits further consideration.

FOOTNOTES TO CHAPTER 5

1. These are Nevada, Ohio, South Dakota, Texas and Washington. In addition, some cities have local corporate income taxes. The large cities are:

Ohio		Michigan	
Akron	1.5 percent	Detroit	2.0 percent
Cincinnati	2.0 percent	Flint	1.0 percent
Cleveland	1.0 percent	Grand Rapids	1.0 percent
Columbus	1.5 percent	Lansing	1.0 percent
Dayton	1.75 percent		
Toledo	1.5 percent	Kentucky	
Youngstown	1.5 percent	Louisville	2.2 percent
Missouri		New York	
Kansas City	1.0 percent	New York City	9.5 percent
St. Louis	1.0 percent		
		Oregon	
		Multnomah County	0.6 percent

2. This is different from a retail sales tax, which taxes retail sales regardless of where the goods are produced.

3. Iowa has no business income tax but taxes the gross value of sales. Michigan has a tax on value added (see this chapter, below).

4. An inverse example is provided by the time when tea duties were slashed in the late nineteenth century by the British government: revenues rose because smuggling became unprofitable.

5. "Relatively concentrated" means that employment in these industries employs a higher share of the city's labor force than they do of the nation's labor.

6. Iowa is one exception—it uses a single factor—gross sales.

7. The Multistate Tax Compact and the Uniform Division of Income for Tax Assessment.

8. The Value Added Tax in Michigan replaced not only the corporate income tax, but also a corporate franchise tax, an inventory tax, a business intangible tax, a financial corporations tax, an insurance company and a savings and loan company privilege tax.

9. There are three forms of VAT that differ in the way they treat depreciation:
■ *Consumption VAT:* deducts purchases of capital equipment but does tax depreciation.
■ *Net Income VAT:* taxes capital equipment when purchased but does not tax depreciation (i.e., assumes 100 percent depreciation in the first year).
■ *Gross Product VAT:* Taxes both capital purchases and depreciation.

10. See Becker (1969); Carlson (1977); Cuddington (1978); and testimony before the House Committee on Banking, Currency and Housing by Lowell Harris, George Peterson, Philip Finkelstein, and Arthur Becker, September 28, 1976, reprinted by the Committee in *Rebirth of the American City,* U.S. House of Representatives, Washington, D.C., 1976.

11. In the 1950s, the lot comprised about 10 percent of the cost of a home; today, it is 25 percent (Carlson, 1977).

6
WHAT SHOULD STATES DO ABOUT TAX INCENTIVES?

A direct result of the belief that business taxes really matter has been the proliferation of special tax incentives designed by states and localities to attract new businesses and to encourage expansion and new investment among existing firms. There are no reliable estimates as to how much in tax receipts are currently foregone under these programs. Smokestack chasing is *de rigeur* for states that adopt an aggressive development program. However, the clear conclusion of this chapter is that, for the most part, *firms are rewarded for doing what they would have done even in the absence of the incentive.* The fixation of states and localities on attracting manufacturing firms by whatever fiscal means possible has arisen from the belief that a new firm will yield a fiscal surplus—that is, its contribution to local tax revenues outweighs the costs of providing public services to the firm and its employees (Groves and Riew, 1963; and Kee, 1968). More recent studies, however, have shown that a new firm is not an unmixed blessing. Even in a community with relative high unemployment, 100 new jobs does not reduce local unemployment by 100. At least 50 of those slots are likely to be filled by new inmigrants who will require schooling, streets, sewers, and water. Other jobs might be filled by those not previously in the labor force. Secondary employment—retail and services—will also make demands for public services and do not necessarily yield a fiscal surplus. In fact, Gerweck and Epp (1976) show that secondary employment impacts may halve the net fiscal surplus resulting from a new factory. *When the state abates or exempts local taxes to induce a firm to move in, the net benefits may well become negative.*

The adoption of tax incentives tailored to the wishes of the few Fortune 500 companies that move is based on the mistaken belief that there is a fixed stock of manufacturing jobs in the nation and that the only way a state can improve its relative position is to steal from other states. The behavior is analogous to that of the homeowner who tries to maintain a green lawn by stealing his neighbors turf—at great effort —every time his own land turns brown. It is much easier and more productive to water regularly and apply fertilizer. We should reiterate the conclusions from earlier chapters. There are very few footloose firms. If growth is to be accelerated, then it must come from increasing the local company birth rate or from expansion in existing local companies, especially small firms. *Development efforts must focus upon* **89**

Table 18
Financial Assistance, Tax Incentives, and Special Services Offered by State and Local Governments

FINANCIAL ASSISTANCE

	State Sponsored Industrial Development Authority	Privately Sponsored Development Credit Corporation	State Authority or Agency Revenue Bond Financing	State Authority or Agency General Obligation Bond Financing	City and/or County Revenue Bond Financing	City and/or County General Obligation Bond Financing	State Loans for Building Construction	State Loans for Equipment/Machinery	City and/or County Loans for Building Construction	City and/or County Loans for Equipment/Machinery	State Loan Guarantees for Building Construction	State Loan Guarantees for Equipment/Machinery	City and/or County Loan Guarantees for Building Construction	City and/or County Loan Guarantee for Equipment/Machinery	State Financing Aid for Existing Plant Expansions	State Matching Funds for City and/or County Industrial Financing Programs	State Incentive for Establishing Industrial Plants in Areas of High Unemployment	City and/or County Incentive for Establishing Industrial Plants in Areas of High Unemployment
Alabama	●	●			●	●									●			
Alaska	●	●		●	●	●	●	●							●			
Arizona					●													
Arkansas	●	●			●	●					●							
California		●			●													●
Colorado		●			●													
Connecticut	●	●	●	●	●	●	●	●	●	●	●	●			●	●	●	●
Delaware	●		●	●			●	●			●	●			●			
Florida		●			●													
Georgia	●	●			●	●	●											
Hawaii	●		●		●	●	●								●	●	●	
Idaho																		
Illinois	●	●			●		●	●							●			
Indiana	●				●						●	●			●			
Iowa		●			●													
Kansas		●			●	●												
Kentucky	●	●			●	●	●								●			
Louisiana		●			●	●												
Maine	●		●		●						●	●			●			
Maryland	●	●			●	●					●	●			●	●	●	
Massachusetts		●			●	●			●	●	●				●	●		●
Michigan	●		●		●	●	●	●			●	●			●	●	●	
Minnesota	●	●	●		●	●	●	●	●						●		●	
Mississippi	●	●			●										●		●	●
Missouri		●			●			●							●		●	
Montana		●			●					●								
Nebraska		●			●										●			
Nevada					●												●	●
New Hampshire	●	●	●		●						●	●			●			
New Jersey	●		●	●	●	●	●				●	●			●	●	●	●
New Mexico	●				●	●												
New York	●	●	●	●	●		●	●	●	●					●		●	●
North Carolina																		
North Dakota	●	●	●	●	●		●								●		●	
Ohio	●	●	●		●		●				●	●			●		●	
Oklahoma	●	●	●		●										●		●	
Oregon	●	●	●		●										●		●	
Pennsylvania	●	●	●		●		●		●						●		●	●
Rhode Island	●	●	●		●						●	●			●			
South Carolina	●	●	●		●													
South Dakota					●													
Tennessee	●		●		●		●				●	●			●			
Texas					●		●	●										
Utah	●	●			●													
Vermont	●	●	●		●		●				●	●			●	●	●	●
Virginia	●	●			●													
Washington	●	●			●	●							●				●	
West Virginia	●	●			●		●		●	●					●	●	●	●
Wisconsin					●	●												
Wyoming		●			●													
STATE TOTALS	32	34	29	7	45	21	19	13	8	7	14	13	1	1	29	9	17	10

Table 18 (continued)

TAX INCENTIVES — SPECIAL SERVICES

Corporate Income Tax Exemption	Personal Income Tax Exemption	Excise Tax Exemption	Tax Exemption or Moratorium on Land, Capital Improvements	Tax Exemption or Moratorium on Equipment, Machinery	Inventory Tax Exemption on Goods in Transit (Freeport)	Tax Exemptions on Manufacturers' Inventories	Sales Use Tax Exemption on New Equipment	Tax Exemption on Raw Materials Used in Manufacture	Tax Credits for Use of Specified State Products	Tax Stabilization Agreements for Specified Industries	Tax Exemption to Encourage Research and Development	Accelerated Depreciation of Industrial Equipment	State Financed Speculative Building	City and or County Financed Speculative Building	Cities and or Counties Provide Free Land for Industry	State-Owned Industrial Park Sites	City and or County-Owned Industrial Park Sites	State Funds for City and or County Development Related Public Works Projects	State Funds for City and or County Master Plans	State Funds for City and or County Recreational Projects	STATE TOTALS	
•	•	•	•	•	•	•	•	•	•	•						•	•	•	•	•	21	Alabama
			•	•		•	•		•							•	•	•	•	•	14	Alaska
•			•	•		•	•				•							•		•	11	Arizona
			•	•		•	•					•						•	•	•	13	Arkansas
			•	•		•	•							•	•			•	•	•	9	California
			•	•		•	•				•						•	•	•	•	10	Colorado
	•		•	•	•	•	•	•			•						•	•	•	•	26	Connecticut
•			•	•		•	•	•		•							•				19	Delaware
•			•	•		•	•	•	•			•		•				•			9	Florida
	•		•	•		•	•	•			•						•	•	•	•	14	Georgia
•	•		•	•	•	•	•				•				•			•	•	•	19	Hawaii
			•	•	•	•					•						•	•		•	8	Idaho
			•			•					•						•	•	•	•	14	Illinois
				•	•		•				•				•			•	•	•	17	Indiana
			•	•	•		•				•						•				7	Iowa
•	•		•	•	•	•	•				•				•	•		•			14	Kansas
•	•		•	•	•	•	•				•				•			•	•	•	16	Kentucky
•	•	•		•	•	•	•	•			•			•				•		•	14	Louisiana
			•	•		•	•		•	•	•	•	•			•					16	Maine
			•	•		•	•		•	•		•	•			•			•	•	20	Maryland
•			•	•		•	•				•		•					•	•	•	21	Massachusetts
•	•		•	•	•	•	•	•		•	•		•					•	•	•	18	Michigan
•	•		•	•	•	•	•	•			•		•	•	•			•	•	•	25	Minnesota
•			•	•	•	•	•				•							•	•	•	18	Mississippi
•				•	•		•				•							•			13	Missouri
	•		•	•		•				•		•						•	•	•	12	Montana
•			•	•		•					•				•			•			10	Nebraska
•				•		•					•							•			9	Nevada
•			•	•	•	•	•				•		•				•	•	•	•	19	New Hampshire
•	•		•	•	•	•	•	•			•		•	•			•	•	•	•	24	New Jersey
			•	•		•					•					•		•			8	New Mexico
•	•	•	•	•	•	•	•			•			•				•	•	•	•	27	New York
			•	•		•					•				•	•		•	•	•	10	North Carolina
•	•		•	•	•	•	•			•		•		•				•	•	•	23	North Dakota
•	•		•	•		•	•				•							•	•	•	21	Ohio
•	•		•	•	•	•	•				•							•	•	•	23	Oklahoma
•	•		•	•		•	•				•				•		•	•	•	•	19	Oregon
			•	•	•	•	•				•				•	•		•	•	•	20	Pennsylvania
•	•	•	•	•	•	•	•		•	•		•						•	•	•	18	Rhode Island
			•	•	•	•	•				•					•	•		•	•	15	South Carolina
•	•	•		•	•	•					•					•	•		•	•	12	South Dakota
•		•	•	•	•	•					•					•	•	•	•	•	22	Tennessee
			•	•		•									•			•	•	•	15	Texas
			•	•	•		•											•			7	Utah
				•	•		•		•		•				•	•		•	•	•	22	Vermont
•	•		•	•	•		•					•		•				•	•	•	14	Virginia
•	•	•	•	•	•		•										•	•	•	•	16	Washington
•	•		•	•		•	•										•	•	•	•	19	West Virginia
			•	•	•	•	•								•			•	•	•	13	Wisconsin
•	•			•	•	•	•										•	•	•	•	10	Wyoming
19	10	23	38	41	37	33	44	3	4	9	25	5	29	14	8	47	34	31	38		STATE TOTALS	

SOURCE: Adapted from "The Fifty Legislative Climates," *Industrial Development,* January/February 1978.

...e that the form in which states offer financial services, tax incentives, and special ...ces differ widely. For a full description see the original source.

the overall economic climate, not upon expensive incentives to a few firms.[1]

Business incentive programs are designed not only to attract foot-loose industries but also to encourage existing firms to expand their level of operations to generate jobs locally. However, as we argued in the preceding chapter, high local business income and property taxes have not had much influence on investment decisions, and, therefore, temporary reductions as a reward for purchasing additional equipment are unlikely to have much impact. In fact, we will argue that reducing the tax on the income from capital to create jobs is perverse, since the policy does nothing to reduce the cost of labor. If a state insists on using tax incentives to generate employment, and we cannot hold out much hope for their effectiveness, it should try to counter the impacts of payroll taxes by introducing wage subsidies.

A systematic examination of business incentives is a large undertaking because of their bewildering variety. For example, we argued in the preceding chapter that the double weighting of out-of-state sales and non-membership in tax compacts should be considered as tax incentives. Table 18 lists some of the financial services, tax incentives, and special programs provided by states for firms. The incentives include exemptions from personal and corporate income tax for those firms moving in, guarantees that property taxes will not increase for 5 or 10 years, exemption of new manufacturing equipment from the sales tax, and accelerated depreciation. Special services encompass free land for industry, state funds for research and development, and state help in bidding on federal procurement contracts. Financial assistance runs from tax exempt revenue bond financing to state matching funds for local development efforts. The discussion in this chapter focuses mainly upon tax incentives, but some of these other development measures are also briefly discussed.

A review of aggressive promotion campaigns by states and cities reveals just how internecine the competition has become.[2] New York State advertises that "We're not giving business the business any more. We're giving it a break", Chicago claims to be "Fund City", and San Diego "is zoned for success," according to its $500,000 a year campaign. The Texas Industrial Commission advises, "When the old corporate tax bite eats away profits, CUT OUT FOR TEXAS." In 1977, nearly $7 million was spent in magazines alone, and the number of business promotion ads jumped by 40 percent in the first three months of 1978.

The rivalry for footloose industries has often been cast as the old and established Snowbelt trying to protect its economic base from the aggressive inroads of the tax cutting Sunbelt. The truth is very different. The fiercest rivalry is between adjacent states—a cut-throat regional

struggle that mortgages future tax receipts and places established factories at a disadvantage relative to the brash newcomers. Ohio and Pennsylvania rival for Volkswagen, while steel companies languish. Firms leave New York State for adjacent Connecticut, New Jersey, and Pennsylvania. Most of the states offering twenty or more special programs (cf. Table 18) are in the Northeast.[3] In fact, public pressure for such measures is most intense in states where the economic development rate has been slower than the national average. A recent survey by the Advisory Commission on Intergovernmental Relations (1977) suggests that public support for tax incentives for business is closely related to local economic fortunes and prospects.

Question: Some states have passed laws which give special tax breaks or other incentives to industries that will locate facilities or expand present operations in that state. Do you favor or oppose such a policy?

	Percent of Total U.S.	Percent of Respondents by Region			
		Northeast	North Central	South	West
Favor	50	57	48	52	42
Oppose	36	30	38	30	49
No Opinion	14	13	13	18	9

SOURCE: ACIR, *Changing Public Attitudes on Government and Taxes,* Washington, D.C., 1977.

If this wasteful competition is to cease, state officials must educate their constituents about the futility of these programs.

EFFICIENCY   Do tax incentives work? Do they attract new firms and encourage new investment? There is no evidence that these concessions have had any significant effect on local growth.[4] Tax concessions are ineffective precisely because state and local taxes are, themselves, relatively unimportant as location determinants.

The tax battle is not only waged between states, but between counties and municipalities within a state. County officials offered a new bicarbonate plant a 12 year property tax break for moving to Seneca County, Ohio, yet the corporation's controller was quoted as saying, "The tax abatement was a nice kicker on the end, but we chose Ohio mainly because of its strategic location for distribution and market growth."[5]

Weinstein (1977, p. 75) concludes that:

Taken as a whole, these incentives probably represent a serious misallocation of resources. In the main the government is subsidizing firms   *93* for performing activities they would have undertaken in any case. Furthermore, when one considers that any incentive designed to reduce a company's state or local tax bill will increase that firm's federal tax liability—the superfluity of tax incentives becomes even more apparent. The result is a form of reverse revenue sharing in the amount of 48 cents on the dollar.

Even if local investment expanded by 2 percent as a result of a local investment tax credit, this still means that 98 percent of credits are flowing to firms that would have invested anyway.

Not only are tax incentives ineffective, they are also costly. Harrison and Kanter (1976) estimate that the ten tax incentives offered by Massachusetts cost at least $100 million a year, revenues that could be used to reduce residential taxes or improve local services. In just over a year, New York City has exempted $461 million in properties from $44 million in taxes. St. Louis has exempted nearly $1 billion worth of real estate—half the city's property tax base. By the early 1980s, Michigan's incentives may cost $50 million in state revenues and $30 million in local revenues.

Of course, to determine whether a measure is worthwhile, it is important to compare its benefits with its costs. A local development incentive does not have to be very effective to be worthwhile if its costs are negligible. The few studies that have compared the costs and benefits of fiscal incentives do not provide a very optimistic picture, although they do show that, under some conditions, fiscal incentives may be cost effective. Morgan and Hackbart (1974) concluded that if locally accruing benefits are not less than 50 percent of value added in a local plant and not less than 5 percent of the investment is a result of an incentive, then that incentive may be cost effective from the viewpoint of the state, although, as we argued in Chapter 2, there is no guarantee that the nation as a whole is not worse off.

What of the few firms that may respond to some kind of fiscal incentive?[6] Are they the type of firm that can assist meeting local development goals? In an important article, Harrison and Kanter (1976) argue that the type of firm most likely to respond are firms in highly competitive industries, for whom small differences in costs make the difference between success and failure. Yet, they argue:

... these are the industries that in general pay lower wages, offer worse working conditions, provide less stable employment, and make it more difficult for labor to organize. Thus, incentives that lower costs of doing business appear to be policy instruments—if they work at all—that are most likely to "goose" the sector of the economy with the least desirable jobs, while providing windfall profits to the segments of the business community that needs them the least (p. 59).

In short, tax incentives are ineffective, and what little impact they might have is not necessarily desirable.

EQUITY Not only are tax incentives inefficient, they are also inequitable. First, the incentive will tend to go to large and financially healthy firms, since these firms will be earning a taxable income.[7] Nearly 50 percent of all firms had no federal tax liability in 1971, and 95 percent of all firms had federal tax liabilities of less than $25,000 (Table 19). Unless the incentives take the form of credits, most firms will not be influenced.

Second, why should a new company pay less in taxes than a comparable firm that is well established in the state? State policy makers should be aware that this program may harm their well established firms, by placing them at a competitive disadvantage with newer competitors locating in other tax cutting states.

A third equity problem is that state and local officials often weave

Table 19
Cumulative Distributions of Income Tax Liabilities
for Corporations Filing Income Tax Returns
in 1971, by Sector

Sector	Income Tax Liability		
	0	Below $10,000	Below $25,000
All Industries	49.0	90.5	94.8
Agriculture	53.3	94.2	97.8
Mining	61.2	86.6	91.8
Contract Construction	50.9	91.0	95.3
Manufacturing	48.4	82.4	87.8
Transportation and Communication and Utilities	53.1	90.6	94.5
Wholesale and Retail	43.1	88.7	94.2
Fire	47.3	92.1	95.9
Services	56.5	95.7	98.1

SOURCE: Robert Tannenwald, "Federal Tax Approaches to Regional Development," in Committee on Appropriations, *Patterns of Regional Change*, U.S. Senate, Washington, D.C., October 1977, p. 697.

together a special "development package" for a particular firm that is considering moving in, threatening to move out, or considering a major expansion. Naturally, officials can only do so if the firm is large. Programs can rarely reach down to small firms, even though past experience suggests that such firms are the main source of employment expansion.

A final equity issue is that almost all incentives are offered to the owners of capital; few are offered to labor. We have argued that payroll taxes and minimum wage laws have priced low-skilled labor out of jobs. It is possible to imagine that the long run impact of tax incentives might be to encourage the substitution of capital for labor and therefore to *reduce* the number of jobs, while enhancing the aggregate returns to the ownership of capital. If this impact is explicitly understood, enthusiasm for present tax incentives may diminish.

ADMINISTRATIVE COST The effectiveness of tax incentives might be greater if they were targeted toward smaller firms, which are the main engines of local growth (Schmenner, 1978). However, while it is administratively simple to identify and approach the relatively few large companies that are considering relocation, the market of small firms is impossibly large. There is a much higher failure rate among small firms, and thus the risk of providing a financial assistance/tax incentive package to these firms is high, and the overall administrative cost is likely to be much higher.

OTHER BUSINESS INCENTIVE PROGRAMS As Table 19 graphically shows, the menu offered to the lucky few businesses to arouse the interest of development officials is not limited to tinkering with the tax structure. The enterprising firm can enjoy low leases on publicly-built facilities, low interest rate loans, cash grants, and publicly-trained employees. Are these other measures more effective than tax incentives?

Our overall answer is that most of these programs are not of major importance to influencing company decisions. We can only touch on these programs briefly in this paper.[9]

Tax Exempt Bonds A major problem with state and local efforts to attract or retain industry is that they rely upon tax expenditures—tax exemption of bond interest payments, for example—and that these are very inefficient ways of channeling subsidies to industry. The federal tax structure has exempted the interest from state and local bonds, as well as bonds sold by local public development corporations, from federal income tax.

96

State and local authorities have, for the most part, extended this exemption to local income taxes. There are several problems with this form of capital market subsidy.

First, only a part of the tax receipts foregone by the federal and state treasuries actually go to reduce borrowing costs. The remainder is a subsidy to high income bond holders. Estimates place the personal subsidy at between 25 percent and 30 percent of foregone revenues. Morris (1976) estimates that the tax exemption of bond interest cost the federal treasury $4.8 billion in 1976, of which only $3.5 billion effectively reduced state and local borrowing costs. Intramarginal bondholders—those with very high marginal income tax rates who would have been satisfied with a lower tax free yield—enjoyed a subsidy of $1.3 billion. Total state and local interest payments in that year were approximately $10.5 billion.

Second, the market for tax free bonds has been narrowing as investors turn to alternative shelters. At the same time, public issues have had to compete with pollution control bonds. Commercial banks purchased 90 percent of net purchases in 1968, but only 10 percent in 1975. The lowering of the maximum federal income tax rate on personal income in 1976 may have reduced the number of household buyers. Pollution control bonds, granted tax exempt status in 1969, grew from only $100 million in 1971 to $2.2 billion in 1975, a year when state and local governments issued $31.6 billion in long term debt.

Third, the interest on state and local bonds is much more volatile than on taxable issues. This volatility results from the selling of municipal bonds by banks during periods when alternatives become much more attractive. The price falls and yields rise to induce other investors to absorb these sales. For example, the average yield on Aa municipals rose from 62 percent of the yield on Aa corporate bonds in January 1968 to 73 percent in June of 1970. A similar shift occurred between 1973 and 1975. A period when inflationary expectations rise leads to more rapid increases in public borrowing costs than in private borrowing costs. Soaring interest rates deter necessary public investments.

Local Credit Agencies Slow growth, it is popularly believed, may arise because of a shortage of loanable funds, or because of high interest rates. High interest rates apply nationwide, and although some regional variation is apparent (Straszheim, 1969), it is not significantly related to growth differences. The belief in a "credit-gap" has spawned a number of state and local practices that provide subsidized loans. Loan subsidies may be available through industrial development bonds, statewide industrial credit corporations, or state industrial finance corporations. **97**

Industrial Development Bonds. Mississippi, in 1936, was the first state to authorize local industrial bonds. Local authorities are authorized to issue bonds to construct industrial facilities for lease to private firms. Interest on these bonds is exempt from federal and local income tax.[10] Aided firms pay rentals sufficient to cover the principal and interest on the bonds and facility maintenance. Facilities are generally exempt from state and local property taxation. Bonds may be secured by the taxing power of the issuing government (general obligation bonds) or by the property acquired with the bond revenue (revenue bonds).

Statewide Development Credit Corporations. Maine authorized the first state development credit corporation in 1969, and now 30 states have such corporations. These corporations are state chartered but privately financed, using revenues from stock sales, private borrowing, or from retained earnings. Their loans usually go to small, established manufacturing firms. Although most loans go for plant and equipment purchases, a sizable number do go for working capital. Almost all of these corporations have made profits. In all states except Alaska, local authorities have been permitted to set up development credit corporations.

There are now several thousand local development corporations concentrated in nonindustrialized areas and in industrialized areas with persistent, high unemployment rates. Some operate under the auspices of local chambers of commerce, others under local jurisdictions; some are non-profit corporations, others are organized as profit making corporations. Funds are raised through donations, sale of stock, private borrowing, or from the Small Business Administration. Most funds are used to construct industrial facilities to the specifications of particular firms; these facilities are then leased to the firms. Funds are also used to make working capital loans, purchase land, construct sites, or purchase leases on an anticipatory basis.

State Industrial Finance Authorities. Started in New Hampshire in 1955, there are now 13 states that have authorized such programs. State authorities either guarantee loans made by private lenders or make direct loans from state funds to industry by issuing industrial development bonds (IDBs).

Proponents of IDBs have pointed out that by exempting interest payments from federal taxable income, the rate of return that must be earned is reduced from 15 percent to 10 percent, allowing expansion into more marginal investments. Stober and Falk (1969) point out that the advantage also includes the fact that the local government that builds the facility faces no corporation income tax, and can thus break even if it only makes enough in receipts to cover interest payments. The lease payments it charges to industry are, therefore, less than the implicit lease payments a private firm would have to charge itself.

One problem with the variety of loan programs offered by states and localities is that they are usually administered by a variety of agencies, inhibiting cooperation and proliferating confusion. Milwaukee, by contrast, administers three loan programs—for housing rehabilitation, commercial rehabilitation and small business financing—through one super agency, the Department of City Development. The result has been the successful coordination and leverage of public funds.

Questionnaires that have been used to assess the role of IDBs are rarely convincing. In Alabama, one-third of 54 firms using IDB financing claimed they would have located elsewhere without that incentive, but fully ninety percent of eligible firms failed to take advantage of the provision (Alabama Business Research Council, 1970).

Overall, it appears that these loan subsidies are not cost effective development tools. States and local areas would be better off making direct cash grants to businesses—firms would feel as well off with a cash grant that is less than the foregone tax receipts under the present system—although this may not be politically palatable. Perhaps the answer is to concentrate on infrastructure development and new development finance corporations—policies whose benefits are less tied to a few large corporations.

WHAT CAN STATES DO?

The preceding discussion suggests several areas where states can take action or lobby for federal assistance:

■ First, interstate tax competition should be reduced, perhaps with federal assistance.
■ Second, states should act to reduce interjurisdictional tax incentive competition within their own borders.
■ Third, income tax exemption for development financing bond interest payments should be replaced by interest subsidies.
■ Fourth, states should focus on infrastructure development and cutting red tape rather than on tax incentives.
■ Finally, if special incentives are to be used, they should be in the form of broadly applied wage subsidies rather than capital incentives.

Interstate Tax Competition

It is difficult for the individual state to act. Failure to offer tax incentives may well bring cries from local industry. Political opponents will be given a readily available, if ultimately fallacious, platform. The gubernatorial campaigns during the fall of 1978 echoed with cries for tax breaks. It seems clear that federal legislation is needed to make it hard for states to offer these bribes.

Can the federal government help? Outright prohibition is probably impossible, or extremely difficult, on constitutional grounds. There are, however, some measures that could be implemented:[11]

■ Overall Economic Development Plans prepared by states and municipalities that offer special incentives could be rejected by EDA on the grounds that they fail to treat all companies equally. This would make those areas ineligible for Title II loan guarantees, and, perhaps, for Title IX grants.
■ HUD could reject community development plans on the same grounds, and hold up CDBG and UDAG funds.
■ General Revenue Sharing funds could be reduced for each dollar of local taxes foregone through an exemption or abatement program that did not apply uniformly to all firms.
■ The corporation income tax code could include a federal tax penalty on firms granted special local tax exemptions.

It is difficult to assess the effectiveness of an initiative of this sort. State and local governments may substitute direct expenditures on infrastructure and business services in order to attract businesses. Reduced tax expenditures may influence economic development patterns.

Success depends on how broadly the anti-tax provisions are applied, and how much effort is devoted to enforcing them. Experience with hastily implemented countercyclical programs suggests that local governments can avoid ill-defined and loosely enforced federal regulations (Vernez and Vaughan, 1978). On the other hand, threat of withdrawal of education grants has been used, with some success, to encourage the integration of schools and the provision of special school services. Without a careful review of the relationship between federal enforcement activity and state and local behavior, and more details on how the program would be enforced, it is difficult to predict the outcome. Generally, states should rely less on firm-specific special incentives and more on actions that improve the overall business climate.

States should also rely more on across the board tax cuts and infrastructure development in order to attract industry. Most of these tax cuts should be directed at personal rather than business taxes, in response to taxpayer unrest.

Interjurisdictional Tax Competition States have considerable control over how their component jurisdictions shape their taxes to attract industry. Again, the most important measures are those that redistribute resources among 100 jurisdictions (Chapter 4), but states could also penalize areas that step out of line in an aggressive tax incentive program.

Exemption of Local Municipal and Development Bonds from Income Tax States can do little to reduce reliance on local bond tax exemption, except through outright prohibition. If local public sector borrowing is to be made easier and cheaper, then states must appeal to the federal government to allow the issuing of taxable bonds which are eligible for a federal interest rate subsidy.

Given the prevailing atmosphere of fiscal restraint, it is reasonable to anticipate that an interest subsidy rate of 33-35 percent is politically feasible since this would involve little net increase in Treasury outlays and yet would provide state and local governments with substantial benefits. A report to the House Ways and Means Committee in 1976 estimated that a 35 percent subsidy would, in the long run, save state and local governments about $1.0 billion a year, and cost the Treasury only $140 million annually.

The shift into the taxable market will have a small effect on interest rates—an increase of between 0.01 and 0.03 on corporate rates (*Fortune,* 1973). Table 20 shows benefits of a $1 billion reduction in borrowing costs, both per capita and per $1000 of personal income, by state, and is based on the simplifying assumption that benefits are distributed among states according to their share of total state and local debt. States are grouped according to their fiscal "blood pressure" as calculated by the Advisory Commission on Intergovernmental Relations. It is apparent that benefits would be greatest in fiscally distressed states, states which tend to be located in the Northeast.

The targeting is not precise, however. Among the "low blood pressure" areas receiving high benefits are Alaska, Nebraska, and the District of Columbia. California and the New England states receive little assistance among the "high and rising" states. Actually, the benefits would be more effectively targeted toward fiscal distress than the table suggests. The taxable option will be exercised most readily by those distressed states and cities in the Northeast whose relatively low bond rating has either squeezed them out of the bond market or has left them paying very high rates. The proportional federal subsidy would mean that their subsidy per $1 million of bonds issued would be much higher than elsewhere. The broader market for taxable bonds will also lead to a reduction in the net interest rate they would have paid had they stayed in the tax exempt market, and reduce fluctuations.

The program has several desirable outcomes: it helps fiscally distressed areas; it encourages increased public borrowing at a time when lack of capital spending is viewed by some as nearing a crisis; it is *101*

Table 20
Fiscal Blood Pressure and Benefits Per Capita and Per $1000 of Personal Income of a $1 Billion Reduction in State and Local Borrowing Costs

High and Falling

	per p.c.	$1000
Wisconsin	3.3	.54
Arizona	4.8	.84
New Mexico	2.9	.55
Louisiana	4.9	.94
Wyoming	4.5	.70
Montana	2.7	.48
Oregon	6.7	1.09
Washington	8.9	1.33
Mississippi	3.1	.69
Unweighted Average	*4.6*	*.79*

High and Rising

	per p.c.	$1000
New York	10.0	1.41
Vermont	4.9	.91
Massachusetts	6.1	.92
California	3.7	.53
Hawaii	7.9	1.13
Minnesota	5.0	.81
Maine	3.7	.70
Nevada	4.4	.64
Maryland	6.0	.88
Rhode Island	4.6	.74
West Virginia	4.0	.76
Michigan	4.0	.59
Michigan	4.0	.59
New Jersey	4.7	.64
Delaware	7.7	1.09
Pennsylvania	5.5	.85
Unweighted Average	*5.4*	*.82*

Low and Falling

	per p.c.	$1000
South Dakota	2.0	.40
Iowa	1.9	.31
Colorado	3.3	.51
Utah	2.1	.41
North Dakota	2.5	.43
Indiana	2.0	.33
Idaho	1.3	.24
Kansas	3.8	.59
North Carolina	1.9	.35
Nebraska	7.8	1.30
South Carolina	3.1	.61
Texas	4.0	.66
Oklahoma	3.1	.55
Florida	3.7	.62
Tennessee	4.3	.82
Alabama	3.3	.65
Arkansas	2.1	.44
Unweighted Average	*3.1*	*.54*

Low and Rising

	per p.c.	$1000
Kentucky	4.8	.89
Connecticut	6.4	.86
Alaska	21.9	2.24
Georgia	3.2	.59
New Hampshire	3.3	.57
District of Columbia	14.3	1.74
Virginia	3.3	.52
Missouri	2.5	.42
Ohio	3.2	.51
Unweighted Average	*7.0*	*.93*

SOURCE: States listed in descending order of "Blood Pressure" in each category, from Advisory Commission on Intergovernmental Relations," *Measuring the Fiscal Blood Pressure of the States—1964-1975*, M-111, Washington, D.C., February 1977; and Bureau of the Census, *Governmental Finances, 1976-1977*, U.S. Department of Commerce, Washington, D.C., November, 1978. The calculations assume that the benefits of the $1 billion savings are distributed in proportion to the states' share of total state local indebtedness.

paid for by the relatively affluent; and will tend, in aggregate, to shift spending toward the less affluent.

Infrastructure   States have typically packaged tax and
Development and   financial incentives with infrastructure
Red Tape Cutting   development. Loans and loan guarantee
offers are normally packaged together with considerable public investments in necessary infrastructure.

To attract Volkswagen to Pennsylvania, the auto manufacturer was offered not only a low interest $200 million loan, but also a promise to complete construction on railroads and highways leading to the New Stanton site. Ohio gave Honda grants totaling $2.5 million to help finance the building of rail spurs and publicly-owned water and sewer facilities, and even provided CETA funds to cover employee training costs.[12]

A major advantage of developing local infrastructure rather than offering specific tax incentives is that many firms can benefit from better roads, sewers, water supply, and fire and police protection. Such benefits need not be limited to a few large firms. The state, with its superior resources, can step in and help local communities with their development problems.

The state of Massachusetts, in cooperation with local governments, approached the problem of decaying mill towns by recycling old mills and buildings into housing, shopping centers, and recreational facilities.[13]

There are other alternatives to tax incentives. "City officials here think that businesses want good parking, clean neighborhoods and decent land—not gimmicks," claims William Schneider, Executive Director of the City-Wide Development Corporation in Dayton, Ohio.[14] Tax incentives cannot address the roots of the problems that lead to slow growth and rising unemployment. Infrastructure development (or redevelopment) can.

A major barrier to the effective use of "place enhancing" programs to spur local development is the artificial barrier between "economic development" and "community development" programs. This distinction is fostered, at the federal level, by the separation, and lack of coordination, between HUD's community development focus and EDA's emphasis on economic development, although the types of projects financed by each are quite similar. Planning activities for these programs at the state and local level are often undertaken by separate agencies.[15] These agencies seldom interact.

A second barrier to a coordinated "packaging" approach to solving development problems is the ambivalent role of state governments. While states have primary responsibility for planning and distributing funds for highways and water treatment, and partial responsibility for *103*

EDA regular projects and CETA, local jurisdictions have a major share of LPW, CDBG, and parts of CETA. This approach to fund distribution by the federal government impedes coordinated local development efforts. States would do well to rationalize local development efforts by clearly delineating state and local responsibilities. However, the major responsibility must lay with the federal government, and at present, reorganization efforts seem to have been abandoned.

Thus we must conclude that a packaged infrastructure building approach to local economic development has the most promise, but also that there are significant institutional barriers that prevent the realization of its full potential.

Wage Subsidies[16]

Incentives could be used to create jobs by reducing the cost of hiring additional labor. We have argued that payroll taxes have raised the cost of labor —particularly unskilled labor—and have contributed toward the problem of unemployment. The number of jobs available would increase if this cost were reduced.[17]

A wage subsidizing incentive could take several forms. The simplest form would be modelled on the investment tax credit, and allow a tax deduction for any increase in the firm's payroll. Thus if its payroll increases by $10,000 in a year, the firm may deduct, say, $1,000 from its taxable income. This is analogous to the federal employment tax credit adopted in 1977. This measure naturally provides most of its assistance to growing areas where employment would be expanding anyway, and does little to focus on the hard-to-employ. The new Targeted Jobs Tax Credit is applicable only to the hard-to-employ, and can be taken as a credit as well as a reduction in taxes. It meets many of these objectives. An alternative would be to provide employment vouchers to unemployed individuals, based upon their past income and unemployment experience. An employer could redeem these vouchers—either for cash or reduced payroll taxes—for each week that they provided the worker with a job. The cash value, or subsidy, would decline over time as the subsidized worker gained work experience.

Consider a simple numerical example. Someone unemployed more than thirty weeks and with a household income of less than $6000 in the previous year could present an employer with vouchers worth $75 per week, a subsidy that would slowly decline to zero over a 24 month period. He or she would compete—presumably for unskilled jobs—in the labor market and could secure a job paying close to the minimum wage—$116 for a forty hour week. The employer would be reimbursed for most of the wage costs. If the worker were employed for a full year, the employer would receive tax subsidies of $2808 toward a wage bill of $6032. During the second year, the subsidy would fall to $1078. The program has the advantage of actually increasing the number of jobs available, and in targeting those jobs to the needy. The recently passed targeted jobs tax credit offers federal subsidies of about $1700 for employers hiring eligible workers. States could add to the program, offering reduced payroll or property taxes, and using CETA funds to cover part of the program cost.

A potential disadvantage of a wage subsidy is that employers might fire an employee as soon as the subsidy was reduced to hire a more subsidized worker. This objection is more apparent that real. First, there need be no sudden cut-off of the subsidy. Second, hiring and firing involves costs to the employer. And third, there would be an increase in the number of jobs available. The policy merits much deeper consideration than it has received in the past.

FOOTNOTES TO CHAPTER 6

1. Logically, reducing the death rate of firms could also boost local growth, but death rates do not vary much among areas, and seem fairly intractable to local policies.

2. These slogans were described in a column by James Sterba in the *New York Times,* July 18, 1978.

3. The exceptions are Alabama, Minnesota, and Tennessee.

4. Bird, 1966, parts I and II; Bridges, 1965; Due, 1961; Hellman, Wassall, and Falk, 1976; Hodge, 1979; Gurwitz, 1977; Harrison and Kanter, 1976 and 1978; Morgan and Hackbart, 1974; Mulkey and Dillman, 1976; and Williams, 1967.

5. Quoted in Jerry Jacobs, "Battling for Business," *People and Taxes,* September 1978, p. 9.

6. Some studies have found tax incentives to be cost effective from the viewpoint of local governments. These have tended to ignore the secondary impacts of development, such as population growth. See, for example, Moes (1941); Rinehart (1963); and Sazama (1970).

7. These problems are not present, of course, with property tax incentives, since property taxes must be paid whatever the level of profit of the firm.

8. The concentration of non-taxpaying firms is likely to be greatest in distressed areas, precisely where the stimulus is most needed.

9. Many of these topics are covered in other volumes in this series.

10. Section 107 of the Revenue and Expenditure Control Act of 1968 denies federal tax exemption to industrial development bond issues exceeding $5 million. Such issues fell sharply from $1.6 billion in 1968 to $0.5 billion by 1978. But bonds for water treatment were exempt from the $5 million limit, and by 1976, $4.5 billion in water treatment bonds were issued.

11. For a fuller discussion, see Vaughan (1979).

12. See Cornia, Testa, and Stocker (1978) and Haskins (1977).

13. See Neal R. Pierce, "States as City Savers," *The Washington Post,* 10/11/77.

14. Quoted in "Ailing Cities Spread the Welcome Mat for Business," *U.S. News and World Report,* 12/19/77, p. 76.

15. HUD encourages local jurisdictions to finance planning from CDBG funds (to replace the old 701 planning grants), while EDA is experimenting with developing local planning capacity through 302 planning grants to states and local jurisdictions.

16. Wage subsidies have been recommended by several authors. See Orcutt, who advocated a scheme similar to the one outlined here in an unpublished paper. A more extensive plan has been devised by Bishop (1977). Lester Thurow recently argued the case in the *New York Times,* 1/10/78. See also Roger Vaughan, "Jobs for the Urban Unemployed," in Bryce (1978).

17. Several studies have attempted to measure the elasticity of demand for labor—the percentage increase in the number of employees demanded in response to a given percentage reduction in the cost.

7
WHAT SHOULD STATES DO ABOUT PERSONAL TAXES?

State economic development programs have traditionally focused upon business taxes. However, there is growing evidence that state differences in personal taxes, especially income and property taxes, may be a more powerful, if indirect, influence on growth than differences in business taxes.

The burden of state and local taxes is a composite of a number of taxes. The most important are personal income taxes, property taxes, and sales taxes. In 1977, personal income, property, and sales taxes accounted for over $123 billion—out of $175 billion in total state/local tax revenues (Table 21).[1] Other sources of revenue from households include state-operated gambling operations and fees and charges.

Within this broad total, there are wide variations among states (Table 22). Oregon, Massachusetts, Montana, Alaska, New York, and Wisconsin rely on the personal income tax for at least 40 percent of their total revenues. Louisiana, Maine, Mississippi, New Mexico, and Ohio raise less than 15 percent of their revenue from personal income taxation. Connecticut, Florida, Nevada, South Dakota, Texas, and Washington have no income tax. The result is that per capita revenues in 1977 ranged from $59 in Louisiana to $400 in New York. Residents of some cities also face personal income taxes.[2]

Residential property taxes also vary sharply among states.[3] In 1975, Massachusetts topped all other states, collecting $229 per capita, followed by New Jersey $216, California $202, and Connecticut $199 (Table 22). At the other end of the scale, Alabama collected only $22 per capita, Lousiana $32, Kentucky $37, and Mississippi $38.

Sales taxes range from 7 percent in Connecticut and 6 percent in Pennsylvania and Rhode Island, to only 2 percent in Oklahoma (Table 22). However, many local jurisdictions impose additional sales taxes, so that the rate in New York City is 8 percent, split evenly between state and city. Per capita revenues range from only $65 in Vermont, to $347 in Washington.

Fees, charges and miscellaneous are also a major source of state/local revenue. This category includes everything from inheritance taxes and state gambling revenues to charges for water supply and local tennis courts. Finally, the growing difficulty of increasing tax revenues from regular sources has broken down the traditional moral opposition to gambling. Today, only 5 states (Hawaii, Missouri, Mississippi, Texas, and Utah) ban all forms of gambling. In many *107* states, publicly-run gambling—from casinos and sports betting to parimutuel horse racing and lotteries—are operated as a source of revenue.

Through state organized gambling, the state can create a good or service which is strongly in demand—or at least take over its production from illegal enterprises—and tax it. Only those that wish to gamble need pay the tax. Atlantic City has tried to create a "Las Vegas East" to revive its flagging tourist trade and raise revenues. Mayor Koch of New York City has even proposed—only half tongue in cheek—that the city run a numbers game. It is a politically expedient move.

New Hampshire introduced the first lottery in 1963, and by FY 1973, eight states were operating lotteries (Table 23). But lotteries are, at best, a marginal source of revenue.

EFFICIENCY   The evidence suggests that the collection of this burden of state and local taxes has several efficiency costs:

Table 21
State and Local Revenues from Personal Income Taxes
and Property Taxes, Selected Years

Tax	Tax Revenues ($ Millions)			
	1960	1965	1970	1977
Personal				
Income Taxes	2,536	4,417	12,114	29,245
States	2,282	3,947	9,583	25,493
Localities	254	470	1,531	3,752
Property Taxes	16,238	23,187	36,546	62,335
States	520	657	923	2,260
Localities	15,718	22,530	35,623	60,275
General				
Sales Taxes				
States	4,302	6,711	14,177	30,896
Localities	1,339	2,059	3,068	5,417

SOURCES: *Survey of Current Business*, May 1978; Bureau of the Census, *Governmental Finances, 1976-77*, Washington, D.C., various years.

Income Tax
■ Interstate differences have encouraged the migration of some high income households toward lower taxing states. However, the effect may not be strong and the quality of the research has been relatively weak.
■ High income tax rates tend to be capitalized in high wages, especially among the more mobile labor force groups.
■ Income taxes discourage labor force participation.

Property Taxes
■ High local property taxes used for redistributive programs have encouraged more affluent households to move away from central cities into relatively homogeneous suburban jurisdictions.
■ Fear of reassessment has not been a major deterrent in property rehabilitation decisions, but high rates do discourage investment by depressing values.

Sales Tax
■ High local rates lead to a loss of local retail sales and retail employment.

Fees and Charges
■ Fees and charges may be used to increase efficiency in the use of public services.

Income Tax
It is difficult to prove that local income tax rates influence residential location. High rates can be accompanied by high quality public services that attract migrants. Some evidence does suggest that high tax rates deter net inmigration and affluent households more than low income households, thus leading to a growing concentration of the poor in high taxing locales. But such data are often highly aggregated, and few studies have considered the quality of local public services. There is room for considerable doubt. One reason why personal income taxes may not influence decisions as much as some critics contend is that, for high income households that itemize their federal returns, local taxes are deductible. Thus for these households the burden is reduced by up to 50 percent.

Migrants are sensitive to cost of living differentials in their choice of destination, and local taxes may contribute significantly to these differentials. A number of studies have found that an increase in local taxes per capita of about one percent would have little or no impact on black inmigration in a metropolitan area and might reduce the rate of white inmigration by about 0.3 percent.[4] However, Liu (1977) found the state tax rate had little effect on migration decisions.

Table 22
Characteristics of State/Local Personal Taxes, 1977

State	Personal Income Tax Rate as Percent of Household Income[1] 5,000	15,000	25,000	Per Capital Revenue	Share of State/Local Revenue	Property Tax (1975) Per Capita Revenue	Share of State/Local Revenue	General Sales Tax Rate	Per Capita Revenue	Share of State/Local Revenue	Charges and Miscellaneous Per Capita Revenue	Share of State/Local Revenue
Alabama	0.3%	1.5%	2.3%	96.8	13.2	22	8.1%	4	160.4	21.9	225.5	30.8
Alaska	—	1.6	2.5	615.3	20.4	79	44.5	—	78.5	2.6	679.8	22.5
Arizona	0.6	1.3	2.5	105.4	10.2	106	30.7	4	263.6	25.6	206.6	20.0
Arkansas	—	1.7	2.9	110.0	16.3	35	16.6	3	131.0	19.4	169.9	25.2
California	-0.7	1.1	2.5	240.3	18.2	202	34.7	4¾	239.4	18.1	230.8	17.5
Colorado	-0.5	1.1	2.6	161.3	14.7	97	28.7	3	216.9	19.7	271.6	24.7
Connecticut	—	—	—	84.2	8.0	199	39.3	7	188.2	17.9	166.1	15.8
Delaware	0.8	2.7	4.7	344.5	31.6	53	11.9	—	—	—	287.2	26.3
D.C.	-0.1	2.8	4.6	366.6	30.2	102	19.5	5	201.6	16.6	158.7	13.1
Florida	—	—	—	22.8	2.7	82	24.5	4	164.5	19.2	232.6	27.1
Georgia	—	1.2	2.7	133.3	15.9	72	22.8	3	154.7	18.4	225.7	26.9
Hawaii	-3.4	2.6	4.3	256.2	20.7	86	13.4	4	378.9	30.6	269.3	21.8
Idaho	-1.2	1.8	3.6	159.4	20.2	51	24.7	3	115.4	14.6	182.0	23.0
Illinois	0.5	1.8	2.1	160.5	15.6	117	31.0	4	200.1	19.4	167.0	16.2
Indiana	1.0	1.7	1.8	113.3	13.3	88	28.6	4	197.3	23.1	197.0	23.1
Iowa	1.1	2.4	3.4	186.0	19.0	87	29.5	3	119.6	12.2	237.2	24.2
Kansas	—	1.2	2.0	144.3	14.9	83	31.2	3	147.5	15.2	233.0	24.1
Kentucky	0.5	2.0	2.9	171.6	22.3	37	14.5	5	132.5	17.3	173.4	22.6
Louisiana	—	0.9	1.0	58.7	6.5	32	11.0	3	207.6	23.0	263.1	29.2
Maine	—	0.7	2.1	100.4	12.6	104	29.5	5	154.3	19.4	146.4	18.4
Maryland	0.6	2.3	3.1	317.2	27.5	126	23.2	5	113.6	9.8	253.6	22.0
Massachusetts	-0.5	3.3	4.0	278.7	23.5	229	41.9	5	77.5	6.5	172.4	14.5
Michigan	-1.6	0.8	1.4	268.4	23.6	130	29.3	4	154.6	13.6	255.7	22.5
Minnesota	-6.9	4.8	6.7	303.8	25.8	103	22.9	4	117.4	10.0	278.4	23.6
Mississippi	—	0.7	1.8	74.0	10.0	38	15.6	5	198.1	26.8	214.0	29.0
Missouri	—	1.0	2.1	121.1	15.7	76	25.0	3⅛	151.7	19.7	204.2	26.5

State	(1)	(2)	(3)	(4)	(5)	(6)	(7)	(8)	(9)	(10)	(11)	(12)
Montana	1.0	2.2	3.6	171.0	17.9	95	36.0	—	—	—	229.0	23.9
Nebraska	-1.6	1.3	2.1	132.8	13.1	91	34.4	3	138.2	13.7	256.2	25.3
Nevada	—	—	—	—	—	133	23.4	3	224.0	17.4	344.5	26.8
New Hampshire	—	—	—	49.5	5.8	163	47.8	—	—	—	192.4	22.7
New Jersey	—	1.5	1.7	142.8	12.7	216	41.7	5	125.1	11.1	190.8	17.0
New Mexico	-2.8	0.1	1.4	46.8	5.0	34	11.9	3¾	222.5	23.6	324.6	34.4
New York	—	2.4	4.4	399.9	25.9	181	29.1	4	218.9	14.2	288.3	18.7
North Carolina	0.8	2.5	3.9	179.3	23.9	48	17.2	3	118.2	15.7	155.5	20.7
North Dakota	—	1.1	3.1	109.7	11.2	54	21.3	3	157.4	16.1	342.0	35.0
Ohio	0.2	0.8	1.5	138.7	16.4	86	29.6	4	112.5	13.3	203.1	24.1
Oklahoma	0.1	0.6	1.8	102.7	12.3	41	16.2	2	121.9	14.6	235.4	28.2
Oregon	0.7	2.8	4.3	272.1	25.1	128	32.3	—	—	—	297.5	27.5
Pennsylvania	—	2.0	2.0	220.5	24.0	62	21.9	6	129.2	14.1	149.0	16.2
Rhode Island	—	1.6	2.1	160.7	15.7	150	33.3	6	157.6	15.4	197.0	19.3
South Carolina	0.5	1.7	3.3	136.9	18.3	42	17.0	4	143.2	19.1	204.0	27.3
South Dakota	—	—	—	3.6	0.4	80	35.2	4	159.1	18.5	239.9	27.9
Tennessee	—	—	—	41.5	5.6	52	19.0	4½	216.1	29.0	179.5	24.1
Texas	—	—	—	—	—	68	27.3	4	156.0	18.3	216.1	25.3
Utah	0.4	2.1	3.4	140.8	16.7	65	22.1	4	205.3	24.4	206.5	24.5
Vermont	-0.6	2.3	3.1	177.4	17.9	137	32.8	3	65.0	6.7	190.0	19.5
Virginia	0.5	2.1	3.1	171.2	19.8	83	22.6	3	112.2	13.0	185.3	21.4
Washington	—	—	—	—	—	123	22.8	4.6	347.3	31.3	296.8	26.8
West Virginia	0.9	1.3	1.9	98.9	13.1	39	14.5	3	235.5	31.1	148.4	19.6
Wisconsin	-4.8	3.7	5.6	297.0	27.5	115	27.4	3	142.1	13.2	218.9	20.3
Wyoming	—	—	—	—	—	66	29.4	3	261.8	18.8	387.0	27.8

1. "Effective rates" are computed as the percentage that tax liability is of adjusted gross income (i.e., income after business deductions and other allowable deductions). In computing income taxes, it was assumed that all income was from wages and salaries and earned by one spouse. In computing the state income taxes for the $5,000 class, the optional standard deductions, low income allowances, and optional tax tables were used. For the other income classes (based on deductions claimed on federal income tax returns) the following estimated itemized deductions were assumed: $15,000—$3,830; and $25,000—$5,115. For federal tax computations, the zero bracket amount ($3,200) and the earned income credit applied for the $5,000 class; the zero bracket amount for the $15,000 class. For the remaining class, the following estimated itemized deduction was assumed: $25,000—$5,850; (state itemized deductions with the addition of est. state income taxes and less certain deductions not allowed under federal law). Excludes the following states with limited personal income taxes: Connecticut (capital gains and dividends); New Hampshire and Tennessee (interest and dividends).

SOURCE: Advisory Commission on Intergovernmental Relations, Family Tax Burdens Compared Among States and Cities, Washington, D.C., 1978; U.S. Bureau of the Census, Governmental Finances, various years, Washington, D.C.; "Tax Wealth in Fifty States," State Government News, July 1978.

Table 23
State Lotteries in FY 1973

State	Sales ($ Million)	Sales ($ / Capita)	Administration Costs* ($ Million)	Revenue to State ($ Million)	Revenue to State Percent of States Own Revenues	Prizes
New Hampshire	6.8	9.28	1.2	2.6	0.9	3.0
New York	130.0	7.13	16.2	61.8	0.7	52.0
New Jersey	112.7	15.72	10.2	50.7	1.9	51.8
Connecticut	34.7	11.45	4.6	14.5	1.2	15.6
Pennsylvania	124.4	10.55	12.5	57.5	1.2	54.4
Massachusetts	70.6	12.55	7.9	32.1	1.5	30.5
Michigan	135.7	15.29	12.4	62.2	1.5	61.0
Maryland	40.1	10.22	8.0	16.0	1.0	16.0

SOURCE: Roger E. Brinner and Charles T. Clotfelter, "An Economic Appraisal of State Lotteries," *National Tax Journal*, Vol. XXVIII, No. 4, 1975, p. 396.

*Operating costs, agents' fees and bank fees on other revenues.

Tax differentials are capitalized in wage differentials, although only among the mobile, affluent occupations.[5] Skilled workers who operate in a regionwide, nationwide, or even international labor market demand, and receive, higher wages and salaries for living in high taxing locales. In fact, this may lead to greater interarea cost differentials than do business taxes.

The view that low personal income taxes are an incentive for economic development is well expressed by a Houston Chamber of Commerce official who pointed out that: "Houston has not found the need to stimulate the economy artificially by the granting of special tax moratoriums on property taxes or the offering of industrial bonds through special economic development corporations. The major tax incentive is the lack of a state or local income tax."[6] A similar view is expressed by a businessman who moved his operation from New York to Texas: "I can bring in an executive and he will get a 20 percent boost in income after expenses at the salary he earned elsewhere."[7]

The Advisory Commission on Intergovernmental Relations (1978) concluded that:

The great variation in state use of the personal income tax stands out as the most potentially harmful tax differential in our federal system. There is little prospect in the near future for a substantial reduction in the great variations in state personal income tax burdens unless: (A) the federal government provides special help to the high income tax states thereby enabling them to cut their income tax rules, and/or (B) takes coercive action to encourage non-income tax states and low income tax states to make more effective use of this revenue source.

Property Tax In 1956, Charles Tiebout outlined what emerged as the dominant view regarding the effects of interjurisdictional differences in taxes and services in residential location: "Given . . . . local revenue and expenditure patterns, the consumer-voter moves to that community whose . . . menu of taxes and services best satisfies his set of preferences." The result is a tendency for metropolitan areas and labor markets to fragment into many jurisdictions, each serving a relatively homogeneous population. Population and property values decline in those areas not offering an attractive mix of services at competitive tax prices.

Models derived from the Tiebout hypothesis have been used to analyze patterns of residential location among political jurisdictions in metropolitan areas, and the effect of local public sector activities on local property values.

Different types of households respond differently to local government behavior. Although local government behavior has not significantly influenced the number of households moving to the suburbs, it has contributed to the growing socio-economic segregation between central city and suburbs.

Mayo (1971, 1972) examined the role of four municipal fiscal practices on residential choice: total per capita public expenditures, per pupil education expenditures, school and property taxes, and proportion of the municipal budget allocated to schools, recreation, highways, police, and fire. He found that, "the influence of . . . public services and taxes . . . probably canot be considered a major locational factor (p. 237), "although definitive test of the hypothesis must "await the development of better data on (public service) output measures" as well as the "availability of more disaggregated tax data."[8]

However, differences in public sector activities have contributed to the concentration of low income households in central city jurisdictions. Higher income households frequently move to the suburbs seeking to live among others of similar income, in order to minimize the taxes they must pay for redistributive services for the poor, while the poor are attracted to high taxing locales to take advantage of the implicit transfers (Aaronson and Schwartz, 1973; and Bradford and Kelejian, 1973). Net fiscal surplus[9] significantly explains household residential choice (Bradford and Kelejian, p. 567.)

This selective suburbanization results in the fragmentation of municipal jurisdictions and economic segregation (Aaronson and Schwartz 1973). There is little evidence, however, that suburbs are able to main- *113* tain their homogeneity. There is considerable heterogeneity with respect to income among suburban towns, although there is some volitional sorting with respect to education and occupation (Pack and Pack, 1977).

Both the level of property taxes and the quality of the public services affect property values and property investment. Evidence generally indicates that *an increase in taxes leads to a decline in property values, while an increase in the level of public services tends to raise property values* (Oates, 1969). The extent to which changes in local taxes or services are capitalized in property values determines the incidence of the property tax and has important implications for the housing stock and the residential location choices of households. For example, that part of the property tax that operates as an excise tax on housing causes families to buy less. Similarly, real estate developers react to the reduction in the after tax return on investment resulting from a property tax increase by reallocating their capital into alternative investments.

Several studies have found that interarea tax differences, and increases in tax rates over time, are reflected in property values and rents (King, 1973; Mayo, 1973; Smith and Dayak, 1975). King, for example, concludes by distinguishing formal and informal variations in the property tax and by suggesting several circumstances that may determine the extent of tax capitalization in a locale. "The extent of capitalization [would seem to be] critically dependent on the visibility and certainty of tax variations. When differentials arise mostly from assessment vagaries, capitalization is unlikely; but when tax changes occur which are more-or-less uniform and highly visible to potential buyers, capitalization seems probable (p. 96)."

Perhaps the strongest evidence for capitalization comes from studies that have drawn on natural experiments. Wicks, Little, and Beck (1968) tested for changes in market values of homes in a Montana municipality before and after a change in the effective property tax rate. They observed that a $1 increase in a tax bill appeared to reduce sales price by roughly $19, indicating capitalization at a rate of 19:1. Moody (1973) studied the effects of tax changes in the San Francisco area using a fortunate natural experiment in 1962, where residents of San Francisco and its surrounding counties voted whether to support BART and incur the increased property taxes it would require. Although San Francisco opted to participate while neighboring San Mateo County did not, a previously planned transit stop in the border of San Francisco and San Mateo's Daly City was installed. The result is that Daly City residents have access to the subway at no cost in property taxes while their San Francisco neighbors bear the cost in a tax increase of $10 to $15, which depressed sales prices by roughly 114 $900. However, not all of the empirical evidence yields indications of capitalization (Daicoff, 1961; and Mayo, 1972).

The degree to which changes in tax rates or in the level of municipal services are capitalized is greater in the short run—when the supply of housing and public services has not fully adjusted to the tax change. In the long run, market response to such differentials may be evidenced mainly in the quantity and quality of the housing stock. The adjustment problem is further compounded by the fact that, as property values shift and as the composition of the local population changes, the menu of local public services offered by a jurisdiction may also undergo adjustment—a response that Tiebout has hypothesized. A local government obviously tends to adapt its services to suit its residents (Edel and Sclar, 1974).

The general view is that property taxes disrupt the operation of the housing market and act as a disincentive to upgrading and new construction as well as acting as a facilitator of downward transition and blight (Peterson et al., 1973):

> Placing a tax on a good must either raise the price consumers pay for the good or lower the profit producers can earn from supplying it. In either case, the imposition of a tax is likely to lead to a lower level of provision of the good in question. If this reasoning is right, an increase in property tax rates may lead directly to a lower supply of new housing or . . . . it may discourage upgrading and rehabilitation of the current stock and accelerate the decision of landlords in low-income areas to abandon their housing altogether (p. 2).

Peterson et al. conducted an extensive study of intraurban variations in effective tax rates and attempted to assess their effects on upward transitional and stable neighborhoods as well as on downward transitional and blighted neighborhoods. The authors noted substantial variation in tax rates between various types of neighborhoods within a given fiscal jurisdiction. For example, property in stable neighborhoods tended to be taxed at a much lower rate than property in blighted neighborhoods. In general, upward transitional neighborhoods enjoyed the lowest tax rates of all.

> Despite the fact that uniform taxation within each city is mandated by law, the neighborhood variation in several cities exceeds the variation in legal rates adopted by different cities. In Chicago and Baltimore, the sample properties in blighted neighborhoods pay property taxes at a rate ten to fifteen times higher than properties in upward transitional neighborhoods. In these cities, the regressivity of the property tax's effective rate structure is due principally to neighborhood bias in assessments (p. 23).

Although fear of reassessment does not appear to act as a deterrent to investment, the high level of taxation is a major factor (Peterson, *115*

1973; and Sternlieb and Burchell, 1973).

Overall, it appears that the property tax is unpopular, inequitable, and deters residential redevelopment.

Since the property tax falls most heavily on housing, relative to other consumer durables and other types of household investments, critics have argued that it leads to too little investment in housing. But the federal income tax strongly favors housing by allowing the deduction of mortgage interest and local property tax from taxable income and by not taxing the imputed rental income of owner occupied housing. There are no studies that compute the net impact of these two countervailing influences, and how they differ according to household income and local property tax rates.

Sales Tax Sales taxes are used by many large cities and by states as a source of revenue. Central cities have imposed sales taxes to try to take advantage of their position as retail centers. But local differentials in sales tax rates appear to shift retail activity from high taxing to low taxing areas. If suburban centers fail to follow central city sales tax rates, retail trade is diverted away from the central city. Hamovitz (1966) estimated that for each one percentage point increase in the sales tax rate, New York City's retail sales declined by six percent. In a study of 137 metropolitan areas, Mikesell (1970) found that the decline in central city retail sales was between 2 percent and 11 percent in response to one percentage point increase in the central city sales tax rate. The use of the sales tax, especially by local jurisdictions, is therefore limited by the tax rates in competitive retail centers.

Fees and Charges Economic efficiency is ensured when, in the absence of market imperfections, consumers of a good, or users of a service, pay the marginal cost of providing the good or service. Therefore, local governments can encourage the efficient use of public facilities or services by charging a price equal to the marginal cost. Obviously, there are many public goods for which fees and charges are impossible to apply—how could motorists be charged for the use of street lighting? But there are some services where changes are appropriate. Consider the following cases:

■ Charging for the use of tennis courts ensures that those who really want to play are not crowded out by those who do not value the experience as much.
■ Charging for water use encourages users not to waste publicly-supplied water.

116 ■ Charging new homes the true cost of hooking up to the municipal sewer and water system discourages sprawling residential development.

To encourage efficiency in this dynamic context, the revenues should provide the producer of the service with a signal as to whether to expand or contract his level of production. For example, if tennis courts remain crowded when players are paying a fee equal to the marginal cost, then additional courts should be provided. If they are vacant, then perhaps the supply should be reduced. Unfortunately, this feedback information is rarely utilized by state and local governments. Receipts become simply part of general revenues rather than an investment indicator.

User fees are a useful source of additional revenue to states and localities trapped by tax limitation statutes. Los Angeles County is proposing a state law for a fire service fee based upon a building's fire risk classification. Scottsdale, Arizona has no public fire protection—the private service operates on a fee—and the costs are relatively low (Ahlbrandt, 1972). The administrative problems of devising a fee schedule are not insuperable (Pollack, 1972). Fire protection expenditures average about 5 percent of local expenditures; therefore, a fee schedule offers some opportunity for relief. Garbage collection— 3 percent of local expenditures—may also be paid for through a fee.

Perhaps the greatest area where the failure to charge fees has had serious efficiency implications is in residential development. Builders of summer homes in Vermont are required to pay only $19 for an electricity hook up, although the cost to the state is $1350 (National League of Cities, 1975). Neal Peirce notes that as a result of Proposition 13, the expanding suburb of Petaluma near San Francisco now charges developers an "impact fee" of $3000 per acre.[10]

Proposing fees and charges usually encounters two objections. They are administratively clumsy, and they penalize the poor (see below). These objections are not always valid, as we shall see.

EQUITY

The equity of personal taxes has been subject to considerable debate. Some of the major conclusions are:

Income Tax
■ Many states have regressive income tax structures.
■ Certain aspects of the income tax structure—standard deductions and certain exemptions—are regressive.

Sales Tax
■ Although the sales tax is basically regressive, the use of exemptions for food and prescription drugs can reduce its regressivity. But these *117*

exemptions are relatively inefficient.

Fees and Charges
■ Although typically argued to be regressive, fees and charges do not necessarily fall heavily on the poor.

The relative equity of property and income taxation has been debated endlessly and cannot be resolved in this paper. However, we can describe, briefly, some of their relative merits, for it does appear that the two taxes are, in some ways, complementary.

Progressivity. The property tax has traditionally been viewed as regressive, while the income tax is, at best, neutral, and may be progressive. Economists have recently taken a less regressive view of the property tax, and a less progressive view of the income tax, because of the many loopholes that high income earners enjoy. There are no definitive studies of relative progressivity.

Ability to Pay. The income tax tends to be favored because income is a measure of an individual's ability to pay, while the value of property is not. The value of property, however, is strongly correlated with a household's normal, or "permanent," income. Taxable income may be artificially low because of certain tax advantages and thus not an accurate reflection of true income.[11] Again, there is no definite answer as to which tax best measures the true ability to pay.

Value of Benefits Received. It has been argued that since the value of local public services received is related to residential location, taxes should be revised on residential property. However, the relationship between the value of real property and the value of services received is no stronger than that between income and services.

Income Tax

Differences in the rate and progressivity of state and local income taxes have influenced economic development. High taxing states, whose taxes often reflect the high level of locally-financed welfare payments, have lost affluent households.

Effective state personal income tax rates for selected, adjusted household incomes are shown in Table 22. For a household earning $15,000 in 1977, state tax burdens varied from almost zero in New Mexico to above 3 percent in Massachusetts, Minnesota, and Wisconsin. For a family earning $25,000, the range was between 1 percent in Louisiana and 1.4 percent in New Mexico, and 6.7 percent in Minnesota and 5.6 in Wisconsin.

Progressivity is, of course, difficult to define. High income individuals are able to take advantage of tax shelters that range from tax free municipal bonds to the differential treatment of capital gains. However, these options are available in almost all states, so that even though the data presented in Table 22 may not measure true interstate progressivity, they do measure differences in the burden to a given household *among* states.

Many states have little progressivity in their income tax structure. Vertical equity could be improved by increasing the progressivity of the rate (see Chapter 4, above).

Another source of vertical inequity is the practice of granting standard deductions from taxable income, rather than tax credits. For a household with a 10 percent marginal state income tax rate, a $1000 personal deduction is worth $100 in reduced state income taxes (and probably about $500 in reduced federal income taxes). To a family with a 2 percent marginal rate, the deduction is worth only $20. Clearly, it would be more equitable to change from a deduction to a flat tax credit of, say, $40, which would be the same for all households.

Horizontal inequity in income tax structure arises because of the special treatment of certain activities, the most glaring being home-ownership. Two households—one renting and one owning its own home—with equal incomes, family size, and housing units, consuming the same public services, will pay very different federal, state, and local taxes. The argument is that this encourages homeownership which is desirable. But it does so at a massive cost in equity. Federal tax expenditures to those fortunate enough to own their own homes, and have high enough incomes to make itemizing worthwhile, at least equal, if not surpass, federal housing assistance to the poor.

A second major inequity is the deduction of state and local taxes from federal taxable income, originally conceived as a way of helping local areas raise taxes. With only 25 percent of households—the relatively well-off—itemizing, this effectively increases the regressivity of local taxes. This deduction also discriminates against the use of fees and charges by local governments.

Property Tax   There is considerable debate as to the regressivity of the property tax, and how it falls on renters. The weight of the evidence suggests that the tax is regressive, and is, for the most part, passed on to renters in the form of higher rents. This regressivity stems from three factors (Grubb and Hoachlander, 1978):

■ The poor spend a much higher share of their income on housing than the more affluent.
■ Expensive houses are assessed at a lower fraction of market value than low-value houses.
■ Jurisdictions with a high concentration of low income households tend to have higher tax rates than more affluent jurisdictions.

There is little doubt that, among personal taxes, the property tax *119* is regarded as the least equitable. In a Gallup poll, only 10 percent of respondents characterized property taxes as the fairest way of financing state and local services, compared with 43 percent for a sales tax and 36 percent for income tax (11 percent "don't know").[12]

Attempts by states and localities to improve the equity of the tax through homestead exemptions are inequitable for the same reason that standard deductions are inequitable for the income tax. The circuit breaker (see Chapter 4 above) is a much more promising avenue for reform.

Sales Tax   Opponents of the sales tax have long argued that its burden falls most heavily upon the poor. Since the poor rarely itemize their federal tax returns, they are unable to offset local sales taxes against federal income taxes. However, special exemptions such as food for home consumption, clothing, and utilities favor the poor, who spend a large share of their income on these necessities (Schaefer, 1969). Of the 44 states with sales taxes, only 22 (plus the District of Columbia), exempt food purchases; 5 exempt clothing; 16 exempt utility payments; and 37 (plus the District of Columbia) exempt prescription drugs. In addition, 7 states allow a credit against state income taxes for food purchased for home consumption. Some states, therefore, have significant opportunities to improve tax equity by extending sales tax exemptions. Also, Hawaii, New Mexico, and South Dakota extend the sales tax to cover professional services, which increases its progressivity since purchase of these services increases with income.

However, exemptions are a relatively inefficient way of helping the poor since all households benefit, although this may be desirable if the policy is to encourage food consumption against expenditures on other goods. An exemption will always be inferior to income tax credits or cash transfers as a way of reducing regressivity.

Fees and Charges   If there is a charge to enter museums or libraries, or an hourly price for the local tennis courts, then the poor will be discouraged from using these facilities. Public facilities also tend to be used more intensively by the poor—more affluent households belong to private tennis clubs and purchase books. Thus, fees are regressive inasmuch as they are collected disproportionately from the poor.

However, this argument applies only to a limited set of charges. Clearly, summer homes are rarely owned by the poor, and development fees will, primarily, fall on homeowners. A charge for water use (through metering) would probably be progressive. It is also possible to make other charges less regressive—such as free use of tennis courts by low-income groups. Charges are highly equitable in

120

that payments are directly related to the volume of public services consumed.

Gambling The incidence of gambling revenues is regressive. For example, in Massachusetts, those with incomes below $15,000 constituted 86.9 percent of the population but paid an estimated 91.7 percent of the lottery taxes (Brinner and Clotfelter, 1975). However, there is surprisingly little opposition to state gambling on these grounds. This is probably because the alternative is illegal gambling, and the poor gamble in games that are particularly inequitable (e.g., numbers).

WHAT SHOULD STATES DO? States and localities can take a number of steps to improve the efficiency and equity of household taxes.

Income Tax
■ Replace standard deductions with standard tax credits.
■ Remove the tax incentive for homeownership (or extend equal benefits to renters).
■ Introduce inflation indexing.
■ Simplify the tax structure.
■ Eliminate the deduction of local taxes from federal taxable income.

Property Tax
■ Improve the efficiency of assessment.
■ Introduce circuit breakers (see Chapter 4 above).
■ Shift some of the tax burden from improvements to land (see Chapter 5 above).

Sales Tax
■ States without exemptions on food and prescription drugs should consider introducing them.
■ Some consideration should be given to extending the tax to cover professional services.

Fees and Charges
■ States should analyze their programs to determine whether fees and charges would be appropriate for some functions.

Income Tax The first two measures are self-explanatory. But implementation must rest upon changes in federal tax laws if states and local areas are to avoid increased administrative costs. Replacing standard deductions with standard tax credits is a simple step, but one to which federal law- *121* makers have not given much thought. Removing the bias in favor of homeownership is a major political step, and must be viewed as unlikely. The most politically feasible step would be to extend the same privilege to renters, which would preserve vertical inequity while gaining a little horizontal equity.

Inflation Indexing. Although no politician who endorsed inflation would long survive, inflation is not without its advantages to state and local administrators. An 8 percent across the board increase in prices and income increases local tax receipts by a good deal more than 8 percent, allowing programs to be expanded even after paying higher wages and materials costs. In states with progressive tax rates, taxpayers are nudged into tax brackets in which they owe a higher percentage of their income, the real value of standard deductions shrinks, and property prices tend to rise more rapidly than the Consumer Price Index. The Advisory Commission on Intergovernmental Relations estimated that states received an income tax revenue windfall of $1.2 billion in 1978, and by 1982, making certain assumptions about price level and income growth, the bonus could be $11 billion (ACIR, 1979).

A solution to this inflation tax is to index the value of the standard deduction and tax bracket levels to the local consumer price index. Three states have taken steps to do this. In California, tax brackets, credits on personal exemptions, dependence and blindness exemptions, and the standard deduction are raised by 5 percent each year that the increase in the state's CPI exceeds 3 percent. Colorado, the first state to adopt indexing, required the State Assembly to determine the annual inflation factor to index taxes—6 percent in 1978. Arizona indexed for 1978 only.

Indexing may improve the equity of the tax system, although not by a great deal. It may be more useful in acting as a restraint on state budget officers, for it reduces the fiscal bonus that inflation brings.

Deduction of State and Local Taxes from Federal Taxable Income. At present, the federal government foregoes revenues of about $13 billion because of the deduction of state and local taxes from taxable income. This is made up as follows. Non-business state and local taxes (other than property and gasoline taxes) reduced federal income taxes by $8.1 billion in 1977; property taxes on owner-occupied homes reduced income taxes by $4.5 billion; and gasoline taxes reduced taxes by $0.79 billion. This benefit is largely showered on those with incomes high enough to merit itemizing. This should be replaced with an increased grant program to state and local governments so that the benefits can be distributed much more broadly.

Simplifying Collection. There are several ways to improve collection. States can move toward greater uniformity in their definition
of the tax base, and in the special provisions allowed (Shannon,

1976c). This would involve pushing the federal government to adopt some of the changes recommended in this section. The advantages of simplicity must be weighed against efficiency and equity.

Property Tax   The first question that must be faced is whether the property tax should be maintained as a major source of local revenues. The answer seems to be that it should, providing certain changes are made. A basic advantage with local financing of public services is that it does give households a choice in the level and type of public services they receive. Local governments can reflect local preferences.

Assessment and collection practices need considerable improvement. When the International Association of Assessing Officers surveyed their membership in 1973, more than two-thirds characterized assessing practices as relatively or very poor (Almy, 1973). Property should be reassessed frequently and as scientifically as possible to avoid the wild variations in effective rates that presently exist within a jurisdiction. Several steps need to be taken.

First, data should be computerized to enable assessors to estimate the annual change in value in different *types* of property in different *locations*. Second, a "truth in property taxation" process should be mandated by the state, requiring localities to disclose, as prominently as possible: (1) the tax rate that would yield the same revenues as the previous year; (2) the proposed tax rate; and (3) the expenditure increases that have necessitated revenue increases. A policy of this type has been implemented in Florida and can serve to douse some of the anger that has kindled the taxpayers revolt.

John Shannon (1978) adds five more conditions under which, he feels, the property tax can be maintained and improved as the major source of local revenues.

■ A uniform system for administering the property tax; appraising, by professional appraisers, at market value for all taxable property; state supervision of local appraisers; and full disclosure of assessments.
■ State-financed circuit breakers.
■ Full state assumption of welfare and medicaid benefits, so that residents cannot avoid the burden of redistributive programs by moving across jurisdictional boundaries.
■ An intergovernmental "fair play" policy, so that as a state mandates new programs it helps local authorities bear their cost, and also compensates them for revenue losses resulting from state mandated property tax exemptions.
■ A moderate appetite for public goods and services.

To this list we should add shifting some of the tax burden from *123* improvements onto land, and greater efforts to reduce interjurisdictional fiscal disparities.

Sales Tax   Reducing the regressivity of the sales tax should be high on the agenda of those states that do not have exemptions for food. States should also weigh the benefits of income tax credits as an alternative way of assisting low income households.

FOOTNOTES TO CHAPTER 7

1. Property taxes include business property taxes.

2. The following cities with populations greater than 125,000 impose personal income taxes at these rates:

Akron	1.5%	Lansing Mich.	
Baltimore	50% of State Liability	residents	1%
Birmingham	1%	nonresidents	0.5%
Cincinnati	2%	Louisville	
Cleveland	1%	residents	2.2%
Columbus	1.5%	nonresidents	1.45%
Dayton	.75%	Montgomery	1%
Detroit		Newark	0.5%
residents	2%	New York	from 0.9% to 4.3%
nonresidents	0.5%	Oakland	1%
Flint		Philadelphia	4 5/16%
residents	1%	Pittsburgh (City)	1%
nonresidents	0.5%	Pittsburgh (School District)	1%
Grand Rapids		Portland, Ore.	0.6%
residents	1%	St. Louis	1%
nonresidents	0.5%	San Francisco	1.1%
Kansas City, Mo.	1%	Toledo	1.5%
		Youngstown	1.5%

Source: Commerce Clearing House, *State Tax Guide 1978,* Chicago, 1978.

3. These data are state averages across all jurisdictions.

4. See Cebula (1974 a, and 1974 b); Ostrowsky (1978); and Pack (1973). Elderly migrants (over 65) are seen as relatively insensitive to tax rates (Barsby and Cox, 1965, and Debua, 1974 c).

5. A number of studies have found a positive relationship between taxes and salares. See Izraeli (1973).

6. C ed in ACIR (1978). The right to issue local development bonds has been requested by the Texas Industrial Commission and was subject to a referendum November 1978.

7. Quoted in "Lower Taxes Bring High Employment," *Nation's Business,* October 1976.

8. See also Friedman (1975) and Orr (1975).

9. Net fiscal surplus is defined as the value of local public services received minus the local taxes paid. Differences in the effect of the local public sector according to income are also observed by Mayo (1971 and 1972) and Orr (1975). However, Mayo notes that the influence of educational outlays is "spotty" and confined largely to those with the highest incomes, who tend

to locate in jurisdictions with high educational outlays, usually suburbs (p. 237), a finding reinforced by Friedman's work.

10. Neal R. Peirce, "Proposition 13—A Clamp on Land Use," *Washington Post,* September 15, 1978.

11. Mainly because recent studies have shown that the tax is not shifted completely onto renters, who tend to have lower incomes than homeowners.

12. Cited in "The Big Tax Revolt," *Newsweek,* June 18, 1978. Also, see Shannon (1973).

WHAT SHOULD STATES DO ABOUT THE FISCAL LIMITATION MOVEMENT?

It has been variously described as an earthquake, a landslide, and an avalanche. Constitutional Amendment XIIIA of the California State Constitution was passed on June 6, 1978, the most publicized success of the fiscal limitation movement, and a victory clear enough to have many states and even the federal government thinking twice about taxes and spending (Table 24). John Shannon and Carol Weissert (1978) of the ACIR gave the New York City crisis a 5 on a Richter-like 1 to 10 scale for the state/local finance sector, the 1974-76 recession about 8, and Proposition 13 almost 10. What will be the effects of the movement to limit state and local fiscal behavior? What actions can state governments take? These are the themes of this chapter.

STATE AND LOCAL LIMITATIONS   Limitations can either apply to expenditures or tax revenues, state or local governments, and can arise from either state legislation or from constitutional amendment. A combination of common sense and some knowledge of the local fiscal sector would suggest:

■ If the desire, either of the legislature or the voters, is to limit public sector spending, then an expenditure limitation is much more effective and equitable than a tax limitation. The latter does not limit spending and bestows capital gains on property owners.
■ To be effective, a spending limitation must apply to all levels of government, otherwise its main impact will be to shift functional responsibilities to the nonlimited level.
■ Expenditure limitations should be linked to the rate of growth of the local tax base (business and personal income and wealth). Limiting growth to an arbitrary annual percentage is very disruptive during periods of high inflation and local growth.
■ While limitations may encourage efficiency in government—and there is no evidence as yet—they do so at some cost. The flexibility of the government to cope with economic problems is limited, and equity is reduced.
■ Tax limitations that apply only to the tax rate or level of assessment—the most common of all limitations—are rarely effective in

126

Table 24
Proposition 13: Highlights

Property tax rates are limited to 1 per cent of the cash value plus the rate
    needed to service bond indebtedness approved by the voters before
    FY 1979. Revenues are collected by each county and apportioned
    among county governments, municipalities, school districts and
    special districts in the ratio of their 1978 allocation.

Assessed values will be rolled back to 1975-76 assessment levels and cannot
    be raised by more than 2 per cent annually unless the property is
    sold.

Increases in state taxes will require a two thirds majority in both houses
    of the Legislature, and no new state ad valorem, sales, or trans-
    actions taxes on real property is allowed.

Special taxes, except for taxes on real property, can be imposed by local
    jurisdictions only after approval of two-thirds of the jurisdiction
    voters.

---

reducing revenues, since revenues are the product of rates and assessed
value. Rate limitations can work if the area practices mandatory 100
percent assessment.
■ Tax revenue limitations of the Proposition 13 type[1] are inequitable
and inefficient. While they may express a very real taxpayer grievance,
they do not address the problem effectively.

State Tax and   At the time of writing, ten states have
Expenditure   some form of actual or intended limi-
Limitations[2]   tation on their taxing or spending powers.
    All limitations have been enacted since
    1976.

Arizona   Constitutional   Limits state annual spend-
(1978)   ing to 7 percent of total
    personal income. Future in-
    creases must be approved
    by two-thirds of both
    houses.

California   Constitutional   Any changes in state taxes
(1978)   to increase revenues must be
    imposed by an act passed by
    two-thirds of both houses. *127*

		No new ad valorem taxes on real properties may be imposed.
Colorado (1977)	Statutory	General fund spending may increase by 7 percent, and the reserve fund may be increased by 4 percent. Any surplus revenues must be refunded to taxpayers.
(1978)	Statutory	State personal income tax must be inflation indexed.
Hawaii (1978)	Constitutional	State spending increases are limited by the rate of growth of the local economy. If the general fund exceeds 5 percent of expenditures for two years, taxpayers are refunded.
Illinois (1978)	Non-binding Proposition	Voters approved the proposition that the state should limit state and local spending. No limit yet set.
Michigan (1977)	Statutory	Amounts of over 2 percent of adjusted personal income are deposited in a state stabilization fund and can be withdrawn as personal income declines.
(1978)	Constitutional	State spending increase is limited to the rate of increase in gross personal income.
New Jersey (1976)	Statutory	Spending increase is limited to the increase in state personal income (between 9 and 10 percent in 1978).
North Dakota (1978)	Statutory	State income tax is to be reduced by increasing the amount of income subject to graduated rates.

| Tennessee (1978) | Constitutional | Spending increase limited to the growth of the economy (11 percent in 1978). |

Local Expenditure Limitations Arizona has had a constitutional limit on the growth of local expenditure of 10 percent since 1921. Booming growth and rising prices have necessitated a number of by-pass tactics, with the endorsement of the state legislature.[3] For example, school expenditures are excluded, as are expenditures of federal monies. Localities can also avoid the limit by declaring a fiscal emergency, a practice that is frequently used. The lesson is that limitations that step beyond the boundaries of practicality tend to be eroded. New Jersey has limited local spending since 1976, but has expanded direct state assistance, which mitigates the impact. Texas adopted local spending limits in 1978.

Local Tax Limitations Local limitations on property tax rates and assessments have arisen because taxpayers resent paying more taxes as a result of rising property values rather than as a result of planned increases in local expenditures. There is a sense that a fiscal variant of Parkinson's Law is at work: Government spending expands to absorb the revenues available. The most logical expression of this is the "truth in taxation" provisions passed in Florida, which allows revenues to increase only enough to meet planned expenditures, and requires local assessors to advertise exactly what spending increases have necessitated the raising of rates or assessments.

A major disadvantage of this approach is that it perpetuates existing inequities in assessments unless special provisions are included to allow these to be redressed.

But tax limitations do not meet these grievances in an efficient or equitable manner.

THE IMPACTS Full effects of the recent spate of limitations will take years to unravel. They are unlikely to be as disastrous as opponents predict, nor as benign as supporters forecast. Proposition 13 is likely to have the following effects:

■ Property values in California will increase more rapidly than elsewhere.
■ Local governments will seek ways to reduce the costs of public service delivery.
■ The burden of supporting local services will shift from local to state *129*

governments, particularly welfare and education.
- Capital expenditures will fall as bond issues are cut. Private developers will have to meet more of the costs of development.
- Some local services will be cut.
- Federal money will be cut back, and federal income tax receipts will grow.

Property Values   The most pronounced impact will be a rapid increase in property values in California. As C. Lowell Harriss (1978) summarizes:

> Today's owners, in voting essentially permanent reductions in annual property taxes, have enlarged the *net* benefits to be capitalized in valuing real estate. This one-time capital gain . . . absorbs *now* much of the future benefit of the tax cut . . . Future buyers will pay a higher price— higher by enough to offset the tax benefit.

Inflated property values will increase the downpayment necessary to purchase homes, excluding many households from the tax advantages of homeownership.

The lower tax also reduces the cash flow required to hold undeveloped land, encouraging speculative underutilization. The increased property values will also discourage industrial development (an increase of jobs was one of the benefits offered by proponents). But the price of land, as well as the tax rate, are factors considered by business.

The rising value of property over time (it can be reassessed when it changes hands) will swell tax revenues, dampening the restrictive effect on local governments.

Government Efficiency   Local governments will attempt to cut costs. Anaheim Mayor William O. Talley claims that, "It's making us more creative, more innovative than ever before."[4] The city has been processing data for itself and nine neighboring towns, and sharing training facilities for fire and police recruits with the cities of Orange and Garden Grove. Opportunities for shaving costs in this way are limited to a few percentage points at best. In fact, efficiency may be reduced. Expenditures to be cut are the least visible, including research and information dissemination and planning programs that can help reduce costs in the long run. There is also a fear that salary freezes, another immediate threat, will drive out the most productive workers.[5]

Many areas will switch to fees and charges, which could, if properly used, increase efficiency.

State Assumption of   The state of California will take over both
130 *Local Responsibilities*   the full cost and the administration of the

Table 25
Possible Effects of Proposition 13 on Major Federal Programs

Program	Effect
Mass Transit Assistance	To qualify for Section 5 funds from UMTA, assistance from state and local governments to operators must be greater than the average of the previous two years. $50 million out of a total of $120 million is jeopardized. Participation in UMTA capital grants is also in danger if the 20 per cent match cannot be made.
Highway Aid	Federal aid covers between 70 and 90 percent of highway construction and rehabilitation. State projects will not be affected since they are paid for from earmarked state highway user taxes. About half of locally administered outlays come from property taxes which could endanger $200 million in federal aid, but the California state Department of Transportation has indicated it will provide extra funds.
Airport Aid	Some federal aid to general aviation is endangered because local airports do rely on property taxes.
Education	As much as $385 million in federal aid could be lost if local school districts cut back expenditures. If tuition is increased for post-secondary education, federal expenditures in the Basic Education Opportunity Grant program could rise.
CETA	Although CETA Title VI does contain maintenance of effort provisions, it may be possible for local governments to use CETA funds to rehire local workers laid off because of the tax cut. Some of the $80 million used for work experience, public service employment, summer youth and youth employment and demonstration programs could be lost.
Welfare	The elimination of the scheduled cost-of-living increase to AFDC recipients will reduce program costs by an estimated $144 million, and since the federal government pays about half, $71 million of this will accrue to the federal government, although food stamp benefits, 100 percent federally funded, are estimated to rise by $25 million.
General Revenue Sharing	Since there is a lag in data collection, there will be no immediate change in California receipts. If GRS is reauthorized without change in the allocation formula, the reduction in local tax effect would cost California $100 million in GRS funds in FY 1981 or FY 1982.

SOURCE: Adapted from Congressional Budget Office, *Proposition 13: Its Impact on the Nation's Economy, Federal Revenues, and Federal Expenditures,* Congress of the United States, Washington, D.C., July 1978, pp. 17-26.

welfare program, relieving counti. s of an estimated $1.6 billion in expenditures. Cutting welfare was one of the reasons that voters gave for approving the measure. The program is now removed from their direct control. Education is also likely to become an increasing state responsibility. Local limits have made a mockery of post-serrano equalization programs. In one area, state funding to localities will decline. The state financed circuit breaker has become unnecessary, saving the state $643 million annually.

Capital Expenditures   Capital expenditures will decline sharply in California because localities will be unable to offer the necessary "tax base collateral" upon which to issue bonds.[6]

Local Services[7]   Although voters only wanted to cut welfare, and, in fact, favored increasing all other categories of spending, they are likely to experience cuts in several others services—those typically regarded as luxury services by local officials. Summer schools and special services to the handicapped have gone, and arts and recreation programs have been severely affected. The California Arts Council has lost 60 percent of its budget, and the Los Angeles Philharmonic 50 percent.

Federal Taxes   A Congressional Budget Office study
and Expenditures   (1978a) estimates that Californians will pay an extra $1.3 billion in income taxes because of the reduced local taxes for itemization.[8] Table 25 summarizes what may happen to federal grants to California as a result of reduced matching funds.

WHAT CAN   The success in California has led to tax
STATES DO?   limitation movements in the other 49 states and the District of Columbia. However, John Shannon (1978) does not see a tidal wave of abatement. He argues that the Californian experience is relatively unique and will be difficult to replicate in many other places. Few states have as large a surplus, as high property tax rates, as high an overall tax burden (40 percent above the national average), or as rapidly growing property values.

The results of the November 1978 elections were ambiguous. Limitations passed in some states but failed elsewhere. Many "single issue" tax cut candidates lost. Polls taken during the election indicated that voters favored spending cuts rather than tax limitations. There will be a few more successful property tax rollbacks in states where values
132 have soared. There will be pressure for spending limits at all levels of

government. There will also be pressure for more open fiscal policy deliberations. Public sector employment will not grow as rapidly as in the past. And public accountability will be more rigorously pursued. But states should not panic. The solution is not an interstate competition to limit taxation. It is the adaptation of state and local policies to the political climate of the 1980s. The policies discussed in the preceding chapters provide a basis upon which states can improve the equity and efficiency of their fiscal practices. The appropriate response is not a mindless "more frugal than thou" stance, but a carefully thought-out reform of the ways taxes are collected and expenditures determined.

FOOTNOTES TO CHAPTER 8

1. Property tax receipts will decline from an estimated $10.3 billion to only $3 billion.

2. Much of the data in this section comes from National Governors' Association, 1978a.

3. See Bruce Koon, "Living with Limits," *Wall Street Journal,* 11/3/78.

4. Quoted in Peter Nye, "What Happened in California," *Nation's Cities,* August 1978.

5. James Ring Adams, "Coping with Proposition 13," *Wall Street Journal,* 10/10/78.

6. Proposition 13 limitations excluded revenues necessary to service existing debts from the 1 percent tax limitation.

7. See Peter Nye, op. cit.; Clint Page, "The Impact of Proposition 13," *Nation's Cities,* August 1978; Stephen J. Sansweet, "Proposition 13's Impact on the Arts," *Wall Street Journal,* 7/14/78; and U.S. Conference of Mayors, *The Taxpayers' Revolt and the Arts,* Washington, D.C. 1978.

8. This is allocated as follows: $490 million from owner occupied residential property (compared with a property tax reduction of $2341 million); $179 million from owners of residential rental property (against a tax savings of $1200 million); 28 million from commercial and industrial property (a tax savings of $1916 million); and $361 million from agriculture ($944 million).

BIBLIOGRAPHY

This paper covers a very broad array of topics. This bibliography allows the interested reader to pursue some of these topics in greater depth. It is organized, broadly, along the major issues covered in the text. Sources that provide a useful summary of each issue are marked with an asterisk.

While there is no single source that provides an overview to all aspects of state and local fiscal behavior, the interested reader may find Maxwell and Aronson's *Financing State and Local Governments,* published by the Brookings Institution in Washington, D.C. (1977), a useful place to start. For an up-to-date discussion of recent changes in fiscal policy and of topical issues, the Advisory Commission on Intergovernmental Relations (ACIR) publishes an annual *Significant Features of Fiscal Federalism.* This, and the many other publications of the Commission, are invaluable sources. Finally, the Municipal Finance Offices Association in Washington, D.C. has published a *Compendium of Current Research on State and Local Finance and Financial Administration,* which contains essays summarizing the state of the art in major areas together with a thorough index and description of ongoing research, which they plan to update regularly. This can put fiscal practitioners in touch with those conducting relevant studies.

Data is a constant problem for those wishing to understand what is happening in the state and local public sector. The U.S. Bureau of the Census in Washington, D.C. conducts a census of state ands local governments every five years. The most recent, in 1977, is not yet published, and thus we rely upon 1972 data. The Census Bureau also publishes a less thorough, but still useful, *Governmental Finances.* The most recent edition, published in the fall of 1978, covers FY 1977. The ACIR also conducts surveys of local governments on relevant issues, and is the source of a great deal of data. Its journal, *Intergovernmental Perspective,* often contains useful summaries of ongoing projects. For an up-to-date description of state tax codes and revenues, see the *State Tax Guide,* revised annually by the Commerce Clearing House in Chicago. The Tax Foundation in Washington, D.C., compiles tables on governmental fiscal behavior biennially, in *Facts and Figures in Government Finance.* The next issue is due in the summer of 1979. Economic and demographic data are available in the *Survey of Current Business,* published monthly by the Bureau *134* of Economic Analysis, U.S. Department of Commerce. One or two issues annually deal with state and local government behavior in a disaggregated manner.

Allocation of Taxable Income
ACIR, 1975; Hellerstein, 1975 and 1977; Cahoon and Brown, 1973.

Assessment and Collection
Almy, 1973; D.C. Tax Revision Commission, 1978; Hellerstein, 1977; Shannon, 1971 and 1977; Stolz and Purdy, 1977.

Circuit Breakers (see Property Tax Relief)

Economic Development
  Components of Change: Allaman and Birch, 1975; Birch, 1978; Jusenius and Ledebur, 1976 and 1978; Ledebur, 1978; Wolman, 1978*.
  Location Determinants: Burns, 1977; Chinitz, 1960; Dorf and Emerson, 1978; EDA, 1971; Fields, 1976; Fuchs, 1962; Fulton, 1971; Harris and Hopkins, 1972; Huntington and Kahn, 1976; Jones et al., 1975; Kemper, unpublished; Moses and Williamson, 1967; Olvey, 1972; Perloff et al., 1973; Steinnes, 1977; Stone, 1976; Struyk, 1972; Struyk and James, 1975; Thompson, 1965; Vaughan, 1977*; Weinstein and Firestine, 1978; Wheat, 1973.

Exempt Property (see also Incentives)
Hellman and Sifniotis, 1978; Peterson, 1973; Pfister, 1976.

Federal Aid
ACIR (Fiscal Federalism); Barro, 1978.*

Federal Assumption
Barro, 1978; Hamilton and Rabinovitz, forthcoming*.

Fiscal Capacity
ACIR, 1971 and 1977a; Akin, 1973; Barro, 1978; Manvel, 1971.

Fiscal Crises
ACIR, 1973b; Aronson and King, 1978; Barro, 1978.

Gambling
Brinner and Clotfelter, 1975; *Gambling in America,* 1977; Suits, 1978.

Incentives (See also Exempt Property and Taxes and Business Location)
Bird, 1966; Bridges, Parts I and II, 1965; Cornia, Testa, and Stocker, 1978*; Falk et al., no date; Harrison and Kanter, 1976 and 1978; Hellman, Wassall, and Escowitz, 1973; Hellman, Wassall and Falk, 1976; Jack Fawcett Associates, 1976; Moes, 1961; Morgan and Hackbart, 1976; Mulkey and Dillman, 1976; Rinehart, 1963; Ross, 1953; Sazama, 1970; Sherman and Willett, 1969; Stober and Falk, 1967; Surrey, 1970.

135

Incidence (see also Investment, Taxes and Business and Residential Location)
  Business Taxes: Bahl and Shellhammer, 1969; Harberger, 1962; Pechman, 1966; Stockfish, 1961; Vasquez and deSeve, 1977.
  Income Tax: Lile and Soule, 1969; Moscovitz, 1972; Pechman and Okner, 1974*.
  Property Tax (see also Property Values...): Aaron, 1975; Arnott and MacKinnon, 1977; Black, 1977; Break, 1975; McClure, 1977*; Mieszkowski, 1972*; Netzer, 1973; Pechman and Okner, 1974; Peterson et al., 1973; Polinsky and Rubinfeld, 1978; Zimmerman, 1973.
  Sales Tax: Schaefer, 1969.

Industrial Development Bonds
  Alabama Research Council, 1970; Jack Fawcett Associates, 1976; Sazama, 1970; Stober and Falk, 1969.

Inflation and Income Taxes
  ACIR, 1976; ACIR, 1979; Greytak and Jump, 1975.

Investment (see also Public Services, Taxes and Business and Household Location)
  Becker, 1969; Beckman, 1974; Hodge, 1979; Peterson, 1973 and 1978*; Sahling, 1978; Sternlieb and Burchell, 1973.

Limitation of Taxes and Expenditures
  Expenditure: ACIR, 1977b; Fuches, 1978; National Governors' Association, 1978b*; Shannon and Weissert, 1978.
  Taxes: ACIR, 1977b; Barkume, 1976; CBO, July and October 1978; Fuchs, 1978; Harriss, 1978; Levy, 1975; National Governors' Association, 1978b*; Neufield, 1977; Shannon and Weissert, 1978.

Municipal Bond Interest Tax Exemption
  Ackerman and Ott, 1970; Fortune, 1973 and 1975; Morris, 1976; Peterson and Galper, 1975; Shaul, 1977*; Vaughan, 1979.

Property Tax Relief
  ABT, 1975; ACIR, 1973a; Bendick, 1976; Cook, 1973; Gold, forthcoming*; Grubb and Hoachlander, 1978; Shannon, 1973.

Property Values, Rentals, and Property Taxes
  Coen and Powell, 1972; Daicoff, 1961; Edel and Sclar, 1974; Hamilton, 1972 and 1973; Heinberg and Oates, 1970 and 1972; Hyman and Pasour, 1973; Moody, 1974; Oates, 1969; Orr, 1968 and 1972; Smith, 1970; Smith and Keyak, 1975; Vaughan and Vogel, 1979*.

Public Services and Residential Location
  Ellickson, 1976; Friedman, 1975; Mayo, 1971 and 1973; Miller and Tabb, 1973; Moody, 1974; Oates, 1969; Orr, 1968 and 1972; Vaughan and Vogel, 1979*.

Resource Taxation
  Gaffney, 1967; Stinson, 1977*; Wead and Koepf, 1976; USDA, 1978.

Revenue Prediction (see also Tax Rate Determinants)
  Auten and Robb, 1976; Bahl and Gretak, 1976*; Greytak and Cupoli, 1978.

Site Value Tax
Archer, 1973; Carlson, 1977; Cuddington, 1978; D.C. Tax Revision Commission,

1978; Finkelstein, 1975; Lindholm, 1977; Lynn, 1977; Oldman and Teachout, 1977; Peterson, 1973 and 1978*; Pollock and Shoup, 1977.

Stabilizing Influence of Taxes
Williams et al., 1973.

State Aid
ACIR, Fiscal Federalism; Barro, 1978; National Governors' Association, 1978a.*

Suburban Exploitation
Bradford and Oates, 1974; Greene, Neenan, and Scott, 1976*.

Taxes and Business Location
Intrastate: Cameron, 1969; Fuller, 1978; Grieson et al., 1977; Hamovitch, 1966; Levin, 1974; Mikesell, 1970; Roniger, 1978; Vaughan, 1977*.
Interstate: Due, 1961; Hodge, 1979; Morgan, 1967; Schmenner, unpublished; Vaughan, 1977*; Williams, 1967.

Taxes and Residential Location
Interstate: Bradford and Kelejian, 1973; Ellickson, 1976; Fuller and Towles, 1977; Hamilton, 1972 and 1973; Heinberg and Oates, 1970 and 1972; James, 1976; Laidler, 1969; Mayo, 1971 and 1973; Vaughan and Vogel, 1979*.
Interstate: Cebula, forthcoming, 1977, 1976, 1974a, b, and c; Greenwood, 1975; Pack, 1973; Vaughan and Vogel, 1979.

Taxes and Wages
Izraeli, 1973.

Tax Base Determinants
Bahl and Greytak, 1976; Barro, 1978*; Booth, 1978; Gerweck and Epp, 1974; Gerard, 1974; Greytak and Cupoli, 1977; Groves and Riew, 1963; Halstead, 1978; Kee, 1968.

Tax Base Sharing
Bahl and Puryear, 1976*; Bahl and Vogt, 1975; Barro, 1978; Fischel, 1976.

Unemployment Insurance
Ehrenberg and Oaxaca, 1976; Feldstein, 1976.

Value Added Tax
Aaron, 1968; ACIR, 1978.

Wage Subsidy
Bishop, 1977; Vaughan in Bryce, 1979.

BIBLIOGRAPHY

Aaronson, J. Richard, and Eli Schwartz, "Financing Public Goods and the Distribution of Population in a System of Local Governments," *National Tax Journal,* Vol. 26, No. 2, June 1973, pp. 137-160.

Aaron, Henry J., *Who Pays the Property Tax: A New View,* Brookings Institution, Washington, D.C. 1975.

_____, "Differential Price Effects of a Value Added Tax," *National Tax Journal,* Vol. 21, No. 2, 1968, pp. 162-175.

ABT Associates, *Property Tax Relief Programs for the Elderly,* prepared for U.S. Department of Housing and Urban Development, Washington, D.C., 1975.

Ackerman, Susan, and David Ott, "An Analysis of the Revenue Effects of Proposed Substitutes for Tax Exemption of State and Local Bonds," *National Tax Journal,* Vol. XXIII, No. 4, 1970, pp. 397-406.

Advisory Commission on Intergovernmental Relations, *Intergovernmental Perspective,* Washington, D.C., January 1979.

_____, *Differential Economic Growth,* Washington, D.C., 1978a.

_____, *Countercyclical Aid and Economic Stabilization,* A-69, Washington, D.C., December 1978 b.

_____, *State Mandating of Local Expenditures,* A-67, Washington, D.C., July 1978 c.

_____, *The Michigan Single Business Tax,* M-114, Washington, D.C., March 1978d.

_____, *Measuring the Fiscal "Blood Pressure" of the States — 1964-1975,* Washington, D.C., 1977a.

_____, *State Limitations on Local Taxes and Expenditures,* A-64, Washington, D.C., 1977b.

_____, *Inflation and Federal and State Income Taxes,* A-63, Washington, D.C., 1976.

_____, *State and Local Doing Business Taxes on Out-of-State Financial Depositors,* report prepared for Committee on Banking, Housing, and Urban Affairs, U.S. Senate, 94th Cong., 1975.

_____, *State-Local Finances, Significant Features of Fiscal Federalism,* M-79, Washington, D.C., 1974a.

_____, *The Property Tax in a Changing Environment,* Washington, D.C., 1974b.

_____, *Financing Schools and Property Relief—A State Responsibility,* A-40, Washington, D.C., January 1973a.

_____, *City Financial Emergencies—The Intergovernmental Dimension,* A-42, Washington, D.C., July 1973b.

_____, *Measuring the Fiscal Capacity and Effort of State and Local Areas,* M-58, Washington, D.C., March 1971.

_____, *Metropolitan Fiscal Disparities,* A-31, Washington, D.C., 1967.

Ahlbrandt, R.S., Jr., "Efficient Output of a Quasi-Public Good-Fire Services," Ph.D. dissertation, University of Washington, 1972.

Akin, John S., "Fiscal Capacity and the Estimation Method of the Advisory Commission on Intergovernmental Relations," *National Tax Journal,* Vol. XXVI, No. 2, 1973, pp. 275-291.

Alabama Business Research Council, *Industrial Development Bond Financing: Business and Community Experiences and Opinions,* University of Alabama Press, 1970.

Allaman, Peter M., and David L. Birch, "Components of Employment Change for States by Industry Group, 1970-72," Joint Center for Urban Studies of M.I.T. and Harvard University, September 1975.

Almy, Richard R., "Rationalizing the Assessment Process," in George E. Peterson, ed., *Property Tax Reform,* The Urban Institute, Washington, D.C., 1973.

Archer, R.W., "Site Value Taxation in Central Business District Redevelopment," The Urban Land Institute, Washington, D.C., 1972.

Arnott, Richard J., and James C. MacKinnon, "The Effects of the Property Tax" A General Equilibrium Simulation," *Journal of Urban Economics,* Vol. 4, 1977, pp. 389-407.

Aronson, J. Richard, and Arthur E. King, "Is There a Fiscal Crisis Outside of New York," *National Tax Journal, Vol. XXIX, No. 4, 1976, pp. 422-435.*

Bahl, Roy W., and David Greytak, "The Response of City Government Revenues to Changes in Employment Structure," *Land Economics,* Vol. 52, Nov. 1976.

Bahl, Roy W., and David Puryear, "Regional Tax Base Sharing: Possibilities and Implications," *National Tax Journal,* Vol. 29, Sept. 1976, pp. 328-335.

Bahl, Roy W., and Kenneth L. Shellhammer, "Evaluating the State Business Tax Structure: An Application of Input-Output Analysis," *National Tax Journal,* Vol. XXII, No. 2, 1969, pp. 203-216.

Bahl, Roy W., and Walter Vogt, *Fiscal Centralization and Tax Burdens,* Ballinger Publication Company, Cambridge, Mass., 1975.

Barkume, Anthony J., "Criteria for Voting Judgments on a Property Tax Initiative: An Analysis of the Watson Amendment," *National Tax Journal,* Vol. XXIX, No. 4, 1976, pp. 448-460.

Barro, Stephen M., *The Urban Impacts of Federal Policies: Vol. 3, Fiscal Conditions,* R-2114-KF/HEW, The Rand Corporation, April 1978.

Becker, Arthur P., *Land and Building Taxes: Their Effects on Economic Development,* Madison, University of Wisconsin Press, 1969.

Beckman, John W., *Industry in New York: A Time of Transition,* The 1976 Report of the Select Committee of the Economy, New York State Legislative Document No. 12, 1974.

Bendick, Marc, Jr., "Designing Circuit-Breaker Property Tax Relief," *National Tax Journal,* Vol. XXVII, No. 1, 1976, pp. 19-28.

Bergin, Thomas P., and William F. Eagen, "Economic Growth and Community Facilities," *Municipal Finance*, Vol. 33, May 1961, pp. 146-50.

Birch, David L., "The Processes Causing Economic Change in Cities," U.S. Department of Commerce, unpublished, 1978.

Bird, Richard M., "Tax-Subsidy Policies for Regional Development," *National Tax Journal*, Vol. XIX, No. 2, 1966, pp. 113-124.

Bishop, John, "Vouchers for Creating Jobs, Education, and Training," SR 17, The Institute for Research on Poverty, Madison, Wisc., 1977.

Black, David E., "Property Tax Incidence: The Excise-Tax Effect and Assessment Practices," *National Tax Journal*, Vol. XXX, December 1977, pp. 429-434.

Booth, Douglas, "The Differential Impact of Manufacturing and Mercantile Activity in Local Government Expenditures and Revenues," *National Tax Journal*, Vol. 31, 1978, pp. 33-47.

Bradford, David F., and Harry H. Kelejian, "An Econometric Model of the Flight to the Suburbs," *Journal of Political Economy*, Vol. 81, No. 3, May/June 1973, pp. 566-589.

Bradford, David F., and Wallace E. Oates, "Suburban Exploitation of Central Cities and Governmental Structure," in Harold M. Hochman and George E. Peterson, eds., *Redistribution Through Public Choice*, Columbia University Press, New York, 1974, pp. 43-90.

Break, George F., "Property Taxation: A Reappraisal of Burden Distribution, Incidence and Equity and their Policy Implications," in Arthur D. Lynn, ed., *Property Taxation, Land Uses and Public Policy*. Madison, University of Wisconsin Press, 1975.

Bridges, Benjamin, "State and Local Inducments for Industry, Part I," *National Tax Journal*, Vol. XVIII, No. 1, 1965, pp. 1-14, and "Part II," Vol. XVIII, No. 2, 1965, pp. 175-192.

Brinner, Roger E., and Charles T. Clotfelter, "An Economic Appraisal of State Lotteries," *National Tax Journal*, Vol. XXVIII, No. 4, 1975, pp. 395-403.

Bryce, Herrington, ed., *Revitalizing the City*, Lexington Books, Lexington, Mass., 1979.

Burns, Leland S., and Wing Ning Pang, "Big Business in the Big City," *Urban Affairs Quarterly*, Vol. 12, No. 4, June 1977, pp. 533-544.

Burnes, Honorable John W., "Federal Action to Strengthen State and Local Revenue Capabilities," *National Tax Journal*, Vol. XIV, No. 3, 1971, pp. 363-368.

Cahoon, C.R., and William R. Brown, "The Interstate Tax Dilemma-A Proposed Solution," *National Tax Journal*, Vol. 26, No. 2, 1973, pp. 187-197.

Cameron, Helen A., "Property Taxation as a Location Factor," *Bulletin of Business Research*, Vol. 44, 1969.

Campbell, Alan K., et al., *Urban Options I,* Academy for Contemporary Problems, Columbus, Ohio 1976.

Carlson, Gary E., "Property Taxes: The Implications for Cities: A Case for Land Value Taxation," *Commentary,* August 1977, pp. 12-13.

Cassidy, M.J., "Is a Progressive Tax Stabilizing?" *National Tax Journal,* Vol. XXIII, No. 2, 1970, pp. 194-205.

Cebula, R.J., "The Migration Impact of State and Local Government Policies: A Survey of the Literature in the United States." unpublished.

_____, "An Analysis of Migration Patterns and Local Government Policy Toward Public Education," *Public Choice,* Vol. 33, 1977, pp. 113-121.

_____, "A Note on Nonwhite Migration, Welfare Levels, and the Political Process," *Public Choice,* Vol. 28, 1976, pp. 117-119.

_____, "Interstate Migration and the Tiebout Hypothesis: An Analysis According to Race, Sex, and Age," *Journal of the American Statistical Association,* Vol. 69, 1974a, pp. 876-879.

_____, "Local Government Policies and Migration: An Analysis for SMSAs in the United States, 1965-1970." *Public Choice,* Vol. 19, 1974b, pp. 86-93.

_____, "The Quality of LIfe and Migration of the Elderly," *Review of Regional Studies,* Vol. 4, 1974c, pp. 62-68.

Chinitz, Benjamin, and Raymond Vernon, "Changing Forces in Industrial Re-location," *Harvard Business Review,* January 1960.

Coen, Robert M., and Brian J. Powell, "Theory and Measurement of the Incidence of Differential Property Taxes on Rental Housing," *National Tax Journal,* Vol. 25, June 1972, pp. 211-216.

Congressional Budget Office, *An Analysis of the Roth-Kemp Tax Cut Proposal,* Congress of the United States, Washington, D.C., October 1978.

Congressional Budget Office, *Proposition 13: Its Impact on the Nation's Economy, Federal Revenues, and Federal Expenditures,* Congress of the United States, Washington, D.c., July 1978.

CONSAD Research Corporation, *A Study of the Effects of Public Investment,* prepared for the Economic Development Administration, U.S. Department of Commerce, Washington, D.C., 1969.

Cook, Billy D., "The Circuit Breaker Approach for Granting Property Tax Relief," in ACIR, *Financing Schools and Property Tax Relief—A State Responsibility,* A-40, Washington, D.c., January 1973.

Cornia, Gary C., William A. Testa, and Frederick D. Stocker, *Local Fiscal Incentives and Economic Development,* Academy for Contemporary Problems, Dayton, Ohio, 1978.

141

Cuddington, John T., "Estimating the Impacts of Property Tax Reform," *Land Economics*, Vol. 54, No. 3, 1978, pp. 362-372.

Daicoff, Darwin W., "Capitalization of the Property Tax," Ph.D. dissertation, University of Michigan, 1961.

District of Columbia Tax Revision Commission, *Financing an Urban Government*, 1978.

Dorf, Ronald J., and M. Jarvin Emerson, "Determinants of Manufacturing Plant Location for Nonmetropolitan Communities in the West North Central Region of the U.S.," *Journal of Regional Science*, Vol. 18, No. 1, 1978, pp. 109-120.

Due, John F., "Studies of State-Local Tax Influences on Location of Industry," *National Tax Journal*, Vol. XIV, No. 2, 1961, pp. 163-173.

Ebel, Robert D., "Research and Policy Developments: Major Types of State and Local Taxes," in Municipal Finance Officers Association, *State and Local Government Finance and Financial Management: A Compendium of Current Research*, Washington, D.C., 1978.

Economic Development Administration, *Survey of Industrial Location Determinants*, U.S. Department of Commerce, Washington, D.C., 1971.

Edel, Matthew, and Elliot Sclar, "Taxes, Spending, and Property Values: Supply Adjustment in a Tiebout-Oates Model," *Journal of Political Economy*, Vol. 82, No. 5, 1974, pp. 941-954.

Ehrenberg, Ronald C., and Ronald L. Oaxaca, "Unemployment Insurance, Duration of Unemployment and Subsequent Wage Gain," *American Economic Review*, December, 1976, pp. 754-766.

Ellickson, Bryan, *Econometric Analysis of Urban Housing Markets: A New Approach*, The Rand Corporation, R-2024-NSF, July 1976.

Falk, Lawrence H., et al., *An Industrial Inducement Program for New Jersey*, Rutgers University, Bureau of Economic Research, no date.

Fantus Company, Inc., *The Appalachian Location Research Studies Program: Summary Report and Recommendations*, New York, 1976.

Feldstein, Martin S., "Temporary Layoffs in the Theory of Unemployment," *Journal of Political Economy*, Vol. 84, No. 5, 1976, pp. 937-958.

Fields, G.S., "Labor Force Migration, Unemployment and Job Turnover, *Review of Economics and Statistics*, Vol. 58, 1976, pp. 407-415.

Finkelstein, Philip, *Real Property Taxation in New York City*, New York, Praeger, 1975.

Fischel, William A., "An Evaluation of Proposals for Metropolitan Sharing of Commercial and Industrial Property Tax Base," *Journal of Urban Economics*, Vol. 3, 1976, pp. 253-263.

Fortune, Peter, "Financing P.L. 92-500: The Impact of the Federal Water Pollution Control Act of 1972 on the Municipal Bond Market," Report for the National Commission on Water Quality, Data Resources, Inc., September, 1975.

Fortune, Peter, "The Impact of Taxable Municipal Bonds: Policy Simulations with a Large Econometric Model," *National Tax Journal,* Vol. XXVI, No. 1, 1973, pp. 29-42.

Friedman, Joseph, *Housing Location and the Supply of Local Public Services,* P-5421, The Rand Corporation, April 1975.

Fuchs, Diane "State and Local Tax and Expenditure Limitations," Report for the Tax Reform Research Group, Washington, D.C., June 1978.

Fuchs, Victor R., *Changes in the Location of Manufacturing in the United States Since 1929,* Yale University Press, New Haven, 1962.

Fuller, Stephen S., and Joan E. Towles, "Impact of Intraurban Tax Differentials on Business and Residential Location in the Washington Metropolitan Area," prepared for the D.C. Tax Revision Commission, 1978.

Fulton, Maurice, "New Factors in Plant Location," *Harvard Business Review,* Vol. 49, 1971, pp. 4-17.

Gaffney, Mason, ed., *Extractive Resources and Taxation,* Madison: University of Wisconsin Press, 1967.

Gambling in America, Final Report of the Commission on the Review of the National Policy Toward Gambling, Washington, D.C., 1977.

Gerard, Karen, "New York City's Industrial Tax Structure," unpublished paper, Chase Manhattan Bank, New York, 1974.

Gerweck, John E., and Donald J. Epp, "The Effect of Industrial Growth on the Local Real Estate Tax: an Expanded Model," *Land Economics,* Vol. 50, No. 4, 1974, pp. 397-401.

Goldfarb, Robert S., and Anthony M.J. Yezer, "Evaluating Alternative Theories of Intercity and Interregional Wage Differentials," *Journal of Regional Science,* Vol. 16, No. 3, 1976, pp. 345-363.

Greene, Kenneth V., William G. Neenan, and Claudia D. Scott, "Fiscal Incidence in the Washington Metropolitan Area," *Land Economics,* Vol. 52, No. 1, February 1976, pp. 13-31.

Greenwood, Michael J., "Research on Internal Migration in the United States: A Survey," *Journal of Economic Literature,* Vol. 13, June 1975, pp. 397-433.

Greytak, David, and Bernard Jump, *The Effects of Inflation on State and Local Government Finances, 1967-74,* Occasional Paper No. 25, Syracuse, New York, 1975.

Greytak, David, and Edward N. Cupoli, "Changes in Central City Employment, Resident Decentralization, and Personal Income Tax Revenues," paper presented to the Meetings of the Northeast Regional Science Association, Summer 1977.

Grieson, Ronald E., et al., "The Effect of Business Taxation on the Location of Industry," *Journal of Urban Economics,* Vol. 4, 1977, pp. 170-185.

Groves, Harold, and John Riew, "The Impact of Industry on Local Taxes—A Sample Model," *National Tax Journal,* Vol. XVI, No. 2, 1963, pp. 137-146.

Grubb, W. Norton, and E. Gareth Hoachlander, "Circuit Breaker Schedules and Their Application to California," *Policy Analysis,* 1978, pp. 317-337.

Gurwitz, Aaron, "The Economic Effects of Property Tax Abatement for Industry," unpublished paper, Department of Economics, Michigan State University, 1977.

Halstead, D. Kent, *The Tax Wealth of Fifty States,* National Institute for Education, Washington, D.C., 1978.

Hamilton, Bruce W., *Property Taxes and the Tiebout Hypothesis: Some Empirical Evidence,* Working Paper 1204-23, The Urban Institute, Washington, D.C., February 1972.

Hamilton, Edward K., and Francine Rabinovitz, "Federalization of Welfare: The Financial Effects," in George Peterson (ed.), *Fiscal Choices,* The Urban Institute, Washington, D.C., forthcoming.

Hamovitch, William, "Effects of Increases in Sales Tax Rates on Taxable Sales in New York City," *Financing Government in New York City,* Graduate School of Public Administration of New York University Report to the Temporary Commission on City Finances, New York University, 1966.

Hanna, Frank A., *State Income Differentials,* Duke University Press, Durham, North Carolina, 1959.

Harris, Curtis C., and Frank E. Hopkins, *Locational Analysis,* Lexington Books, Lexington, Massachusetts, 1972.

Harrison, Bennett, "The Political Economy of State Job Creation Business Incentives," *Journal of the American Institute of Planners,* November 1978.

_____, *The Economic Development of Massachusetts,* prepared for the Joint Committee on Commerce and Labor of the Massachusetts State Legislature, November 1974.

_____, *Urban Economic Development,* The Urban League, Washington, D.C., 1974.

_____, and Sandra Kanter, "The Great State Robbery," *Working Papers for a New Society,* Spring 1976, pp. 54-66.

Harriss, C. Lowell, "Property Taxation After the California Vote," *Tax Review,* The Tax Foundation, August 1978.

Hartnett, Harry D., "Industrial Climate in Central Cities," *American Industrial Development Conference Journal,* Vol. 7, No. 2, April 1972, pp. 19-38.

Haskins, Gage B.A., "The Impact of International Trade and Investment Policy on Employment in the United States: A Policy Briefing Paper," prepared for the Department of Housing and Urban Development, November 1977, mimeographed.

Heinberg, John D., and Wallace E. Oates, "The Incidence of Differential Property Taxes on Rental Housing: an Addendum," *National Tax Journal,* Vol. 25, June 1972, pp. 221-222.

_____, The Incidence of Differential Property Taxes on Rental Housing: A Comment and Further Evidence," *National Tax Journal,* Vol. 23, March 1970, pp. 92-98.

Hellerstein, Jerome R., "State Tax Discrimination Against Out-of-Staters," *National Tax Journal,* Vol. XXX, No. 2, June 1977, pp. 113-134.

_____, "Multinational Corporations and Income Allocation Under Section 482 of the Internal Revenue Code," *Harvard Law Review,* Vol. 89, 1976, pp. 1202-38.

_____, "The Unitary Business Principle and Multicorporate Enterprises: An Examination of the Major Controversies," *The Tax Executive,* July 1975.

Hellman, Daryl A., and Costas Sifniotis, "Distributional Considerations of Property Tax Exemption: Analytical Framework," *Public Finance Quarterly,* January 1977, pp. 127-135.

Hellman, Daryl, Gregory H. Wassall, and Herb Escowitz, "The Role of Statewide Industrial Incentive Programs in the New England Economy," *New England Journal of Business and Economy,* Vol. 1, 1973, pp. 10-29.

Hellman, Daryl A., Gregory H. Wassall, and Lawrence H. Falk, *State Financial Incentives to Industry,* Lexington Books, Lexington, Mass., 1976.

Hodge, James H., "A Study of Regional Investment Decisions," Ph.D. dissertation, University of Chicago, March, 1979.

Hogan, Timothy D., and Robert B. Shelton, "Interstate Tax Exportation and States' Fiscal Structures," *National Tax Journal,* Vol. 26, No. 4, 1973, pp. 77-84.

Holcombe, Randall C., "The Florida System: A Bowen Equilibrium Referendum Process," *National Tax Journal,* Vol. 30, No. 1, March 1977, pp. 77-84.

Hyman, David N., and E.C., Pasour, "Real Property Taxes, Local Public Services, and Residential Property Values," *Southern Economic Journal,* Vol. 39, No. 4, April 1973, pp. 601-611.

Izraeli, Oded, "Differences in National Income and Prices Between Cities," Ph.D. dissertation, University of Chicago, 1973.

Jack Fawcett Associates, Inc., *Effectiveness of Financial Incentives on Investment in the Economic Development Administration's Designated Areas,* Economic Development Administration, Washington, D.C., 1976.

James, Franklin, "Income Taxes, Homeownership, and Urban Land Use," Paper presented at the American Economic Association meetings, New Jersey, 1976.

145

Jones, H.C., Mike et al., *An Analysis of the 1973-74 Energy Shortage in the New York Region*, BNL 20133, Brookhaven National Laboratory, New York, 1975.

Jusenius, Carol L., and L.L. Ledebur, *Documenting the Decline of the North*, Economic Development Administration, Washington, D.C., June 1978.

_____, *A Myth in the Making: The Southern Economic Challenge and Northern Economic Decline*, Economic Development Administration, November, 1976.

_____, *Firms in New England: Deaths, Births and Migration*, forthcoming.

Kee, Woo Sik, "Industrial Development and Its Impact on Local Finance," *Quarterly Review of Economics and Statistics*, April, 1968, pp. 19-24.

Kemper, Peter, *Manufacturing Location, Production Requirements, and Market Characteristics*, Unpublished, 1974.

Laidler, David, "Income Tax Incentives for Owner-Occupied Housing," in A.C. Harberger and M.J. Bailey, eds., *The Taxation of Income from Capital*, The Brookings Institution, Washington, D.C., 1969.

Ledebur, Larry, "Regional Location and Performance of Manufacturing in the United States," unpublished, The Urban Institute, October, 1978.

Levin, Sharon C., "Suburban-Central City Property Tax Differentials and the Location of Industry: Some Evidence," *Land Economics*, Vol. 50, No. 4, November, 1974, pp. 380-386.

Levy, Mickey, "Voting on California's Tax and Expenditure Limitation Initiative," *National Tax Journal*, Vol. 28, No. 4, 1975, pp. 426-435.

Lile, Stephen E., and Don M. Soule, "Interstate Differences in Family Tax Burdens," *National Tax Journal*, Vol. 22, No. 4, 1969, pp. 433-445.

Lindholm, Richard M., ed., *Property Tax Reform: Foreign and United States Experience with Site Value Taxation*, Monograph 77-11, Lincoln Institute of Land Policy, Cambridge, Mass., 1977.

Liu, B.C., "Local Government Finance and Metropolitan Employment Growth: A Simultaneous Equation Model," *Southern Economic Journal*, Vol. 43, 1977, pp. 1379-1385.

Loewenstein, Louis K., "The New York Urban Development Corporation—A Forgotten Failure or a Precursor of the Future?" *Journal of the American Institute of Planners*, July 1978, pp. 261-273.

Lynn, Arthur D., Jr., "Legal and Public Policy Aspects of Implementing Site Value Taxation," in Lindholm, ed., *Property Tax Reform*.

Manvel, Allen D., "Differences in Fiscal Capcity and Effort: Their Significance for a Federal Revenue Sharing System," *National Tax Journal*, Vol. 24, No. 2, 1971, pp. 193-204.

146 Maxwell, James A., and J. Robert Aronson, *Financing State and Local Government*,

The Brookings Institution, Washington, D.C., 1977.

Mayo, Stephen K., "Local Public Goods and Residential Location: An Empirical Test of the Tiebout Hypothesis," paper presented to the Metropolitan Governance Committee, Resources for the Future, Washington, D.C. 1973.

_____, "An Econometric Model of Residential Location," Ph.D. Dissertation, Harvard University, Cambridge, Mass., 1971.

McClure, Charles E., "The New View of the Property Tax: A Caveat," *National Tax Journal,* Vol. 30, No. 1, 1977, pp. 69-76.

Mieszkowski, Peter, "The Property Tax: An Excise Tax or a Profit Tax?" *Journal of Public Economics,* Vol. 1, April 1972, pp. 73-96.

Mikesell, John L., "Central Cities and Sales Tax Rate Differentials: The Border City Problem," *National Tax Journal,* Vol. 23, No. 2, 1970, pp. 206-213.

Miller, Stephen M., and William K. Tabb, "A New Look at a Pure Theory of Local Expenditures," *National Tax Journal,* Vol. 26, 1973, pp. 161-176.

Moes, Joe E., "The Subsidization of Industry by Local Communities in the South," *Southern Economic Journal,* Vol. 28, October 1961.

Moody, James, "Measuring Tax Benefit and Capitalization from a Local Rapid Transit Investment in the San Francisco Bay Area," Ph.D. dissertation, University of California at Berkeley, 1974.

Morgan, William E., *Taxes and the Location of Industry,* University of Colorado Press, Boulder, 1967.

Morgan, William E., and Merlin M. Hackbart, "An Analysis of State and Local Industrial Tax Exemption Programs," *Southern Economic Journal,* Vol. 41, No. 2, 1976, pp. 200-205.

Moscovitch, Edward, "State Graduated Income Taxes—A State Initiated Form of Federal Revenue Sharing," *National Tax Journal,* Vol. 25, 1972, pp. 53-64.

Moses, Leon, and M.F. Williamson, "The Location of Economic Activity in Cities," *American Economic Review,* Vol. 57, 1967.

Morris, Frank, "The Taxable Bond Option," *National Tax Journal,* Vol. 29, No. 3, 1976.

Mulkey, David, and B.L. Dillman, "Location and the Effects of State and Local Development Subsidies," *Growth and Change,* Vol. 7, April 1976, pp. 71-80.

Municipal Finance Officers Association, *State and Local Government Finance and Financial Management: Compendium of Current Research,* Washington, D.C., August 1978.

National Governors' Association, *Allocation of State Funds for Jurisdictions,* Washington, D.C., 1978a.

_____, *Tax and Expenditure Limitations 1978,* Washington, D.C., 1978b.

_____, *Targeting of Federal and State Aid to Distressed Cities,* Washington, D.C., forthcoming.

National League of Cities, *The Tax System: Consequences for Urban Policy,* Washington, D.C., 1977.

Netzer, Dick, "The Incidence of the Property Tax Revisited," *National Tax Journal,* Vol. 26, No. 4, 1973, pp. 515-535.

Neufield, John, "Tax Rate Referenda and the Property Taxpayers' Revolt," *National Tax Journal,* Vol. 30, No. 4, 1977, pp. 441-456.

Oates, Wallace E., "The Effects of Property Taxes and Local Public Services on Property Values: An Empirical Study of Tax Capitalization and the Tiebout Hypothesis," *Journal of Political Economy,* Vol. 77, Nov/Dec. 1969, pp. 957-971.

Oldman, Oliver, and Mary Miles Teachout, "Land Valuation Under a Separate Tax on Land," Proceedings of the 70th Annual Conference on Taxation, National Tax Association, Chicago, 1977.

Olvey, L.D., "Regional Growth and Interregional Migration—Their Patterns of Interaction," *Review of Regional Studies,* Vol. 2, No. 2, 1972, pp. 139-163.

Orr, Larry L., "The Incidence of Differential Property Taxes on Urban Housing: Reply," *National Tax Journal,* Vol. 25, No. 2, 1972, pp. 217-220.

_____, "The Incidence of Differential Property Taxes on Urban Housing," *National Tax Journal,* Vol. 21, No. 3, 1968, pp. 253-262.

Ostrovsky, A., "Some Economic Effects and Causes of State and Local Government Commitment to Public Education," *Indian Journal of Economics,* Vol. 60, 1978, pp. 49-58.

Pack, Howard, and Janet Rothenberg Pack, "Metropolitan Fragmentation and Suburban Homogeneity," *Urban Studies,* Vol. 14, 1977, pp. 191-201.

Pack, Janet Rothenberg, "Determinants of Migration to Central Cities," *Journal of Regional Science,* vol. 13, 1973, pp. 249-260.

Pechman, Joseph A. *Federal Tax Policy,* The Brookings Institution, Washington, D.C. 1966.

Pechman, Joseph A., and Benjamin Okner, *Who Bears the Tax Burden,* The Brookings Institution, Washington, D.C., 1974.

Perloff, Harvey S., et al., *How a Region Grows,* Committee for Economic Development, Supplementary Paper No. 17, Washington, D.C., March 1973.

Peterson, George E., "Differential Taxation of Land and Improvements," report prepared for the D.C. Tax Revision Commission, Washington D.C., 1978a.

_____, *Federal Tax Policy and Urban Development,* The Urban Institute,

Washington, D.C., 1978b.

————, "Finance," in William Gorman and William Glazer, eds., *The Urban Predicament,* The Urban Institute, Washington, D.C., 1976.

————, Testimony Before the Committee on Banking, Currency and Housing, U.S. House of Representatives, Washington, D.C., September 28, 1976.

————, and Harvey Galper, "Tax Exempt Financing of Private Industry's Pollution Control Investment," *Public Policy,* Vol. 23, 1975, pp. 81-103.

————, et al., *Property Taxes and Housing in Central Cities,* D.C. Heath and Co., Lexington, Mass., 1973.

Pfister, R.L., "A Re-evaluation of the Justifications for Property Tax Exemptions," *Public Finance Quarterly,* October, 1976, pp. 431-452.

Polinsky, A. Mitchell, and Daniel L. Rubinfeld, "The Long Run Effects of a Residential Property Tax," *Journal of Urban Economics,* Vol. 5, April, 1978, pp. 241-262.

Pollack, W., "Pricing Fire Protection Services," in Selma Mushkin, ed., *Public Prices for Public Goods,* The Urban Institute, Washington, 1972.

Pollock, Richard L., and Daniel C. Shoup, "The Effect of Shifting the Property Tax from Improvements to Land Values: An Empirical Estimate," *Land Economics,* Vol. 67, 1977.

Rafuse, Robert W., "The New York State Personal Income Tax: Essays in Fiscal Analysis," prepared for the New York State Temporary State Commission on State and Local Finances, December, 1974.

Renas, S.M., and R. Kumar, "The Cost of Living, Labor Market Opportunities, and the Decision to Migrate: A Case of Misspecification," *Annals of Regional Science,* Vol. 12, 1978, pp. 65-74.

Rinehart, J., "Rates of Return on Municipal Subsidies to Industry," *Southern Economic Journal,* April 1963.

Roniger, George, *Testimony before the Committee on Taxation and Government Operations,* New York State Senate, 1/26/78.

Ross, D. William, "Tax Exemption in Louisiana as a Device for Encouraging Industrial Development," *Southwestern Social Science Quarterly,* June 1953, pp. 14-22.

Sahlings, Leonard, "Are State and City Corporate Income Taxes Stifling Investment in New York City?" *Federal Reserve Bank of New York,* December 1978.

Samaza, Gerald W., "A Benefit Cost Analysis of a Regional Development Incentive: State Loans," *Journal of Regional Science,* Vol. 10, 1970.

Schaefer, Jeffrey M., "Sales Tax Regressivity Under Alternative Tax Bases and Income Concepts," *National Tax Journal,* Vol. 22, No. 4, 1969, pp. 516-527.

149

Schmenner, Roger, "City Taxes and Industrial Location," unpublished paper, Harvard, 1974.

Shannon, John, "After Jarvis—Hard Questions for State-Local Policymakers," Testimony before the Subcommittee on Intergovernmental Relations of the Senate Committee on Government Affairs, June 28, 1978.

_____, "Property Taxation: Federalism and Federal Policy," in Arthur D. Lynn, Jr., ed., *Property Taxation, Land Use and Public Policy,* University of Wisconsin Press, 1976a.

_____, Testimony before the House Committee on Banking, Currency and Housing, reprinted by the Committee as *The Rebirth of the American City,* Part 2, U.S. House of Representatives, Washington, D.C., 1976b, p. 807ff.

_____, "The Property Tax: Reform or Relief?" in George E. Peterson, ed., Property Tax Reform, The Urban Institute, Washington, D.C., 1973.

, "Federal Assistance in Modernizing State Sales and Local Property Taxes," *National Tax Journal,* Vol. 24, No. 3, 1971, pp. 379-388.

_____, "Federal Assistance in Modernizing State Sales and Local Property Taxes," *National Tax Journal,* Vol. 29, No. 3, 1976c, pp. 379-388.

_____, and Carol S. Weissert, "After Jarvis: Tough Questions for Fiscal Policymakers," *Intergovernmental Perspective,* Vol. 4, No. 3, 1978.

Shaul, Marnie, *The Taxable Bond Option for Municipal Bonds,* Academy for Contemporary Problems, Columbus, Ohio, October, 1977.

Sherman, Roger, and Thomas D. Willett, "Regional Development Externalities, and Tax-Subsidy Combinations," *National Tax Journal,* Vol. 22, No. 2, 1969, pp. 291-300.

Smith, David Mitchell, "Neoclassical Growth Models and Regional Growth in the U.S., *Journal of Regional Science,* Vol. 15, No. 2, 1975.

Smith, V. Kerry, and Timothy A. Keyak, "A Comparison of Tax Capitalization Effects on Owner Occupied and Rental Housing in the United States," *Applied Economics,* Vol. 7, 1975, pp. 167-174.

Smith, R. Stafford, "Property Tax Capitalization in San Francisco," *National Tax Journal,* Vol. 23, No. 2, June 1970, pp. 177-193.

Stanfield, Rochelle L., "There are Surpluses in the Statehouses—But Can They Last Forever? *National Tax Journal,* 1/21/78, pp. 95-99.

Steinnes, Donald N., "Causality and Intraurban Location," *Journal of Urban Economics,* Vol. 4, No. 1, 1977, pp. 59-79.

Sternlieb, George, and Robert W. Burchell, *Residential Abandonment: The Tenement Landlord Revisited,* Center for Urban Policy Research, Rutgers, The State University of New Jersey, 1973.

Stinson, Thomas F., *State Taxation of Mineral Deposits and Production,* Interagency Energy Environment Research and Development of the USDA and EPA, Washington, D.C., 1977.

Stober, William J., and Lawrence H. Falk, "Industrial Development Bonds as a Subsidy to Industry," *National Tax Journal,* Vol. 22, No. 2, 1969, pp. 232-243.

_____, "Property Tax Exemptions: An Inefficient Subsidy to Industry," *National Tax Journal,* Vol. 20, No. 4, 1967.

Stockfish, J.A., *A Study of California's Tax Treatment of Manufacturing Industry,* California's Economic Development Agency, Sacramento, 1961.

Stolz, Otto C., and George A. Purdy, "Tax Simplification and Efficiency Through Federal Collection," report by the Advocates and Analysts, Arlington, Va., June, 1977.

Stone, Donald B., *Industrial Location in Metropolitan Areas,* Praeger, New York, 1976.

Struyk, Raymond J., "Spatial Concentration of Manufacturing Employment in Metropolitan Areas," *Economic Geography,* Vol. 48, No. 2, 1972, pp. 189-192.

_____and Franklin James, *Intermetropolitan Industrial Location: The Pattern and Process of Change in Four Metropolitan Areas,* Lexington Books, Lexington, Mass., 1975.

Suits, Daniel B., "Gambling Taxation in the District of Columbia," paper prepared for the D.C. Tax Revision Commission, Washington, D.C., 1978.

Surrey, Stanley S., "Tax Incentives as a Device for Implementing Government Policy: A Comparison with Direct Government Expenditures," *Harvard Law Review,* Vol. 83, No. 4, January 1970, pp. 705-738.

U.S. Department of Agriculture, *State Taxation of Mineral Deposits and Production,* Rural Development Research Report No. 2, Washington, D.C., 1978.

Vasquez, Thomas, and Charles deSeve, "State/Local Taxes and Jurisdictional Shifts in Corporate Business Activity: The Complications of Measurement," *National Tax Journal,* Vol. 30, No. 3, 1977, pp. 285-298.

Vaughan, Roger J., "Federal Policy and Local Fiscal Conditions," paper presented at HUD conference on the urban impacts of federal policies, Washington, D.C., February 1979.

_____, *The Urban Impacts of Federal Policies: Vol. 2 Economic Development,* The Rand Corporation, R-2028-KF/RC, July 1977.

_____and Mary E. Vogel, *The Urban Impacts of Federal Policies: Vol. 4, Population and Residential Location,* The Rand Corporation, R-2205-KF/HEW, March 1979.

Vernez, Georges, and Roger Vaughan, *Assessment of Countercyclical Public Works and Public Employment Programs,* The Rand Corporation, R-2214-EDA, *151*

September, 1978.

Vernez, Georges et al., *Regional Cycles and Employment Effects of Public Works Investments,* The Rand Corporation, R-2052-EDA, January 1977.

Wead, Jim, and Lois R. Koepf, *Coal: State Severance Taxes and the Distribution of Revenue,* Lexington, Kentucky, Council of State Governments, 1976.

Weicher, John W., "Determinants of Central City Expenditures: Some Overlooked Factors and Problems," *National Tax Journal,* Vol. 23, No. 4, 1970, pp. 379-396.

Weinstein, Bernard L., "Tax Incentives for Growth," *Society,* Vol. 14, No. 3, 1977, pp. 73-75.

_____, and Robert E. Firestines, *Regional Growth and Decline in the United States,* Praeger, New York, 1978.

Wheat, Leonard F., *Regional Growth and Industrial Location,* Lexington Books, Lexington, Mass., 1973.

White, Michelle J., and Lawrence J. White, "Tax Subsidy to Owner-Occupied Housing: Who Benefits?" *Journal of Public Economics,* Vol. 3, 1977, p. 111-126.

Williams, William V., et al., "The Stability, Growth, and Stabilizing Influence of State Taxes," *National Tax Journal,* Vol. 26, No. 2, 1973, pp. 267-273.

_____, "A Measure of the Impact of State and Local Taxes on Industry Location," *Journal of Regional Science,* Summer 1967, pp. 49-59.

Wisconsin Department of Revenue, *Corporate Tax Climate: A Comparison of 15 States,* Madison, Wisconsin, December 1975.

Wolman, Hal, "Components of Employment Change in Local Economies," Report 1264-02, The Urban Institute, Washington, D.C., 1978.

Zimmerman, Dennis, "Expenditure-Tax Incidence Studies, Public Higher Education, and Equity," *National Tax Journal,* Vol. 26, No. 1, 1973, pp. 65-70.

Part II

TAXES AND GROWTH
BUSINESS INCENTIVES AND
ECONOMIC DEVELOPMENT

Michael Kieschnick

INTRODUCTION

Since the early years of U.S. economic history, state governments have sought to influence the pace and composition of economic development. Over time, they have used tax policy, regulatory policies, direct expenditures and public persuasion in efforts to increase income and employment for state residents. These policies have received mixed support from both economists and the businesses they are intended to benefit.

After a decade of slow economic growth, an increasing number of states are turning to manipulations of their overall tax structure and explicit tax incentives to induce industrial development. Hardly a legislative session goes by in each state without a new tax incentive proposal being debated and quite frequently adopted.

A tax incentive represents the expenditure of public funds for economic development purposes. As such, its costs and benefits need to be evaluated just as one would evaluate public works, job training programs, or direct loans to businesses. Proponents of tax incentives have argued that taxes are an important barrier to business expansion, and that tax reductions can be targeted to investment or employment increases to stimulate development. Opponents have argued that taxes at the state and local level are of little importance in business investment decisions, so that tax incentives represent windfalls to businesses which would have invested or hired in any case.

With a few notable exceptions, academic economists have opposed the use of state tax incentives, characterizing them as ineffective. Even if incentives are effective in influencing the location of investments, many economists condemn them as leading to a misallocation of resources. For the most part, the vigor of economists' verbal opposition has been overwhelmed by the interests of state legislators and their business constituents in adding to the number of incentives. A few economists, focusing on the competition among states for new businesses, have concluded that the provision of subsidies under competition leads to an improved allocation of resources— particularly labor—and should be encouraged and expanded in depth.

For the most part, this study will assume that the broad goals of development policy are agreed upon—an increase of employment and income for in-state residents. Largely ignored will be issues of the quality and distribution of employment opportunities among individuals or communities within the state. To render the study manageable, the examination of policies will be limited to attempts by *155* states to use specific automatic provisions within their state corporate income tax to influence business investment decisions. The policy question addressed in this study is, "Should a state, given its present tax levels and structure, its present expenditure policy, and its present regulatory policy, adopt tax incentives intended to increase business investment within its borders?"

The study combines a conceptual essay, a review of the academic literature, and new empirical work. While the existing literature is voluminous, most is conceptually or methodologically flawed, and is better presented within the context of a more appropriate framework. The study consists of five chapters. Chapter One presents an overview of the level and composition of present state and local taxes, along with a review of existing state business tax incentives. Chapter Two considers the use of tax incentives as a public investment in a benefit/cost framework. Chapter Three is a literature review of existing empirical studies on the effects of state business tax incentives. Chapter Four presents new empirical research developed as part of this study. Finally, Chapter Five summarizes the findings and considers the implications of the study for state policymakers.

1

THE STRUCTURE OF
STATE TAX SYSTEMS

Researchers seeking analytical simplicity would do well to avoid the field of state taxation of business. The number of different taxes, tax base definitions, and lack of publicly available data present far more difficulties than are found in federal taxation.

As can be seen in Table 1 below, the relative importance of particular taxes has changed quite dramatically at the state level over the past decades. In particular, the state property tax has declined to the extent that property tax revenues are now overwhelmingly a local revenue source. States have significantly increased the use of general and selective sales taxes. Personal income taxes have steadily increased in importance. As a percentage of state revenues, the corporate income tax has remained relatively stable, generally fluctuating between 5 and 9 percent.

THE ISSUE OF
TAX INCIDENCE

It is well understood by most economists, but very few political figures, that the entity which writes the check to the state Department of Finance is not necessarily the same entity which bears the tax burden. There is extraordinary disagreement over the incidence of corporate income taxes, with some arguing that all corporate income taxes are a burden on shareholders, others arguing that such taxes are shifted forward to consumers, and others arguing a more eclectic position—with the burden shared among shareholders, consumers, and workers depending on characteristics of the relevant factor and demand markets. If all state/local taxes on businesses are shifted forward to consumers, state tax incentives should have little or no incentive effect. If they are all borne by shareholders, there may be a significant incentive effect from reducing such taxes.

The issue of incidence substantially complicates the task of apportioning the state and local tax burden between individuals and businesses for purposes of interstate tax comparisons. The Advisory Commission on Intergovernmental Relations (hereafter ACIR) has periodically issued estimates of the amounts of state and local taxes initially paid by businesses, carefully avoiding the issue of eventual incidence. Their estimates considering the states as a whole are displayed in Table 2 below. The share of taxes initially paid by business has declined from 36.8 percent in 1957 to 30.6 percent in 1977. Over the *157*

Table 1

State Taxes by Source—Selected Years 1940–1980
(In Percent)

Year	Total Excluding Unemployment Taxes	Individual Income Taxes	Corporate Income Taxes	Death and Gift Taxes	General Sales Taxes	Selective Sales Taxes	Property Taxes	Motor Vehicle Licences	All Other
1940	100.0%	6.2%	4.7%	3.4%	15.1%	34.0%	7.8%	11.7%	17.0%
1950	100.0	9.1	7.4	2.1	21.0	33.8	3.9	9.5	13.1
1960	100.0	12.2	6.5	2.3	23.9	28.8	3.4	8.7	12.1
1962	100.0	13.3	6.4	2.5	24.9	30.4	3.1	8.1	11.6
1964	100.0	14.1	7.0	2.7	25.1	28.9	3.0	7.9	11.4
1966	100.0	14.6	6.9	2.8	26.8	27.7	2.8	7.6	10.8
1968	100.0	17.1	6.9	2.4	28.7	25.6	2.5	6.8	9.9
1970	100.0	19.1	7.8	2.1	29.6	24.0	2.3	6.2	9.0
1972	100.0	21.7	7.4	2.2	29.4	22.7	2.1	5.6	8.9
1974	100.0	23.0	8.1	1.9	30.5	21.1	1.8	5.1	8.7
1976	100.0	24.0	8.1	1.7	30.6	19.2	2.4	4.9	9.0
1978	100.0	25.7	9.5	1.6	31.1	16.6	2.1	4.3	9.0
1980 (Est.)	100.0	26.4	9.7	1.5	31.6	15.3	1.9	4.0	9.6

SOURCE: Table 52, *Significant Features of Fiscal Federalism: 1979–1980 Edition*, M-123, Advisory Commission on Intergovernmental Relations, Washington, D.C., October, 1980.

Table 2

State and Local Taxes with an Initial Impact on Business By Type of Tax 1957, 1962, 1967, 1977

Tax	Amount (in millions)				Percent of Total			
	1977	1967	1962	1957	1977	1967	1962	1957
Total, excluding unemployment taxes	$53,520	$19,900	$14,478	$10,553	100.0%	100.0%	100.0%	100.0%
Property (real and personal)	21,288	10,298	8,156	5,808	39.8	51.7	56.3	55.0
Sales and Gross Receipts	15,062	4,076	2,694	1,902	28.1	20.5	18.6	18.0
Corporate Net Income	9,902	2,479	1,332	1,043	18.5	12.5	9.2	9.9
Severance	2,168	577	451	388	4.1	2.9	3.1	3.7
License and other	5,100	2,470	1,845	1,412	9.5	12.4	12.7	13.4

SOURCE: Table A-1, *Regional Growth: Interstate Tax Competition*, Report A-76, Advisory Commission on Intergovernmental Relations, Washington, D.C., March 1981.

past twenty years, property taxes on businesses have declined in relative importance but remain the single largest tax. Sales taxes paid by business and corporate income taxes have generally increased. For the most part, the income and sales taxes are state levies while the property taxes are local levies. Unemployment taxes are relatively large, but are levied on crudely determined actuarial grounds, and so are relatively less important determinants of interstate tax differentials.

When disaggregated, as in Table 3 below, it is clear that the share of state and local taxes paid by business varies significantly among states. In West Virginia, businesses pay 45.4 percent of state/local taxes, while in Nebraska, businesses pay only 19.0 percent of state/local taxes.

RELATIVE IMPORTANCE OF STATE/LOCAL TAXES ON BUSINESS

As a share of sales or income, or relative to some base such as employment, how important are state and local taxes initally borne by business?

As shown in Table 4 below, there are substantial differences among states in terms of the tax burden per employee. In 1977, Alaska imposed about $4,273 per private nonagricultural employee, while South Carolina imposed only about $475. Alaska is clearly an extraordinary case, with only six other states imposing a burden of over $1,000 per employee. The median tax burden per employee in 1977 was $669. Such figures do not accurately represent the tax burden of any single employer, since firms in different industries have very different capital/labor ratios, profitability, and other factors which influence relative tax burden.

For manufacturing firms, it is possible to construct a "hypothetical" firm, complete with balance sheets and income statements, with which to calculate the state and local taxes which would be paid in each state. The results of one such study are shown in Table 5 below. In 1980, the hypothetical firm would have had an average (unweighted) state and local tax burden of $184,798 on sales of $6,919,920 (or 2.7 percent of sales). This reflects quite a wide range, with North Dakota imposing $892,070 (with the great majority in local property taxes) and Nevada only $59,340.

Much of this variation reflects the differences in local property tax rates. However, there is also substantial variation among states in the corporate income tax structure. As seen in Table 6, a number of states do not tax corporate income at all (Wyoming, Washington, Texas, South Dakota, Nevada). Among states with proportionate taxation, the rate varies from 3 to 12 percent. Among states with progressive corporate tax structures, the rate varies from 1 to 10.5 percent. The base *160* for determining taxable income also varies substantially. Alabama,

Table 3

Taxes With an Initial Impact on Business as A Share of Total State and Local Taxes[1]

Ranked in Decreasing Order of Percent Share

1977

1. West Virginia	45.4%		27. Pennsylvania	29.4
2. Alaska	42.5		28. North Carolina	29.1
3. Wyoming	39.2		29. Virginia	28.4
4. Tennessee	34.9		30. Idaho	27.6
5. Washington	34.5		31. Utah	27.5
6. Delaware	34.2		32. Oregon	27.5
7. Connecticut	33.4		33. Rhode Island	26.9
8. Texas	33.0		34. Vermont	26.6
9. Kansas	32.9		35. Arkansas	26.5
10. Ohio	32.8		36. South Carolina	26.1
11. Alabama	32.0		37. Georgia	25.7
12. Illinois	32.0		38. Hawaii	25.3
13. D.C.	31.9		39. New Mexico	25.0
14. Arizona	31.8		40. Maine	24.6
15. Missouri	31.2		41. Minnesota	24.5
16. Florida	30.9		42. Maryland	24.1
17. California	30.9		43. Oklahoma	23.7
18. Colorado	30.7		44. Massachusetts	23.6
19. Nevada	30.4		45. Michigan	23.5
20. New York	30.4		46. North Dakota	23.4
21. New Hampshire	30.1		47. Kentucky	23.3
22. Montana	29.9		48. South Dakota	22.1
23. Louisiana	29.8		49. Iowa	21.5
24. New Jersey	29.8		50. Wisconsin	22.3
25. Mississippi	29.7		51. Nebraska	19.0
26. Indiana	29.6			

[1]Excluding severance taxes

SOURCE: Business taxes, excluding severance taxes, derived from Table A-2, *Regional Growth: Interstate Tax Competition.*

Arizona, Iowa, Louisiana, Missouri, and North Dakota allow a firm to deduct all or part of its federal tax liability in arriving at state taxable income. Most states simply adopt the federal definition of taxable income, thus incorporating federal depreciation provisions, while some begin with sales and use separate (and frequently unique) depreciation provisions. States also differ in the manner in which they determine taxable income for those corporations whose activities are spread among a

Table 4

Business Taxes per Nonagricultural Private Employee Ranked in Decreasing Order

1977

1.	Alaska	$4,273	27.	Virginia	$ 667
2.	New York	1,221	28.	Nevada	664
3.	Wyoming	1,185	29.	North Dakota	636
4.	California	1,074	30.	Idaho	629
5.	Arizona	1,058	31.	Ohio	627
6.	West Virginia	1,049	32.	Tennessee	623
7.	Washington	937	33.	Mississippi	621
8.	Montana	893	34.	Rhode Island	615
9.	New Jersey	867	35.	New Mexico	611
10.	Delaware	836	36.	Utah	609
11.	Hawaii	807	37.	Wisconsin	597
12.	Kansas	802	38.	Alabama	594
13.	Colorado	791	39.	Missouri	591
14.	Illinois	787	40.	Indiana	582
15.	D.C.	779	41.	Maine	567
16.	Maryland	765	42.	New Hampshire	558
17.	Connecticut	762	43.	South Dakota	536
18.	Vermont	722	44.	North Carolina	529
19.	Florida	697	45.	Iowa	528
20.	Oregon	692	46.	Oklahoma	526
21.	Pennsylvania	692	47.	Kentucky	517
22.	Massachusetts	687	48.	Georgia	513
23.	Minnesota	674	49.	Arkansas	497
24.	Michigan	672	50.	Nebraska	495
25.	Louisiana	670	51.	South Carolina	475
26.	Texas	669			

SOURCE: Business taxes, excluding severance taxes, derived from Table A-2, *Regional Growth: Interstate Tax Competition.* Private employment taken from Table 1, "Employees on nonagricultural payrolls for states and selected areas by industry division," various issues, *Employment and Earnings,* U.S. Department of Labor, Bureau of Labor Statistics.

Table 5

Ranking of States by State and Local
Tax Burden on a Hypothetical
Average Manufacturing Corporation

1980

State	Tax Liability	State	Tax Liability
1. Massachusetts	$387,630	26. Maine	$147,980
2. New York	378,840	27. Hawaii	144,950
3. Rhode Island	325,900	28. South Carolina	144,340
4. Pennsylvania	325,720	29. West Virginia	143,100
5. Mississippi	273,640	30. Nebraska	141,700
6. Connecticut	270,120	31. Oregon	141,120
7. Kansas	229,110	32. Idaho	138,300
8. Indiana	226,800	33. Delaware	136,070
9. New Hampshire	214,640	34. Illinois	130,530
10. Wisconsin	209,580	35. Colorado	125,500
11. Vermont	209,000	36. South Dakota	123,840
12. Iowa	199,620	37. Florida	121,170
13. Virginia	196,390	38. Alaska	116,230
14. New Jersey	188,920	39. Michigan	107,800
15. Ohio	188,420	40. Arkansas	107,700
16. D.C.	180,800	41. North Carolina	103,360
17. California	171,510	42. Utah	94,720
18. Texas	170,920	43. Washington	93,530
19. Missouri	161,780	44. New Mexico	89,830
20. Georgia	160,790	45. Oklahoma	89,650
21. Tennessee	160,430	46. Kentucky	80,000
22. Maryland	157,100	47. Louisiana	77,480
23. Minnesota	155,910	48. Alabama	65,770
24. Arizona	151,130	49. Wyoming	65,640
25. Montana	150,660	50. Nevada	59,340
		51. North Dakota	57,700

SOURCE: Calculated on the basis of a hypothetical manufacturing firm with a gross sales of $6,919,920.Details are available in Appendix I. Tax rates and methods based on *All States Tax Handbook*, 1980. The calculations do *not* include the effects of temporary tax incentives.

number of states (and sometimes countries). Most states allocate income for a multistate company according to a formula based on sales, employment, and assets. Typically, national (or worldwide) income is allocated to a state based on a formula using the share of the firm's total employment, sales, and assets which are located within the *163* state. The weight attached to each factor varies, although the most common weighting procedure uses even weights. If all states allocated income in the same manner, all companies would pay taxes on 100 percent of their income, although at different rates in different states. As will be discussed in greater detail in Chapter 3, the existence of multistate firms, and the ambiguity over defining their actual income in a given state, tremendously complicates the development of an accurate measure of state tax burdens (and hence a measure of interstate differences). Equally profitable firms as measured nationally can be treated quite differently in the same state because of a different interstate allocation of out-of-state assets, sales, or employees.

THE BENEFIT SIDE OF TAXES

Most studies which attempt to relate state taxation to investment or location behavior neglect the benefits which businesses receive from state and local expenditures. The use of tax funds to train workers in schools and provide for highways and public protection all benefit businesses. Hence, differences in tax rates in some way reflect differences in service levels. However, taxes are also used for redistributive purposes and for activities which do not benefit businesses. If the relationship between tax burden and services was on an accurate fee-for-service basis, a firm could choose its location at least partially based on the cost per unit of services and on the state capacity to provide those services.

States differ dramatically in their mix of expenditures (see Table 7 below), while businesses certainly differ in their need for services. Some firms depend heavily on workers trained in public schools, while others are dependent on public highways. Others may prefer workers with little education at lower wages, or ship by rail. Few businesses demand higher welfare expenditures, although the welfare system may serve to support low-income workers who are frequently laid off from cyclical industries. As a percentage of state personal income, there are dramatic differences in state redistributive expenditures on welfare (see Table 7). An ideal analysis of taxation and industrial development must either adjust the tax level for redistributive expenditures, or include them in a separate analysis.

POSSIBLE INCENTIVE EFFECTS OF STATE TAXATION OF BUSINESS

As a byproduct of its revenue-generating function, state and local taxation may affect the economic decisions of businesses and households. While it is relatively easy to conceptually identify these incentive effects, it is far more difficult to quantify them. In the absence of empirical estimates of the responsiveness of various economic decisions to specific taxes, this

164

Table 6

State Corporate Income Tax Rates: 1980

State	Rate (%)	State	Rate (%)
Alabama	5.0	Montana	6.75
Alaska	5.4 (+4.0)*	Nebraska	4.5–4.95
Arizona	2.5–10.5	Nevada	—
Arkansas	1–6	New Hampshire	8.0
California	9.6	New Jersey	7.5
Colorado	5.0	New Mexico	5.0
Connecticut	10.0	New York	10.0
Delaware	8.7	North Carolina	6.0
D.C.	9.0**	North Dakota	3.0–8.5
Florida	5.0	Ohio	4.0–8.0
Georgia	6.0	Oklahoma	4.0
Hawaii	5.85–6.435	Oregon	7.5
Idaho	6.5	Pennsylvania	10.5
Illinois	4.0	Rhode Island	8.0
Indiana	3.0	South Carolina	6.0
Iowa	6.0–10.0	South Dakota	—
Kansas	4.5 (+2.25)*	Tennessee	6.0
Kentucky	4.0–5.8	Texas	—
Louisiana	4.0–8.0	Utah	4.0
Maine	4.95–6.93	Vermont	5.0–7.5
Maryland	7.0	Virginia	6.0
Massachusetts	9.5	Washington	—
Michigan	2.35	West Virginia	6.0
Minnesota	12.0	Wisconsin	2.3–7.9
Mississippi	3.0–4.0	Wyoming	—
Missouri	5.0		

*Surcharge

**A 10 percent surcharge is also imposed.

SOURCE: *All States Tax Handbook,* 1980 (Prentice-Hall). Where a range is given, the state has a progressive income tax. Highest and lowest rates are shown. Federal taxable income is used as a base except in Alabama, Arkansas, California, D.C., Louisiana, Minnesota, Mississippi, Oregon, South Carolina, Utah, and Wisconsin. All or part of federal income tax paid is deductible in Alabama, Arizona, Iowa, Louisiana, Missouri, and North Dakota.

Table 7

State Expenditures for Selected State-Local Functions From Own Revenue Sources, By State, 1977–1978 In Relation to State Personal Income

State	Local Schools	Highways	Welfare	Health and Hospitals
United States	2.24%	0.74%	0.93%[1]	0.74%[1]
Alabama	2.90	1.00	0.44	1.03
Alaska	5.06	1.05	1.24	0.76
Arizona	2.58	0.89	0.38	0.55
Arkansas	2.40	1.30	0.68	0.63
California	1.83	0.40	1.70	0.59
Colorado	2.06	0.51	0.64	0.64
Connecticut	1.34	0.49	0.93	0.70
Delaware	3.63	0.68	0.87	0.70
Florida	2.46	0.56	0.31	0.52
Georgia	2.23	1.08	— *	1.25 *
Hawaii	3.29	0.39	1.52	1.34
Idaho	2.27	1.59	0.66	0.51
Illinois	2.01	0.66	1.29	0.52
Indiana	2.41	0.90	0.32	0.60
Iowa	2.13	1.41	0.86	0.59
Kansas	2.09	0.90	0.80	0.55
Kentucky	2.98	1.80	0.90	0.57
Louisiana	2.85	1.17	0.58	1.07
Maine	2.57	1.13	1.01	0.64
Maryland	2.26	0.81	1.21	0.89
Massachusetts	1.92	0.57	1.85	0.74
Michigan	2.36	0.70	1.33	0.70
Minnesota	3.39	0.94	0.93	0.72
Mississippi	2.64	1.38	0.68	0.85
Missouri	1.54	0.88	0.51	0.63
Montana	3.33	1.20	0.36	0.76
Nebraska	0.89	1.29	0.43	0.67
Nevada	1.52	0.72	0.26	0.45
New Hampshire	0.38	1.13	0.58	0.85
New Jersey	2.05	0.27	0.77	0.56
New Mexico	4.18	1.28	— *	1.04 *
New York	2.25	0.40	0.84	1.06
North Carolina	3.34	1.14	— *	1.04 *
North Dakota	2.33	1.29	0.54	0.63
Ohio	1.73	0.73	0.83	0.73
Oklahoma	2.68	1.02	0.59	0.58
Oregon	1.53	1.02	1.01	0.67
Pennsylvania	2.44	0.70	1.64	0.88
Rhode Island	1.87	0.36	1.70	1.53

(Continued on following page)

Table 7 (cont'd)

State	Local Schools	Highways	Welfare	Health and Hospitals
South Carolina	2.88	0.78	0.61	1.16
South Dakota	0.71	1.19	0.57	0.82
Tennessee	2.12	1.01	0.58	0.63
Texas	2.51	0.64	0.36	0.63
Utah	3.38	0.63	0.65	0.83
Vermont	1.70	0.73	0.83	0.80
Virginia	1.74	1.17	0.54	1.00
Washington	2.72	0.87	1.04	0.43
West Virginia	3.17	1.84	0.63	0.72
Wisconsin	1.94	0.77	1.17	0.73
Wyoming	1.51	1.87	0.24	0.62

*Public welfare expenditures for Georgia, New Mexico, and North Carolina are included with health and hospital expenditures. Data necessary for separations are not available for FY 1978.

SOURCE: Table 21, *Significant Features of Fiscal Federalism, 1979–1980 Edition.* M-123, Advisory Commission on Intergovernmental Relations. Washington, D.C., October 1980.

section will simply identify the direction of reasonably expected effects.

Corporate Net Income Tax   Income taxation of business profits can have incentive effects on the location of investments, the magnitude of investments, and the capital/labor ratio selected. Since income taxes are based on the accounting definition of profits, instead of the economic definition, they are in part a tax on the return to capital and management factors of production. As such, interstate differentials in income tax rates should be expected to reduce the level of investment in high tax states, lower the capital/labor ratio, and reduce the number of projects in high tax states. A state whose sole taxation of business was through an income tax should differentially attract firms which have unstable profits, because they would have no tax liability in bad years—in contrast to states where the principal business tax was a property tax, which applied regardless of income.

Sales Tax   Both the level and the tax base for a sales tax are of interest. If applied to business purchases, a sales tax directly increases the cost of operation. However, in almost all states, business inputs which are used in a manufacturing process are exempted from the sales tax. Naturally, the higher the rate, the larger the potential impact.   *167*

Real and Personal   While the property tax is not a major
Property Taxation   contributor to state revenues in the great
                                majority of states, it is important in a few
states, and dominant in many local communities. The important point
to understand is that in the short run property taxes fall most heavily
on immobile capital. Hence, in a state which taxes real property (land
and structures) and personal property (plant and equipment) as well as
inventory, the most significant impact will be on land prices and the
level and composition of fixed investment. Because of the mobility of
inventories, many states have fully or partially exempted inventories
from property taxation. Real property taxation is to some degree
capitalized in land prices, although there is substantial uncertainty in
the empirical literature as to the degree. If land markets were perfect,
all land prices would fully reflect property tax differences, so that there
would be no geographical incentive effect.

Personal Income Tax   For completeness, it is useful to mention
                              several of the possible incentive effects of
personal income taxation. Higher personal tax rates are sometimes
thought to lead to interstate migration toward low-tax states, reduced
work effort, reduced personal savings, and for unincorporated
businesses, a lessened rate of new business formation.

STATE TAX
INCENTIVES FOR
NEW AND
EXPANDING
INDUSTRY

States offer a number of tax incentives to
new and expanding manufacturers (see
Table 8 below for details on two state incentives), where an incentive is a con-
scious and automatic feature of the tax
code, which is conditioned upon a hiring,
purchase, or investment decision. As of 1980, the most popular state
incentives were sales tax exemptions for raw materials used in
production (forty-six states), sales tax exemptions on new equipment
(thirty-one states), and a variety of general investment and
employment income tax credits (fifteen states).

State corporate income tax credits include both investment and
employment tax credits, and a few states combine investment and
employment credits. A typical employment credit allows a reduction in
state taxes based on some proportion of new wages and salaries.
Others condition the credit on personal characteristics of the new
employees. (For example, Massachusetts gives tax credits for hiring
individuals who were receiving unemployment insurance or public
assistance, or were participants in a job training program. Such
targeted incentives are excluded from this study.) Investment tax
credits are usually based on the value of depreciable investment, with
168 the size of the credit sometimes increasing with the depreciable life of

Table 8

Selected State Tax Incentives for New and Expanding Industry

State	Corporate Income Tax Exemption	Sales Tax Exemption	Sales Tax Exemption on New Equipment
Alabama		x	
Alaska		x	
Arizona			
Arkansas		x	
California			
Colorado	o	x	
Connecticut			
Delaware	o	x	
D.C.			
Florida		x	
Georgia		x	
Hawaii			
Idaho		x	
Illinois		x	
Indiana		x	
Iowa			
Kansas	o		
Kentucky			
Louisiana	o	x	
Maine	o	x	
Maryland		x	
Massachusetts	o	x	
Michigan		x	
Minnesota			
Mississippi		x	
Missouri	o	x	
Montana	o		
Nebraska			
Nevada			
New Hampshire			
New Jersey		x	
New Mexico	o		
New York	o	x	
North Carolina		x	
North Dakota	o		
Ohio		x	
Oklahoma	o	x	
Oregon		x	
Pennsylvania		x	
Rhode Island	o	x	
South Carolina		x	
South Dakota			
Tennessee	o	x	
Texas			
Utah			
Vermont		x	
Virginia		x	
Washington			
West Virginia	o	x	
Wisconsin		x	
Wyoming			

SOURCE: Compiled from state promotional literature, various issues of *State Tax Review* (Commerce Clearing House), and *Industrial Development*.

the asset. Sales tax exemptions are frequently very narrowly targeted to politically influential industries, but most states also have broad-based incentives applying to all new machinery and equipment intended for expansion, replacement, or new facility.

States have significantly increased their use of these tax incentives since the late 1960s (see Table 9 below). The number of states offering sales tax exemptions for machinery and equipment has gone from eighteen to thirty-one in twelve years, while the number of broad-based income tax credits has increased from none in 1968 to fifteen in 1980. Casual inspection reveals that much of the increased use of these incentives came after the early 1970s. The early 1970s were years in which many state legislatures concentrated on environmental issues, and took a generally skeptical approach to industrial development. The 1974 recession seemed to have dramatically increased the interest of state governments in using all available tools to increase employment and income. However the recent proliferation of tax limitation measures may act to reduce interest in revenue-losing tax incentives.

Table 9

Increased Use of State Tax Incentives

Year in Full Effect	General Investment and Employment Income Tax Credits	Sales Tax Exemptions for New Equipment
1980	15	31
1979	11	31
1978	8	—
1977	7	27
1976	6	27
1975	5	25
1974	5	23
1973	5	25
1972	5	21
1971	4	23
1970	1	23
1969	1	21
1968	0	18

SOURCE: Compiled from state promotional literature, various issues of *State Tax Review* (Commerce Clearing House), and *Industrial Development*.

The particular incentives available vary both in size and in the nature of the base activity eligible for subsidy. Table 10 presents a summary of the general development incentives available at the state level as of December 1980.

While it is extremely easy to determine the availability of specific tax incentives by reference to trade journals and various proprietary tax guides, it is far more difficult to estimate the frequency of their use or the magnitude of the initial revenue loss to state governments. In contrast to the federal government, which is required to publish an annual supplement to the budget in which it estimates the magnitude of tax expenditures in a number of programmatic areas, only three state governments make such estimates. California, Michigan, and Maryland has each published estimates of the tax expenditures in their budgets, although none has state-level industrial tax incentives. Hence, no estimates exist of the recent magnitudes of state revenue losses from various incentives.[1]

All locally exempted property simply does not appear in many records. Similarly, exemptions from sales tax collections are not recorded anywhere. Theoretically, it is possible to determine the claims for employment or investment tax credits on state corporate returns. However, in conducting this study, no state was willing to reveal such figures or allow access to corporate tax returns.

Clearly, a necessary step toward good public policy is to periodically evaluate business tax incentives. One of the reasons that tax incentives can be repeatedly proposed and passed is the general (and specific) lack of evaluations of their effectiveness. For those firms which benefit from tax incentives, and their representatives, it is clearly attractive for tax subsidies to remain an off-budget item, since quantification is a necessary first step toward evaluation. The new research reported in Chapter Four should provide a partial guide to those interested in future and more detailed evaluations.

FOOTNOTES TO CHAPTER 1

[1]In writing this book, the author was initially promised access to state corporate income tax records in a number of states. This cooperation was eventually withdrawn.

Table 10

State General Tax Incentives Designed to Stimulate Manufacturing

State	General Description of Incentive
Colorado	$50 credit per new employee and $50 credit per $100,000 depreciable investment in new or expanded manufacturing facility, available for up to ten years.
Delaware	$75 credit per new employee and $185 credit per $100,000 investment in new or expanded manufacturing facility with at least 25 employees, available for ten years.
Kansas	$50 credit per new employee plus $50 credit per $100,000 investment in a new or expanded manufacturing facility, available for up to ten years.
Louisiana	$100 credit per new employee in a manufacturing facility (larger credits for certain individuals and certain areas). State can also lower taxes to meet lower state taxes offered elsewhere.
Maine	10% credit for depreciable investment. Total investment must be at least $5 million.
Massachusetts	3% credit for depreciable investment in manufacturing facility.
Missouri	$100 credit per new employee plus $100 credit per $100,000 new investment in expanding manufacturing facility. For new plants, parallel credits are at $75.
New Mexico	3.75% credit of value of new machinery and equipment used in manufacturing.
New York	4% credit for depreciable investment in new or expanded manufacturing facility.
Montana	1% credit for wages paid new employees in new or expanding manufacturing facility.
North Dakota	1% credit of wages for new employees in manufacturing facility for first three years, .5% for fourth and fifth years.
Oklahoma	.5% credit for depreciable investment in manufacturing facility which increases employment.
Rhode Island	2% credit for depreciable investment in manufacturing facility.
Tennessee	.2% credit for industrial machinery, increasing to 1.0% after July 1984.
West Virginia	10% credit for depreciable investment with 1% increments available for ten years.

SOURCE: Compiled from promotional literature of various states and issues of *State Tax Review* (Commerce Clearing House)

2

INDUSTRIAL TAX INCENTIVES
AS A PUBLIC INVESTMENT

State corporate tax incentives intended to induce additional investment or employment are public investments, and should be analyzed within the framework of a large body of public finance literature. The decision rules for such public investment are well known: the investment should be made if (1) the rate of return on the tax incentive, adjusted for risk, exceeds the social opportunity cost of capital, or equivalently (2) the net present value of the stream of benefits and costs arising from the investment is positive. Additional public investments can be justified until the last dollar of subsidy has a return just equal to the cost of capital and the net present value is zero.

These principles are well known among economists, but somewhat obscure among development officials and elected representatives. Rather than develop a full discussion of public investment rules, this paper will serve simply to highlight some issues of particular concern to tax incentives: (1) the key question of uncertainty about the effect of the subsidy; (2) the difference between automatic subsidies and negotiated subsidies; and (3) the different costs and benefits taken into account by a private firm, a state development official, and a national observer.

THE IMPACT OF UNCERTAINTY ON THE PUBLIC INVESTMENT DECISION The public investment decision should count only the costs and benefits resulting from investment or employment which would not have occurred without the tax subsidy. All other investment or hiring decisions should be excluded from consideration. There is an unfortunate tendency among some advocates of state tax incentives to assume that all businesses which receive a subsidy on the basis of an investment or hiring decision would not have done so in its absence. In some cases, the investment or hiring would have taken place, but at a lesser volume or level. In others, the investment or hiring would not have taken place at all. Any public investment or social benefit-cost analysis must make some judgment about the sensitivity of investment or hiring with respect to the subsidy. Alternatively, some estimate of the proportion of subsidized investment or hiring which would not have taken place in the absence of the subsidy can be used. While many local property tax incentives *173* are discretionary, meaning local officials can bargain with company representatives over the existence, depth, and length of property tax abatements, most state tax incentives are automatic. All a firm must do, if it has made an investment or hired new workers, is fill out a form, and it will automatically receive the tax credit. Because the state does not seek to determine, at the time of the tax credit, whether or not the investment would have been made in any case, the state faces uncertainty in that it does not know the true effect of the incentives. This is true uncertainty, where not even the proportion of investment affected is known, as opposed to risk, in which the proportion is known, but there is uncertainty about which specific investments make up the affected proportion.

The state also bears uncertainty with respect to the magnitude of benefits and costs for those firms which are actually induced to invest or hire more. Just as an equity investor in a business faces risk with respect to the future profitability of the firm, the public investor's return will depend on the future growth, profitability, and employment of the subsidized business. Similarly, as will become clear below, the state cannot know with certainty the extent to which the employment generated by a project will benefit in-state residents, the previously unemployed, or out-of-state residents. Some of this risk can be diversified by the public investor through the portfolio effects of subsidizing a large number of companies, some of which will succeed and others fail. However, the state cannot diversify away the effects of business cycles (and does not have access to future markets to diversify across time).

These distinctions between uncertainty and risk, and diversifiable and undiversifiable risk, should directly influence the public investment decision. As discussed above, the decision to invest is based in part on the required rate of return (or opportunity cost of capital). A great deal of literature and experience in financial markets states that a major investor, with investments in a diversified portfolio, should be much less concerned about risk than a small investor with an undiversified portfolio (see Daniels and Kieschnick, 1979 for more on this point). If the state views its collection of individual tax incentives to specific firms as an investment portfolio, what rate of return should it require? Clearly the state is a "large investor," and will have a diversified portfolio—at least among manufacturing firms within the state. However, even a large public investor should be concerned about true uncertainty—not knowing even a guess about the effectiveness of its incentives—and business cycle risk. Accordingly, the state should seek a higher return on its "portfolio" of incentives than it would if it were investing in low-risk Treasury bills.

174

THE INFLUENCE OF AUTOMATIC VERSUS NEGOTIATED SUBSIDIES

Traditional investment decision rules call for making incremental investments until the last dollar of investment has a marginal net return of zero. At that point, the net benefits of the program (or net development impact) will be maximized. To carry out such a decision rule, however, the investor (whether public or private) must face a schedule of independent investment opportunities, each with an associated expected rate of return. With no constraint on the amount invested, the investor simply invests in projects in order of return until the next project has an unacceptable rate of return.

If state tax incentives are provided on the basis of negotiations between public developers with a subsidy fund and a set of private firms, this underlying picture has a great deal of relevance. Based on the results of the negotiations about level of subsidy, investment and hiring practices, and public services to be provided, the public investor would simply invest in all those projects whose expected return was sufficient. Marginal decision rules could be used. Of course, factors other than public benefit may enter into negotiations, as political figures, consultants, and "deal packagers" seek to influence the subsidy decision.

However, the great majority of state tax incentives are provided automatically, rather than through negotiations. So long as a firm meets certain criteria, and actually makes the investment or hires an additional employee, the tax incentive is provided. No assessment of the expected return on each project is made. In this case, the decision to provide public subsidies is an all-or-none (lumpy and discontinuous) decision. Legislators or elected officials must make the decision to implement a subsidy program based on an assessment of the average return and must assume that the marginal decision rule will be violated. It is impossible to predict whether or not the tendency would be to overinvest or underinvest (thus foregoing valuable investments).

DIFFERING PERSPECTIVES OF THE FIRM, A STATE, AND SOCIETY

The evaluation of an investment opportunity will be critically influenced by which costs and benefits are counted. In many situations, a private firm, a state government, and society as a whole would make different decisions about the same investment project because they include or ignore different benefits and cost.

From the point of view of a private business, only direct revenues and costs are included in the calculation of a net profit estimate. The existence of a tax incentive will alter the net profits of a given investment by reducing the tax costs in a given state. This may make a *175* previously unacceptable investment acceptable, or may simply increase the profitability of an already chosen investment opportunity. However, the private firm is not interested in whether or not personal income in the state of its choice is increased or decreased, or who obtains any new jobs, or whether or not the tax incentive made a difference in the location decision—so long as it does reduce costs.

A single state government should incorporate different costs and benefits into its decisionmaking process. The benefits to the state include net increases in income due to induced investment or hiring, reduced welfare or transfer payment costs, and any increased tax revenues from the expanded economic activity. If the tax incentive does not induce greater investment or hiring, there are no net benefits to the state although there will be to the private firm. The costs to the state include the revenue initially foregone through the subsidy to all subsidized investments or hirings—not just those which are changed— and any increased public service costs or new infrastructure required by induced investments and hirings.

From the point of view of a single state, investments which are merely shifted from one state to another count as much as those investments which would have occurred in no location without the subsidy. A somewhat more difficult conceptual question arises in determining whether or not to count wages and salaries paid to workers who are brought in from out of state to work in induced projects. Such wages and salaries provide no direct benefits to the then current voters/citizens of the state where the subsidy decision (whether automatic or negotiated) was made. At a minimum, there are important distributional questions if a tax subsidy is borne by initial residents while the benefits are borne in part by immigrants.

If a state maintains its level of services (and hence budget) while providing tax incentives, the taxes borne elsewhere must increase. The losses sustained by other taxpayers to compensate merely represent a transfer from those subsidized to those paying higher taxes. In this case, there is no direct tax loss to the state. The benefit-cost decision then must be determined on the basis of relative induced changes in economic activity due to the changed composition of taxes.

This relative incentive effect is illustrated in Figure I below. Consider a state which has two classes of firms—stable (those which are not considering expanding, locating, or leaving the state) and marginal (those which are considering investment decisions). With a uniform tax rate on corporate income, and investment demand equations which are a function of the after-tax cost of capital $s+t$, the stable firms will invest $\bar{I}_2$ and the unstable firms will invest I_2. In each case, the mere existence of taxes, assuming some elasticity of investment with respect to taxation, means that investment is foregone. For the stable firms, the lost investment is equal to $\bar{I}_1 - \bar{I}_2$, where $\bar{I}_1$ is the amount which would have been invested with no taxation of capital.

For unstable firms, the lost investment is $I_1 - I_2$, where I_2 is the amount which would have been invested with no taxation. If the state introduces a tax incentive by placing no taxes on the marginal firm, and shifts them all to the stable firm (in that ideal world in which the firms could be so identified), the relative incentive effects must be compared. So the stable firms must pay a cost of capital of $s+t'$ while the unstable firms have a cost of capital equal only to s. Now, given the demand curves, an additional amount of investment is lost in the stable firms, equal to $\bar{I}_3 - \bar{I}_2$, while investment in unstable firms is increased by $I_1 - I_2$. If the increased investment exceeds the reduced investment, the state is better off (assuming away, for the moment, the other costs involved). If the increased investment from marginal firms is less than the reduced investment from stable firms, the state is worse off for shifting taxes. This indicates the importance of accurately targeting incentive policies not only in lowering taxes for firms with elastic investment responses, but in raising them (or perhaps reducing services) for those with inelastic investment responses.

Figure 1

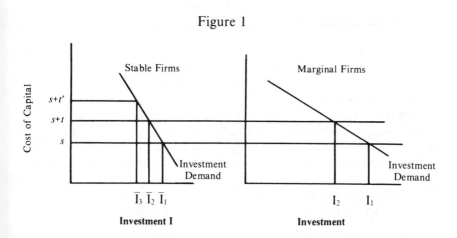

A true social cost-benefit decision is indifferent to the location of the investment. Thus, if investment is simply shifted in location, but not in amount, the result is no net increase in economic welfare. Only if the tax incentive serves to correct labor market failures, which will be discussed in more detail in a following section, can the zero-sum investment outcome produce increased net benefits. For the most part, a social analysis of tax incentives will thus count only the incremental investment at the national level. This will result in reducing the percent of investments having received subsidies which will be counted as *177*

benefits, because those which merely shift location are eliminated. However, since the social analysis is also indifferent to the previous residence of newly hired workers, it will not eliminate in-migrants to a state from the benefit side. Thus, a larger proportion of the wages and salaries for those investments which are induced will be counted. Most analysts believe that the reduction in the share of investment counted outweighs the increase in wages and salaries counted for each induced investment, thus lowering the attractiveness of state incentives when evaluated at a national level.

When an incentive to one firm, or one class of firms, is offset by increases in taxes to another class of firms, the benefits depend on the relative incentive effects, just as in the single state analysis. In terms of the graphical presentation, the elasticity of investment with respect to state taxes becomes smaller when viewed from the national perspective.

COMPETING JUSTIFICATIONS FOR TAX INCENTIVES

When considered from the perspective of a single state, a review of the voluminous arguments in the academic, political, and business press suggests five different justifications for state tax incentives for investment or employment:

1. equalizing interstate tax differentials, which may serve as an inducement for a firm to select an alternative business location;
2. serving as a wage subsidy to offset the effects of wage rigidity or labor immobility;
3. lowering the cost of capital to induce greater overall capital formation, independent of location choices;
4. serving to redistribute income from labor to capital under the politically acceptable guise of providing development incentives; and
5. serving as a "signal" to out-of-state businesses that the state has generally "pro-business" regulatory and spending policies.

Equalizing Interstate Tax Differentials

All other things being equal, a rational firm with perfect foresight and operating in perfect markets will prefer to produce in states with the best combination of taxes and business services. If possible, a firm will avoid states in which it perceives that its tax burden exceeds the value of services provided, and seek those where value exceeds the tax burden. A relatively tiny percentage of taxes are on a user charge or fee for service basis, so that there is generally little direct connection between revenue sources and service funding.

178   Unfortunately, there is little relevant evidence to indicate whether

state-provided services in general are typically higher or lower in value than state-imposed taxes. It is perfectly possible that all states presently provide businesses with services whose value exceeds the tax burden (or the converse). All of the empirical work dealing with the issue of the fiscal impact of new industrial development has been concerned with local impacts (for a good review of this literature, see Reigeluth, et al., 1979). The literature, while quite mixed in quality, indicates that there is a wide variety of experience, with some specific projects providing significant surpluses and others requiring significant subsidies. The result depends not only on the existence of tax subsidies for the firm, but on whether or not the firm's labor force requires the construction of new infrastructure. Naturally, the provision of tax subsidies reduces the likelihood of a fiscal surplus, and the use of an underutilized local labor force increases the likelihood of a fiscal surplus. Since state business taxes are not precisely (and could not be) on a fee for service basis, there will always be some firms with above average service needs with a lower than average tax "price" for services and some firms with a higher than average tax "price" for services. Unless tax incentives are negotiated, they cannot be used to selectively provide reductions to firms facing higher than average tax prices, if such firms can be identified.

The provision of selective income tax credits based on new investment or employment is usually seen as a less costly alternative to general business tax reductions. Reductions are offered only to those firms actually considering an action which might create new income. A general reduction in business taxes sufficient to influence this limited number of firms to the same degree would be far more costly to the state because of the windfalls to firms not considering investment or employment decisions.

The value of the attempt to increase economic activity by equalizing "price" differentials depends critically on the elasticity of the investment or employment response to the subsidy. The larger the proportion which are actually influenced, and the larger the average size of their reaction, the higher the return on the state public investment. There is a significant body of literature addressing the relative influence of different factors—including taxes—on the industrial location decision, which will be reviewed in the next chapter.

Offsetting Labor Market Failures The wage rigidity and labor immobility arguments have been made most forcefully by Moes (1961) and Rinehart and Laird (1972). They argue that the existence of unemployment in a community indicates that wages are insufficiently flexible for workers unwilling to move to areas with job openings. That is, local wage rates are too high relative to the marginal productivity of labor given the *179* relevant capital/labor ratio and other cost factors in an area. They argue that tax policy is frequently the only public policy to offset "high" wages. Many of these arguments were developed before the increasingly prevalent set of alternative labor market policies seen in the 1970s: training to upgrade skills (which might be seen as increasing the value of workers relative to "high" wages), job placement programs to better match workers with available jobs (which serves to help workers break out of "informal" networks of information about job openings), and relocation subsidies, by which workers can be induced to relocate from depressed areas into growing areas. Where tax subsidies are used to offset wage rigidities, they should be well targeted to only those workers whose labor market value is less than their wages, with the upper limit on the subsidies equal to the difference between wages and market value.

Both authors generally address the practice of local property taxes, rather than state subsidies. They suggest that only communities with unemployment will offer subsidies. The degree of competition among communities and the magnitude of the unemployment problem will determine the level of subsidy. They assert that the present level of local subsidy is too low (since unemployment remains), and suggest that if competitive subsidization were allowed to take its full course, equilibrium would occur when all communities are at full employment.

These arguments rely heavily on investors shifting their desired capital/labor ratio in response to wage subsidies. If the capital/labor ratio was relatively constant among locations, wage subsidies which were successful in influencing the location of investment would simply redistribute unemployment, rather than increase overall employment.

Buchanan and Moes (1962) have suggested that newly employed workers be subject to an "income-added" tax to provide subsidies to new and expanding firms. Under some circumstances, the subsidies involved in such a scheme could be quite large. For example, consider the case of a town with 100 unemployed workers, each completely unwilling to relocate. A firm is considering locating in the town and offering employment to these workers, but has forced them to compete with other communities in offering subsidies. The jobs available offer salaries of $10,000 per year and will be available indefinitely (that is, there is no threat of failure or relocation). If workers consider such income as the return on an investment from a subsidy, and their alternative investment opportunities return 10 percent per year, what will each worker be willing to offer as a subsidy? Under extreme competition, and placing no value on leisure, the workers would be willing to bid up to about $100,000 per job in an up-front subsidy. No state presently offers subsidies of anywhere near this magnitude (for reasons to be discussed below).

Lowering the Cost of Capital To Increase Investment There is now substantial discussion about the appropriate national tax policy to induce additional corporate investment in fixed structures, plant, and equipment. This reflects considerable uncertainty about the influence of tax policy on the level (as distinct from the location) of investment. If, as argued by some economists, the "wedge" between private and public return on investment caused by taxation of business income causes capital to flow into less taxed areas or consumption, it is also possible that reductions in the level of state taxation of business income will increase investment. Corresponding to this "income" effect due to reduced income taxation is the "substitution" effect of simply reducing the labor content of production and increasing the capital content due to the investment tax credit. There is no consensus as to the relative importance of the two effects at the national level, and little study of the issue at the state level.

There are two possible ways in which lowering the taxes on capital income might influence the amount of investment without changing the capital/labor ratio. First, a firm may simply decide that additional production can be justified at the lower tax rates, and add an additional machine, assembly line, or structure to expand output. Because state corporate income taxes are substantially lower than federal income taxes, the level of additional justifiable output is likely to be quite small. Unless small increments of output are easily matched with small amounts of new capital (i.e., investment plans of corporations would have to be quite "divisible" at the margin), it is unlikely that small incentives would influence the amount (as opposed to the location) of investment. Alternatively, the increased cash flow due to lowered taxes may not have any influence on the project which generates the tax incentive, but may make possible an additional investment at some other location or time.

Using Tax Incentives to Redistribute Income from Capital to Labor Some observers, notably Kanter (1977) and Harrison and Kanter (1978), focus on the effects of state tax incentives on functional distribution of income. They note the near consensus of surveys of business decision-makers that taxes and tax incentives have very little influence on location or investment decisions at the state level. Yet, under the influence of business arguments that tax relief will increase employment (or reduce employment losses), legislators continue to offer additional incentives. They argue that tax incentives, wrapped in the politically palatable guise of job creation, merely serve as an acceptable way to increase the share of income going to capital. The argument does not particularly depend on the motivations of legislators, who could simply believe the *181* claims of business representatives. *If* tax incentives have little or no influence on corporate behavior, the validity of the Kanter/Harrison argument depends crucially on the incidence of state taxes on corporate income. Kanter and Harrison assume that such taxes fall solely on shareholders. As noted above, there is nothing approaching a consensus on this issue. Given the debate in this area, it is equally possible to argue that the tax incentives provide relief to consumers, in the absence of any effect on investment or employment.

Tax Incentives as a *"Signal" to Out-of-State* *Investors*
A final justification frequently asserted by development practitioners is that while tax incentives do not offer cost savings sufficient to affect corporate decisions, they do serve as a signaling device of the "business climate" in a state. This argument focuses on the psychological aspects of corporate decisions, as well as on the cost to the firm of obtaining accurate information about public services, regulations, political attitudes, and future tax levels. Because of these costs, and because businessmen enjoy public attention, states find that tax incentives are an inexpensive way to signal firms of a state's interest in development. From the point of view of firms, it is far easier to check on the existence of tax incentives through the quick perusal of easily obtainable tax guides or industrial development publications than to examine in detail the attributes of each potential location. This argument offers a plausible justification for the proliferation of a large number of tax incentives whose value to a firm, in terms of percentage of investment or wage bill covered, is extraordinarily low. The primary weakness of the argument is that it is similarly inexpensive for other states, with less attractive attributes, to offer inexpensive incentives as well. If a competitive environment exists, other states would rapidly have to offer larger incentives or provide nontax signals. In general, it appears that nontax signals have been the favored response, as state recruiting teams have become increasingly important in providing direct contact with industrial prospects.

THE EFFECT OF THE DISTRIBUTION OF BENEFITS AND COSTS ON THE PUBLIC INVESTMENT DECISION
Since automatic tax incentives must be approved by the state legislative body and governor, their presence indicates at least majority legislative approval, if not popular approval, for their use. Leaving aside the use of tax incentives to redistribute income directly, legislators and governors must believe that the rate of return on the investment is higher than the opportunity cost (recognizing that it is unlikely to be thought of or analyzed in this way). However, of a least

equal importance as the expected rate of return is the expected distribution of benefits and costs.

The actual public investment decision is determined by the interaction between the political structure of the state, the fiscal structure, and the distribution of benefits and costs. If the distribution of benefits and costs are quite unequal, the fiscal structure and the political structure of the state must serve to redistribute costs and benefits. If not redistributed, even subsidies with a very high expected rate of return will face major political obstacles in passage.

Vaughan (1980) has suggested that elected bodies, in the aftermath of Abscam, be selected in a competitive bidding process. Each person running for office would offer his/ her proposals for bid by competing interests, with the person receiving the largest dollar amount of bids winning. Thus, with a tax incentive proposal to be considered in the next legislative session, all voters would consider the likely distribution of costs and benefits to themselves, taking into account the effects of lost or altered revenues, the new jobs, the effects on suppliers, and similar direct and indirect effects. Each voter would then tender bids to candidates supporting or opposing the proposal based on their position on the tax subsidy. If a number of conditions are met, proposals with net benefits will win, and those with net losses will lose. The most important of these conditions are:

1. accurate information about the magnitude and incidence of costs and benefits;
2. perfect capital markets so that those who might gain benefits after a tax subsidy but who are without assets or income before the subsidy can borrow funds for bidding; and
3. separation of each issue facing the legislature from all others in the voting (bidding) process.

Clearly these conditions are not met. The existence of this study indicates that the first condition is not met. Capital markets are clearly inefficient for those without current assets or income. Candidates for office must offer positions on a variety of issues, which are then inseparable in voting.

When elections are not conducted in this manner (and they are not), and these conditions are not met, the political process substitutes other mechanisms to transform an expected return on public subsidies into votes for and against the proposal. For the most part, tax incentives are not widely discussed, and are rarely issues in a majority of the legislators' election campaigns. Thus, legislators are dependent upon lobbying, legislative research, and their own beliefs about the likely rate of return.

The interaction of these factors determines whether or not the *183* subsidies offered (and not offered) are insufficient or overly generous. Particularly in the absence of accurate information about the expected rate of return, the relative political strength of those who expect to gain (typically businesses) and those who expect to lose (typically taxpayer organizations, social service beneficiaries, and unions) through offsetting taxes or program cuts in the legislature determines the existence, magnitude, and targeting of incentives.

With most tax incentives, the costs (increased offsetting taxes or program cuts) are more diffuse than the benefits (lower tax bills for some firms and increased employment in some cases). This should impart a bias toward greater subsidies if concentration increases the ability to organize political support. On the other hand, the failure of most state and local tax systems to capture many of the benefits and redistribute some portion of them to those who face net costs will result in greater political obstacles. The political obstacles increase as the distribution of costs and benefits becomes more unequal. Thus, it is impossible to predict in general whether the political process produces a bias toward or against subsidies without knowing the specific tax system and political structure of each state.

POSSIBLE NATIONAL JUSTIFICATION FOR STATE TAX INCENTIVES

The previous section considered possible justifications for instituting state tax incentives when viewed solely from the perspective of a single state. This section attempts to determine the conditions under which state tax incentives will result in an increase in national benefits. The primary basis of the discussion is viewing the use of state tax incentives as a competitive game among states, with tax structures the primary method of competition.

Following Rinehart and Laird (1972), the game starts in some state with unemployment due to wage rigidity or labor immobility. Only in such areas will there be a positive return to tax incentives. With subsidies, additional investment will occur in labor-surplus regions, with capital/labor ratios for the incremental investment being lower than in other areas. Thus, the redistribution of incremental investment creates additional national employment.

The game continues when another state with its own excess labor pool observes the success of the first state in creating new employment (perhaps achieved in part by attracting firms which would have located in the second state). The entry of the second firm into the game, by offering competing incentives, lowers the initial advantage of the first state. The process continues, with other states adding incentives (thereby entering the game) so long as the value of the new employment 184 they expect to be generated exceeds the loss of tax revenues from the initial subsidy. The competitive process should go through an unending series of maneuvers, reflecting the changing balance as each new state enters and as national factors influence relative unemployment rates among states. In theory, the process should continually move states toward full employment situations, thereby providing overall national benefits along with benefits for each state.

Factors Limiting the Process of Competitive Subsidization Casual observation indicates that not all states with unemployment offer tax incentives, and those states with tax incentives continue to have unemployment. Either the process of competitive subsidization never reaches equilibrium because of continually changing macroeconomic conditions (as discussed above), or firms do not respond to incentives as assumed, or information and structural problems limit the competitive process.

There are two major instances when the competitive process does not work simply because firms do not react as assumed. In the first case, firms may change their location but not their capital/labor ratios. In this situation, competitive subsidization is a zero-sum game, with investment and employment merely shifted from one location to another. Many opponents of state tax incentives consider this to be what usually occurs. In the second case, few if any firms react at all, simply accepting the reduced taxes without changing their behavior. Thus, employment and investment is not shifted, only the tax burden is altered.

If subsidized firms do react as assumed, there are a number of factors which should serve to limit the competitive process. Among the most important are the lack of adequate information, inadequate transfer mechanisms, the effect of increased taxes on other sectors of the economy, and political concerns over equity in the structure of tax systems. Lack of adequate information will occur whenever businesses are unaware of incentives or legislators are unaware of their asserted benefits. Inadequate transfer mechanisms refer simply to the difficulty in obtaining political support for subsidies to selected firms when there is a distinct possibility that they will be raised for other firms or for individuals. As discussed above in reference to the targeting of incentives to responsive firms, if the incentives result in additional taxes on firms or individuals who are sensitive to higher taxes, the benefits of the initial subsidies may simply be canceled out. These firms or individuals may hire fewer people or spend less, thereby offsetting any additional hiring in the originally subsidized firms. Finally, in addition to these economic arguments, there frequently exists political opposition to tax incentives based solely on standards of fairness in the design of tax systems.

185

There currently exists strong political and analytical disagreement over the likely rate of return on tax incentives, the distribution of any benefits and their certain costs, and their fairness to nonsubsidized firms and individuals. When these disagreements are coupled with significant problems in transferring benefits from those subsidized to those not subsidized through the tax system, and political systems which do not act on Vaughan's Abscam model but on frequently more random methods, it is quite clear that "market" for state tax incentives is quite inefficient. However, it is impossible to predict whether or not the net effect of the inefficiencies is that too many incentives exist or too few.

3

A REVIEW OF
THE EMPIRICAL LITERATURE

A theoretical discussion of the effect of state tax incentives is insufficient to guide decisionmakers in choices about whether or not to institute, amend, or repeal such incentives. Further empirical information is required to make sensible development policy.

From a policy perspective, it would be valuable to have answers to the following empirical questions:

1. What is the relevant weight of state and local business taxes compared to such factors as wages?
2. How much do state and local taxes on business vary between states?
3. What is the current level of state tax expenditures in support of industrial development?
4. What types of firms are receiving which types of tax expenditures?
5. What is the elasticity of investment with respect to state taxation of business?
6. What proportion of firms considering investment are aware of state tax incentives?
7. What proportion of firms considering investment seriously consider locating in another state?
8. Is the primary effect of state tax incentives on the location or the amount of investment?
9. What is the expected rate of return on state tax incentives?

A number of these questions do not appear to have been asked in previous studies. In particular, there have been no estimates of the current level of state tax expenditures, the types of firms receiving tax incentives, the proportion of firms aware of the incentives, the proportion of firms choosing among states for a new investment, or the relative effect of tax incentives on location and the amount of investment. The remaining questions have been addressed in at least one study, but the conclusions are generally limited to a few states or are flawed by the research methodology.

This chapter will primarily review the existing empirical literature. Ideally, the empirical literature should be shaped by underlying theoretical considerations. The key theoretical issues relate to the methods by which firms make the location portion of an investment decision, so a brief section will review several frequently neglected *187* aspects of the location decision. Following this discussion, the chapter will review studies in five different areas:

1. studies reviewing different methods of measuring the business tax burden;
2. studies attempting to determine the relative share of state and local business taxes on business scales or profits and compare that share to other factors such as wages;
3. studies using surveys and interviews with business decisionmakers to evaluate the relative importance of different factors thought to influence the manufacturing location decision;
4. studies using statistical techniques to determine the relative importance of tax differentials in the manufacturing location decision; and
5. studies using case studies to evaluate the rate of return on particular firms' receipt of state tax incentives.

SELECTED THEORETICAL ASPECTS OF THE BUSINESS INVESTMENT DECISION

In the simplest neoclassical approach to investment, a firm faces a schedule of independent investments, each with known costs and revenues. Under competitive markets (including capital markets), a firm will undertake all investments in which the discounted cash flow is positive at the after-tax cost of capital. When a firm faces revenues and costs which are certain but vary spatially, under similar circumstances it will undertake each investment whose return exceeds the cost of capital. Where a firm faces some discontinuity in the availability of capital, or lacks management capacity to undertake all investments of acceptable return, it will choose investments in order of return.

Search Costs

An important qualification to these models of business investment and location behavior is that information about prices, markets, and costs is costly for both the present and future. This costly process of acquiring information will directly affect location decisions. A profit maximizing process of investment decisionmaking requires accurate information about each project at each possible location. If the costs of search increase less than proportionately to project size, firms undertaking smaller projects could be expected to search less than those undertaking larger projects. Similarly, since information obtained in a search for new locations by a multiplant firm can be used by units other than the prospective venture, we should expect multiunit firms, controlled for size, to search more widely than single-unit firms. This type of behavior has been confirmed in survey research by Oster (1979). It implies that many firms will not be located at the site of least-cost production excluding search costs. Further, the existence of search costs helps to explain the observation that the great majority of relocations of firms are within a relatively short radius of the prior location (see Schmenner (1978), Wolman (1979), and Jusenius and Ledebur (1977)).

The Effect of Uncertainty Firms which expect their operations to last for more than a short period of time and having a discount rate of less than infinity will be concerned about future as well as present costs and demand. At some expenditure, uncertainty about present costs can be reduced to a low level. However, most future costs are uncertain with any degree of search (although contracts can be used to reduce uncertainty). Presumably, firms use some conceptual model to predict future prices and costs, which incorporates present trends as well as the effects of their own investment and hiring decisions on markets.

A project with net revenues that are less certain at one location than another (but with the same expected level) will have a higher cost of capital at the less certain location. It is likely that most firms feel more confident (i.e., have more information at a lower level of search costs) at present locations than at distant alternative locations which may be less costly. This aspect of uncertain futures, when added to the cost of search for present information, leads to a potentially large bias to expansion at present sites for existing firms and for new firms to be started in areas familiar to the entrepreneur. Willingness to search and choose new locations over existing ones should increase with company and venture size, as returns to scale are realized.

Several State Location Searches One method used by firms to reduce search costs is to make location decisions in several stages. Surveys and interviews with business decisionmakers indicate that most large firms tend to select a location in at least two states (see McMillan (1969), and Vaughan (1977)). A region (perhaps a state or larger) is first selected on the basis of such factors as the size of the potential market, the general level of labor costs, or the existence of a reliable supply of a natural resource. Within that region, a number of communities will be examined in much greater detail, with specific information collected on the cost and availability of different types of labor, land, transportation, taxes, and other spatially varying factors. This sort of two-stage process clearly reduces the amount of costly information that would be required relative to a full investigation of all sites, including those in areas that could be eliminated in the first round and *189* those that are comparable to the sites in the selected region, but aren't worth the cost of a two-region search.

Implications for These considerations indicate that em-
Empirical Research pirical investigations should, where possible, differentiate between firms which are start-ups, expansions, and new branch plants. In addition, the relative influence of tax burdens may vary at different stages of the location choice—hence, surveys should clearly specify the level of location choice being examined.

TECHNIQUES OF MEASURING DIFFERENCES AMONG STATE TAX BURDENS

"The measurement of comparative state and local tax burdens constitutes one of the more formidable if not wholly intractable tasks in the field of public finance. This is usually recognized by students of taxation despite the fact that special tax committees, industrial development agencies, and representatives of business and sundry other special interest groups are continually "proving" that the tax burdens in their respective states or communities are either higher or lower than those prevailing elsewhere."

So began a piece which appeared in 1961 (Zubrow, 1961). For the most part, relatively little progress has been made in developing a measure agreed upon by economists. This has not slowed the proliferation of comparative and econometric studies relying upon one measure or another.

The most typical methods of comparing state tax burdens for the past two decades has been to compare state and local taxes per capita or per $1,000 personal income using all state and local taxes, or to construct "hypothetical corporations," which are then subjected to prevailing state and local tax rates. Each of these methods overlooks major difficulties if a measure is to be used as representative of the tax burden faced by a firm considering a location choice. The major problems to be considered are those of incidence, offsetting levels of benefits, excessive levels of aggregation, assumptions of factor proportions, temporal variations in taxes, and fiscal interactions among states for firms which do business in more than one state. These problems are considered in order below.

We have previously noted that the signer of the check to the state Department of Finance is not necessarily the party which actually bears the costs of taxes. If a firm was able to pass along all tax costs to workers through lower wages and to consumers through higher prices, it would be indifferent to its tax burden and no measure of tax burden would be relevant to a location choice. For the firm whose
190 shareholders absorbed all of the tax burden, the relevant measure is the

taxes actually paid by the corporation facing the location choice. If the tax burden is partially shifted to workers or consumers, the effect of the tax is to reduce effective wages or demand in other sectors, and a broader measure of tax burden is required. While never explicitly stated, an agnostic assumption on incidence of state and local taxes might justify a broad measure of the tax burden, such as state and local taxes per capita or per $1,000 of personal income. Unfortunately, individual taxes within the state and local tax structure are certain to have varying patterns of incidence. For example, the property tax can be separated into a national average tax and local variations, each with separate patterns of incidence. Severance taxes on coal or oil clearly have different patterns of incidence than personal income taxes. The sales tax in a state like Nevada, which is heavily dependent on out-of-state visitors, will be more readily "exported" to nonlocal taxpayers than in most states. All of these factors severely complicate the task of constructing an appropriate measure of tax burden.

As previously discussed, there is at least some relationship between the level of taxes and the level of public services provided. This relationship is affected by the presence of economies of scale, relative wage levels among public jurisdictions, relative levels of efficiency, the mix of public expenditures among those which provide direct benefits and those which are primarily redistributive in nature, and such factors as weather and the influence of the state's congressional delegation in obtaining federal services and grants. No one has yet devised an appropriate measure of the benefits rendered to a business by location, sector, or taxes paid. Under some circumstances, it is equally likely that a high tax state which efficiently provided services with little redistributive spending would be more attractive than a low tax state with few benefits.

One of the most important drawbacks to the use of tax measures based on "hypothetical" firms is that they necessarily obscure many differences among individual firms. What is typically done is to use publicly available figures for the total balance sheets and income statements of different categories of manufacturing firms to construct average balance sheet and income statements. Average state and local tax rates are then applied to the average financial statements to obtain average tax burdens, which are then compared among states. Such studies necessarily assume away much of the diversity among business firms in profitability and composition of taxable assets. The distortion which results from the use of average figures clearly diminishes if less-aggregated types of firms are used in the calculations. Thus, there is likely to be less variation if electronics firms were compared with other electronics firms in terms of profitability and types of assets than there would be if electronics firms were combined in a category with steel mills. A second form of aggregation which leads to some *191* distortions is the use of average state and local tax rates. Differences do exist among communities within a state in terms of local property tax rates, and such differences are lost in the process of developing an average tax burden for the entire state. Finally, in those states which have graduated corporate income taxes, lumping firms of the same size together, even within the same industry, will mean that the measure of taxes overestimates the taxes actually faced by small firms and underestimates it for large firms. Clearly, subject to data constraints (which are quite severe in most cases), more detailed categories of businesses are preferable to more aggregated categories.

The taxes paid by a corporation may vary substantially over time even if the tax rates on businesses remain unchanged. If the relative proportion of business profits and assets changes over time—perhaps as a new firm or new plant is built and comes into profitable operation—a state with both property taxes and income taxes will levy a changing stream of taxes. Most hypothetical tax comparisons, by selecting an average corporation, implicitly use a comparison of firms at one point in time. It is at least conceivable that firms place widely varying emphasis on the relative tax rates at different periods in the business life-cycle. For example, a high income tax rate will cause little burden to a firm in its initial unprofitable years, while high property taxes could cause substantial harm. In contrast, as the firm becomes quite profitable, the property taxes may become less important, but high income tax rates could be seen as a substantial obstacle.

The primary use of measures of interstate tax burdens is to determine the relative importance of state and local taxes in the business location decision. The use of hypothetical firms to measure tax burdens assumes that it is reasonable to place the same firm in all fifty states, without changing the relative proportions of labor, land, or depreciable assets. Ironically, if businesses actually believe state and local taxes to be important, they may change not only their location but their composition of assets and their capital/labor ratio to minimize tax liabilities once a location is chosen. In fact, in one state a firm may choose to use fewer machines but more workers due to the ratio of taxes on capital to wage costs, while in another it may purchase less land but put more capital into plant and equipment because of the differing assessment ratios on types of property. This factor has not been studied, and it is very difficult to obtain detail at the level of the individual firm to carry out such a study. In the meantime, all methods currently available to compare states implicitly assume that a firm does not change its factor proportions.

Finally, there exists interaction among the fiscal systems of each state. Vasquez and deSave (1977) have stated that the "particular distribution of a firm's existing activities among states and localities can have such a dramatic effect on its after-tax rate of return on marginal investments that broad generalizations about the fiscal interaction of jurisdictions may be impossible to make." This is because of variations in the way in which states use the distribution of sales, assets, and employment to determine taxable income. Vasquez and deSave argue that to truly understand the tax effects of a particular location, knowledge is required of the *present* distribution of plants, employees, and the distribution of sales. However, their argument is weakened by the lack of any evidence that corporate decision-makers understand the implications of interstate taxation practices. A reasonably exhaustive review of the literature generally available to businesses from private sources did not turn up awareness of the issue or proposed responses to it. Nonetheless, an interesting result of the research of Vasquez and deSave, not mentioned in their prose but clear in their empirical results, is that the marginal return may vary somewhat among investments as the pattern of existing activity is altered, but the *ranking* of states is quite stable. It thus may be more appropriate to use the ranking of states to compare different locations rather than to use the single estimate of taxes paid derived from hypothetical firms.

A REPRESENTATIVE SAMPLE OF INTERSTATE TAX COMPARISONS

Having reviewed the limitations of interstate tax comparisons, it is still possible to gain some indication of the order of magnitude of interstate tax differentials by examining a small number of studies done as part of state development efforts. In particular, several studies have attempted to relate the magnitude of interstate tax differentials to wage differences or total operating cost differences. A recent example of the hypothetical firm method of calculating state business tax burdens is furnished in a study performed by the major accounting firm Price Waterhouse under contract to the State of Missouri in 1978 (see Table 11). The state furnished Price Waterhouse with balance sheet and income statements, as well as other operating assumptions, for a "typical" manufacturing firm. Using information about tax rates and bases for twenty states thought to compete with Missouri for new investment, the projected tax burden during the first year of operation was calculated. While the Price Waterhouse report noted that the taxes were for a "typical" manufacturing firm rather than any specific industry or firm, Missouri clearly should hope that the caution is disregarded by those firms who read the report, as Missouri appears with the second lowest tax total. Among the twenty-one states compared in the study, there was considerable variation in average tax burden.

However, without knowing the relative importance of state and local taxes on business, it is difficult to interpret the results. The State *193* of Ohio attempted to put interstate tax comparisons on a somewhat different basis by calculating state and local business taxes per $1,000 dollars of business profit. To facilitate comparisons, a recent study (Cornia, Testa, and Stocker, 1978) for the same year, estimated wages per $1,000 of business profit. These results appear in Table 12 below. These figures must be interpreted quite cautiously. The study assumed that profits were distributed among the states in direct proportion to nonagricultural private employment. Then total wages and total state and local business taxes in each state were used to arrive at the ratio of taxes and wages to profits. This procedure was necessary because no figures exist on actual business profits at the state level due to the fundamental ambiguity resulting from multistate firms.

There appears to be substantial variation among states in terms of the tax burden as a share of profits. The relative weight of wages is clearly much larger than that of business taxes. When calculated on an

Table 11

State of Missouri Comparative Summary Business Tax Liabilities

State	1978 First Year Total	% Higher Than Lowest State
Michigan	$389,094	—
Missouri	436,072	12.07%
Arkansas	456,660	17.36
Oklahoma	487,416	25.27
Kentucky	496,838	27.69
Iowa	526,318	35.27
Texas	555,145	42.68
Tennessee	555,784	42.84
Nebraska	574,936	47.76
New Jersey	576,158	48.08
Massachusetts	590,952	51.88
Ohio	592,811	52.36
Indiana	615,333	58.15
Minnesota	618,621	58.99
California	625,882	60.86
Kansas	659,352	69.46
New York	660,604	69.78
Wisconsin	672,309	72.79
Illinois	681,406	75.13
Connecticut	717,351	84.36
Pennsylvania	790,471	103.16

SOURCE: Summary table from *State Tax Comparison Study*, Price, Waterhouse and Co., 1978.

unweighted basis, business taxes averaged $21.6 per $100 profit, while wages averaged $379.3 per $100 profit. Clearly, equal percentage differences in average wages would be viewed with far more importance in the location decision than equal percentage differences in state and local business taxes by a business seeking to minimize would be costs. The standard deviation (again unweighted) of business taxes is $5.6, while the standard deviation for wages is $48.0. Thus, the variation among states in terms of wages is about 8.6 times greater than for taxes. This means that small differences in wage costs will usually be of much more importance to businesses than small differences in tax

Table 12

State and Local Taxes on Business Per $100 Profit and Wages Per $100 Profit: 1974

State	Taxes	Wages	State	Taxes	Wages
Maine	$21	$317	North Dakota	17	304
New Hampshire	15	324	South Carolina	18	317
Vermont	20	339	Georgia	16	326
Massachusetts	23	382	Florida	19	342
Rhode Island	23	324	Kentucky	14	366
Connecticut	27	397	Tennessee	15	323
New York	33	385	Alabama	15	350
New Jersey	25	396	Mississippi	20	284
Pennsylvania	23	386	Arkansas	14	299
Ohio	21	481	Louisiana	38	442
Indiana	18	457	Oklahoma	20	343
Illinois	23	445	Texas	23	357
Michigan	31	557	Montana	28	405
Wisconsin	24	440	Idaho	20	344
Minnesota	28	431	Wyoming	32	N/A
Iowa	14	400	Colorado	21	405
Missouri	16	382	New Mexico	27	308
North Dakota	19	323	Arizona	24	394
South Dakota	16	336	Utah	22	405
Nebraska	12	347	Nevada	22	464
Kansas	19	353	Washington	26	416
Delaware	23	461	Oregon	19	385
Maryland	21	336	California	32	409
Virginia	18	334	Alaska	19	490
West Virginia	26	400	Hawaii	20	375

SOURCE: "State and Local Fiscal Incentives and Economic Development," Cornia, G., Testa, A., and Stocker, F., Urban and Regional Development Series No. 4, Academy for Contemporary Problems, Columbus, Ohio, 1978.

burdens (this may indicate that the competition among states on the basis of taxes is more fierce than competition in labor markets). If tax incentives are viewed as a means to offset wage differences, they would typically have to be very large—much larger than those currently in use.

Williams (1967), in a more detailed study of relative costs of doing business in a number of states, constructed average costs structures, including a measure of state and local tax burden, for manufacturing industries in the upper Midwest. The study was conducted with a focus on Minnesota, and used industries at the level of detail described by the two- and four-digit industries of the Standard Industrial Classification (for example, primary metals is a two digit industry, while gray iron foundries, within primary metals, is a four digit industry). For each industry, states were ranked in terms of total average cost with and without state and local business taxes. With taxes included it was found that taxes ranged from 1.82 percent down to .26 percent of the value of shipments (or sales). In the industry with the greatest tax advantage for Minnesota, taxes as a percentage of the value of shipments were only one-fourth the level of the highest state in the ranking. In the area of greatest tax disadvantage, the Minnesota tax burden was nearly five times as high as the state with lowest tax ranking.

Such figures must be viewed in the context of other cost differences. The Williams study attempted to do this by determining the effect on the overall cost ranking of eliminating all state and local taxes. Among the more aggregated two-digit industries, the rankings of states changed in only two cases, and then by only one position. Among the more detailed four-digit industries, the ranking changed only ten times out of thirty-eight industries. Thus, in the majority of industries, state and local taxes did not appear to distort the relative cost structure of competing states (even without taking into account the possibility that the tax differences reflected different preferences for state and local services).

Williams also evaluated the effect on Minnesota's ranking of eliminating the Minnesota business taxes while retaining those of other states. In some ways, this is similar to the provision of tax incentives by one state without a response from others. As seen in Table 13, Minnesota would change total cost ranking in two of the two-digit industries, and in twenty of the thirty eight four-digit industries. However, it is quite unlikely that Minnesota would be able to drop business taxes without a competitive response, without dropping valuable business services, or without significantly increasing personal taxes to the point that it influenced wage costs.

In an interesting exercise, Williams calculated the magnitude of the
196 tax reduction required for Minnesota to improve its competitive

Table 13

The Effect of Tax Reduction on Minnesota's Relative Cost Position

Industry	Net Change in Ranking if only Minnesota's Taxes Eliminated	% Tax Reduction Needed to Improve Rank One Position	Industry	Net Change in Ranking if only Minnesota's Taxes Eliminated	% Tax Reduction Needed to Improve Rank One Position
Two-Digit Industries			Motors and generators	1	69
Lumber and wood products	0	—	Fabricated plate shops	3	39
Stone, clay, and glass	0	—	Trucks and tractors	0	243
Machinery, except electrical	0	—	Sporting goods	1	33
Pulp and paper	0	299	Knit outerwear	1	30
Petroleum and coal	0	564	Fabricated structural steel	1	14
Fabricated metal products	0	156	Concrete brick and block	0	129
Transportation equipment	0	136	Games and toys	0	155
Printing and publishing	5	21	Candy	0	155
Rubber products	0	214	Machine tools	0	130
Chemicals	1	70	Bolts, nuts, etc.	1	32
Primary metals	0	133	Truck and bus bodies	3	14
Food and kindred products	0	136	Drugs	0	321
Four-Digit Industries			Nonferrous foundries	1	72
			Grain mill products	1	35
Malt Liquors	0	—	Book printing	0	337
House furnishings	0	—	Mattresses and springs	2	53
Screw machine products	0	—	Food products machinery	1	95
Millwork plants	0	1,285	Meat packing	8	34
Wood preserving	1	46	Prepared animal feed	1	39
Printing Machinery	0	195	Wood furniture	5	2
Boat building	0	112	Upholstered furniture	0	618
Grease and tallow	0	333	Lithography	1	22
Underwear	0	1,253	Sheet metal work	4	10
Prefabricated wood buildings	2	62	Bakery products	3	11
Shoes	0	842	Commercial printing	2	45
Gray iron foundries	0	167			

SOURCE: Tables 2 and 3, "A Measure of the Impact of State and Local Taxes on Industry Location," Williams, W., Journal of Regional Science, Vol. 7, Summer 1967, no. 1.

position with regard to at least one other state (allowing for reductions of greater than 100% or a net subsidy). As shown in Table 13, in many cases large multiples of present taxes would be required in tax reductions or refundable tax credits to offset nontax interstate differentials.

STATISTICAL APPROACHES TO MEASURING THE INFLUENCES OF TAXES[1]

There exists a variety of statistical approaches available to examine the relationship between state and local taxes on business and investment and employment. The goal of using statistical approaches is to force a researcher to specify more precisely what he expects to find, and to seek empirical evidence to confirm or deny the expectation. There is a danger that simple statistical approaches will neglect the complexities inherent in business investment decisions, and find misleading results. The most appropriate method of statistical investigation in this area is to correctly specify an equation with investment or employment by state and industry as the dependent variable—with independent variables representing as many of the factors thought to influence the business decisions as can be quantified—and estimate the coefficient of the variable representing state business tax burden. If the equation is properly specified, and the tax variable accurately captures differences among states, the elasticity or investment or employment with respect to taxes can be derived. However, as discussed previously, there are significant difficulties in properly specifying the equation, capturing offsetting benefits of taxation, and measuring the tax burden. With very few exceptions, empirical work in industrial location has been carried out without explicit discussion of these problems.

The earliest statistical attempt to relate taxation to state development appeared in *An Econometric Model of Postwar State Industrial Development* (Thompson and Mattila, 1959). In part, this study is important because it is frequently cited as a basis for asserting that state taxes do not significantly influence state industrial development. The study attempted to explain differences among states in manufacturing employment growth over the period 1947-1954. The methodology employed incorporated both simple correlations and ordinary least squares regression equations. Their dependent variables were both absolute and percentage employment growth in manufacturing industries at the two-digit level of sectoral detail. As independent variables, they tested changes in state population, changes in state personal income, average manufacturing wages, percent of the work force in unions, average educational levels, overall manufacturing investment by state, industry investment by state in 1947, and industry employment in 1947. To test the importance of state tax burdens, they used two alternative variables: state and local taxes as a percent of state personal income in 1953, and an estimate of state and local taxes paid per nonagricultural business employee in 1953. Neither measure attempts to separate out taxes with an initial impact on business. A major conceptual problem arises in attempting to explain growth over a period beginning in 1947 with tax burden measures for 1953. Unless relative taxes did not change among states over the time period, this method must assume that businesses could accurately forecast future taxes, since businesses making investment and employment decisions in 1947, 1948, 1949, 1950, 1951, and 1952 did not have access to 1953 tax information.

Thompson and Mattila first examined simple correlations between each of their employment variables and each independent variable. In the case of the tax burden variables, the only significant negative correlation was found for the apparel industry and taxes per employee. The importance of this finding is minimized by realizing that both New York and New England, relatively high tax areas, were losing a significant portion of their apparel industry in this same time period. The relative importance of taxes, of course, cannot be separated using simple correlation methods.

Thompson and Mattila also estimated regression equations with ordinary least squares. Again, the only industry with a significant and negative coefficient between employment growth and tax burden was the apparel industry (although their t-statistic in this case was only 1.74). These overall regression results have been widely cited as demonstrating the insignificance of state and local taxes in influencing the relative rates of state development and interstate industrial location choices.

Campbell (1965) employed similar correlation methods to come to similar conclusions. In this study, simple correlations were calculated between development indicators such as income per capita, production per capita, and percent employment growth, and tax measures such as per capita state and local expenditures and per capita taxes. Unfortunately, the tax measures employed 1962 information to be correlated with 1959 development indicators, implicitly assuming excellent forecasting ability among the business community. In all cases, Campbell found positive and significant correlation coefficients, and concluded that taxes measured in per capita terms move with economic activity. The study concluded that the frequently assumed negative relationship between high taxes and economic activity does not exist. This is a somewhat strong conclusion given the methodological problems in the study.

Sacks (1965) sought to relate a more narrow version of tax burden to development with similar methodologies. This study defined a set of state and local taxes as business taxes, and developed measures of *199* business taxes per capita, business property taxes per capita, and business taxes as a percent of total taxes. As development indicators, he used per capita income received and per capita production. In all cases, Sacks found significant and positive correlation coefficients between tax measures and development indicators. The study concluded that no evidence exists to indicate that high business taxes or a high business share of total taxes are a deterrent to economic development.

Struyk (1967) examines two hypotheses: (1) that regions with low taxes will grow more rapidly than other regions with high taxes, and (2) that regions with higher public services will grow more rapidly than regions with lower public services. He uses the growth of fifty cities in twenty four states as the units of observation. For the period 1950-1960, the study attempted to explain the growth of population and per capita income in terms of the levels and percentage change in per capita state taxes and per capita local taxes. Struyk found a significant and negative coefficient for the total state and total local taxes growth rate variable in explaining changes in population growth (because the study did not report actual coefficients or equations, it is not possible to be more specific). The tax variables had insignificant and inconsistent coefficients when used to explain changes in income. In *separate* regressions, Struyk attempted to relate public expenditures as a measure of service levels (no differentiation by type of service) and growth. No consistent results were found. Thus, Struyk reported that tax differentials influenced population growth but not income growth, and that expenditure levels had no observable effect on growth.

Carlton (1979) attempted to determine the relative importance of a number of factors in the location choices of new companies and new branch plants in the plastic products, electronic transmitting equipment, and electronic components industries. Instead of using investment or employment as the dependent variable, Carlton used the event of a new company or new plant as the unit of observation. The time period used was 1967-1975, and the geographical unit of observation was an SMSA. The number of urban areas in the sample ranged from twenty-eight for electronic transmitting equipment to forty-two for plastic products.

For births of new firms, Carlton estimated coefficients with a conditional logit equation to predict the probability of births in each urban area. Independent variables included were wage rates, electricity costs, natural gas costs, person-hours of activity in the local industry at the beginning of the period (as a measure of "potential" entrepreneurs and agglomeration economies), the number of engineers (with a similar motivation as existing activity), unemployment rates (as a proxy for local demand), and four tax variables. The local property tax rate, the state personal income tax rate, the state corporate income tax rate, and an index reflecting the number of incentives (both fiscal and financial) were tested.

Carlton found that the birth rate in all three industries was very responsive to local wage rates. Electricity and natural gas costs were also significant and negative. Existing activity and the number of engineers—intended to measure agglomeration economies and the availability of entrepreneurs—were both significant and positive in sign.

In no case was the coefficient for either personal income tax rate or corporate income tax rate negative and significant. In two cases, the corporate income tax rate was *positive* and significant. Similarly, the coefficients on local property tax rates were not significant for any of the industries. The coefficients for the incentive index were generally *negative* but usually insignificant.

A similar approach was taken for new branch plants. In this case, all coefficients for each tax measure were insignificant. Wages were relatively less important and energy costs relatively more important than for new companies. The level of existing activity exerted a positive and significant influence on new branch plants, indicating that agglomeration economies existed.

Hodge (1978) examined the investment patterns of the apparel, furniture, and the electronics industry in forty-two cities over the period 1963 to 1975. Using pooled time series and cross-section data, Hodge's work is unique in that it includes a variable intended to capture the proximity of a city to the sources of demand for the industry. (The index was constructed using private data on sales patterns in major urban areas and the distance from each city to those urban areas.) Hodge's equation also included as dependent variables a wage cost variable, a rent index, the national growth rate of the industry, a building cost index, the national cost of capital, a supply index constructed in a manner similar to the spatial demand index, and three variables to capture tax and incentive patterns. He included the local property tax rate, the state corporate income tax rate, and an index of incentives (similar to that constructed by Carlton).

Hodge's results varied substantially among the industries. For the furniture industry, he estimated a significant and negative coefficient for both the local property tax and the state corporate income tax rate. He estimated the elasticity of investment with respect to local property tax rates at –0.35 and the elasticity with respect to state corporate income tax rates at –0.29. For the apparel industry, he found a significant and negative coefficient for the local property tax, implying an elasticity of –0.54 (although this may partially reflect the heavy weight of New York City, with a great loss of apparel and high property tax rates over his study period). The coefficient for the state corporate income tax rate was insignificant. For the electronics *201* industry, the tax variables were all insignificant. For all industries, the coefficient on the incentive index was insignificant. Hodge noted that his findings may simple reflect an increase in the capital/labor ratio under the influence of property taxes rather than an effect on the location of investment.

Genetski and Chin (1978) represents one of the most flawed but politically significant attempts to relate state and local taxation to economic development. This study, an unpublished paper done in the research unit of the Harris Bank of Chicago, has been cited by the *Wall Street Journal* in editorials on regional policy.

The study attempted to find a relationship between growth in per capita personal income by state relative to national growth income, and relative growth in total state and local tax receipts as a percent of total state personal income. The study was cross-sectional, with changes measured over seven-year periods.

When relative income growth was regressed against relative tax levels, no significant relationship was found. State income growth appeared to be independent of the level of taxation by state and local authorities. When relative income growth was regressed against *changes* (from 1969-1976) in relative state and local tax burdens, their adjusted R^2 increased to .25. Finally, they regressed relative income growth versus changes in relative tax burden from an earlier period— 1967-1974. In this case, their adjusted R^2 increased to .59. On the basis of this evidence, they argued (and the *Wall Street Journal* asserted) that relative income growth responded, with a three year lag, to relative changes in the state and local tax burden. Thus, a state which has high taxes, but reduces them slightly, will increase its growth relative to a state which has low taxes but increases them slightly.

The Genetski and Chin study suffers from fatal flaws, and is an excellent example of the use of simple statistics for political purposes. In their preferred regression, with lagged tax changes, most of the change in relative income must occur before the relevant workers, consumers, and businesses have the information about the tax change that is supposed to be influencing their behavior. Even ignoring this flaw, the use of relative changes in taxes to predict relative changes in income tells a story about the behavior of economic entities inconsistent with other observed behavior: the study asserts that economic decisionmakers ignore the level of their taxes and focus only on the direction of relative change. In effect, all decisionmakers must assume that the direction of change will continue and have a discount rate which approaches zero, in that history (as embodied in the present tax rate) is of no effect. A third flaw is the exclusion of a number of other possible variables, such as population migration, land costs, wages, climate, crime, energy costs, and any number of other factors of potential importance in explaining the general direction of economic development. As is well understood, the exclusion of relevant variables will cause bias in the estimated coefficients for remaining variables. Genetski and Chin excluded variables which all observers would agree have some effect, so that *by definition* their coefficient on the tax variable is biased. In which direction the bias exists is impossible to determine without further study. Finally, it is possible to tell an entirely different story than assumed by Genetski and Chin. It is quite possible that it is previous slow relative growth which causes changes in relative tax rates rather than the reverse. To test this possibility, we ran a number of alternative regressions (the detailed results are available from the author). In these regressions, the relative change in tax burden was used as the *dependent* variable, and regressed against relative change in income, with income changes lagged three years. In a number of time periods, this reverse relationship appears to be as strong as the one described by Genetski and Chin. Undoubtedly both factors are at work. However, given the conceptual and methodological errors of the underlying study, it is not possible to infer *any* conclusions about the true relationships between state and local taxes and economic development. To assert, as the *Wall Street Journal* does, that research now shows that relative changes in tax burden will lead to increased development is completely without justification and can be understood only as a rhetorical statement.

Summary of Statistical Investigations   Only limited conclusions can be drawn from previous statistical research in this area. Few studies have focused directly on investment or employment. Most other studies, such as those of Campbell, Sacks, Genetski and Chin, and Struyk, are fundamentally flawed in methodology, either through sole reliance on simple correlation or by excluding variables known to be important. Thompson and Mattila, Carlton, and Hodge approach the issue more directly and with fewer methodological flaws. None sufficiently address the difficult issue of developing an appropriate measure of state and local taxes on business. Of these studies, only Hodge found a significant and negative effect of state corporate income taxes on the investment of any sector (in his case furniture). Only Hodge and Carlton attempted to explicitly measure the influence of incentives (through the construction of an incentive index) on investment, and they detected no significant effects. However, it is not possible to place a great deal of confidence in these results, since there is no information on the relative size or targeting of the incentives. Only if businesses took an extremely naive view of incentives, and considered them without determining their relative size or eligibility, would such an aggregate index be an acceptable measure.   *203*

EVIDENCE FROM SURVEYS AND INTERVIEWS

In terms of simple number, the largest body of evidence relating tax structure to economic development comes from surveys and interviews with businesses. There is substantial controversy over the value of evidence gained in this manner because of a number of weaknesses with the methods usually used.

The typical survey instrument and methodology consists of drawing up a long list of factors which the researcher believes may influence industrial location. The survey is sent to a firm, which in some cases has recently located in a limited geographical area, and in other cases has no particular geographical orientation. The firm is asked to rank the factors in terms of importance, or state whether or not they had any influence, or place the factors into such categories as critical, significant, modest importance, and no importance. The results are used by public development agencies or private advocacy groups to recommend (or rationalize) changes in development policy. Some factor such as taxes or tax incentives is usually included so that local development officials can determine whether or not taxes or lack of incentives are deterring investment.

At least six substantial criticisms have been levied against survey methods. First, the questions asked tend to make a substantial difference in the answers obtained. In particular, different answers are obtained if, "What factors should be considered in a location decision?" is asked rather than "what factors were considered in your location decision?" Second, if questions are asked about a past location decision in a given geographical area, the sample is restricted to those firms which found the area acceptable, rather than to those firms which considered the area. Third, there is usually no information contained in the survey to indicate the position of the respondent, and it probably makes a difference whether it was the director of labor relations, the real estate manager, the corporate treasurer, or the president of the company. Fourth, the specific factors included in the survey usually contain at least some ambiguity in their interpretation (to be stated precisely would lengthen the survey instrument beyond what most respondents would consider filling out). Fifth, it can be presumed that there is an incentive for strategic behavior on the part of respondents when questions of public policy such as tax policy are asked. If a respondent believes legislators or elected officials will be influenced by the survey, there is an incentive to answer by exaggerating the importance of taxes. Sixth, few surveys include questions about the process of geographical selection, or differentiate between selction of a region versus selection of a specific site. While both logic and industrial location analysts indicate that larger firms search for new locations in a multistate process, almost no surveys attempt to separate out these stages in their questions. Finally, it is difficult to interpret the results of most surveys in an anlytical manner. Learning that a certain portion of respondents considered taxes "of moderate importance" in choosing a location gives relatively little information about the magnitude of the response to changes in tax levels or incentives.

The best review of surveys undertaken prior to 1964 is provided in Morgan (1964). This study reviewed twenty-four survey and interview studies of firms in all areas of the nation. Morgan found general consensus among the survey results. Even though there was considerable variation in the specific questions asked, the types of firms in the sample, and the areas of the country, taxes and financial inducements were consistently ranked in the bottom one-fifth or one-tenth of factors mentioned by respondents. In Morgan's review, surveys were examined from the point of view of whether the results indicated that taxes or financial inducements were ranked of primary significance, some significance, or little significance by the average respondent. As shown in Table 14 below, in the thirteen surveys which specifically included incentives, such inducements were, on average, always of little or no importance. Overall business taxes, as distinct from incentives, were included in all seventeen surveys. They were considered of primary importance (along with wages, markets, and availability of raw materials) in one survey, of some significance in three surveys, and of little significance in the remaining thirteen surveys.

Table 14

Relative Importance of Location Factors in 17 Surveys

	Number of surveys in which a factor was described as of:		
Factor	Primary Significance	Some Significance	Little Significance
Markets	16	1	0
Labor	10	7	0
Raw Materials	10	6	0
Transportation	7	10	0
Taxes	1	3	13
Financial Incentives	0	0	13

SOURCE: Table 2, "The Effects of State and Local Tax and Financial Inducements on Industrial Location," Morgan, W. unpublished Ph.D. dissertation, University of Colorado, 1964.

Further insight can be gained by examining some of the actual numbers underlying Morgan's review. Even in cases where the overall rating in a survey is that taxes are of minor importance, some firms may have been substantially influenced by interstate tax differences (although it should be noted that most of the surveys reviewed by Morgan did not attempt to determine the stage of the location decision at which various factors became important). In a study of 253 businesses which had located in Colorado between 1948 and 1957, 12.7 percent indicated that they had given some consideration to state and local taxes. In a survey of 752 firms locating in Florida in 1956 and 1957, only one firm mentioned state and local taxes as the primary factor influencing its location choice. When 102 Georgia firms were asked what Georgia should do, in 1956, to attract more firms, only three firms mentioned tax concessions. In a survey of 118 firms which located in Maryland between 1946 and 1951, only four firms considered state and local taxes to be significant in their decision. In a survey of 241 (primarily new) New Jersey firms in 1958, 34 percent stated that business taxes were very important in their location decisions (this was the survey in which taxes were determined to be of primary significance). Of 166 firms locating in Oregon between 1948 and 1953, 3 percent mentioned that state and local taxes strongly influenced their choice. In a national survey by *Business Week* in which 283 firms were asked which factors *should* be considered in a location decision (not which were considered for a specific decision), 14 percent considered state and local taxes to be of some importance. In a study of 350 Texas firms in 1953-1954, five firms ranked state and local taxes among the five most important factors in their choice. These figures should not be taken as estimates of the proportion of firms which would not have located in some area if taxes were higher or incentives not offered. These proportions are at best an upper bound on the estimates for that question.

Morgan also reviewed seven studies based on personal interviews with corporate decisionmakers. Such interviews share many of the shortcomings of mail surveys, but typically have the advantages of clearly identifying the appropriate decision-maker and not restricting possible answers to those preselected by the researcher. However, as in the surveys, there was general agreement among the interview studies. As seen in Table 15 below, markets were considered to be the most important factor, followed by labor, raw materials, and transportation. In not one of the interview studies reviewed by Morgan were either taxes or financial incentives considered of primary or secondary importance.

In an early study not reviewed in Morgan (1964), Mueller and Morgan (1962, unrelated), used personal interviews to determine the factors underlying the locational choices of manufacturing firms in

Table 15

Relative Importance of Location Factors in 7 Interview Studies

Number of studies in which a factor was described as of:

Factor	Primary Significance	Some Significance	Little Significance
Markets	6	1	0
Labor	3	4	0
Raw Materials	3	4	0
Transportation	0	6	1
Taxes	0	0	7
Financial Incentives	0	0	7

SOURCE: Table 4, "The Effects of State and Local Tax and Financial Inducements on Industrial Location," Morgan, W. unpublished Ph.D. dissertation, University of Colorado, 1964.

Michigan. The study differentiated between factors which the firms felt *should* be important in locating a plant and factors which had been important in locating the specific plant of the corporate decisionmaker. In ranking factors, executives were asked to name the five factors which should be of most importance. Six factors were named by firms representing at least 50 percent of employment in the sample. In order of mention, they were labor costs, proximity to markets, availability of skilled labor, industrial climate, the tax bill, and proximity to raw materials. The tax bill was mentioned among the five most important factors in firms representing 52 percent of sample employment.

Mueller and Morgan obtained very different results when executives were asked to report the factors that influenced their specific plant to be located in Michigan (as opposed to the choice of a particular site within Michigan). With this question, nontraditional factors become far more important. Personal reasons were a main reason for firms with 50 percent of the employment to locate in Michigan, with the relative importance of personal reasons declining with firm size. A better tax situation was mentioned by firms representing only 1 percent of sample employment, primarily among the larger firms. Local incentives were mentioned by firms representing only 2 percent of sample employment, again concentrated among larger firms.

Stafford (1974) conducted in-depth personal interviews with a small number of manufacturing firms which had recently located in Ohio. No initial list of factors was used, with only the statements of the *207* manufacturers indicating the relative importance of location factors. Of fourteen factors mentioned in the interviews, taxes were mentioned least frequently, and were seen as unimportant in choosing either a region or a specific site.

Inc. magazine (1980) conducted a survey of its readers to determine the factors influencing their future location choices. Firms were asked to select the three most important considerations in selecting a future site (note no distinction was made between stages of the location selection process). Various labor market factors were mentioned in the top three by 65.1 percent of the respondents, with the availability of skilled labor most important. Market location was mentioned by 56.1 percent of the respondents, with access to established markets viewed as more important than access to new markets. Transportation facilities were seen as important by 58 percent of the respondents, with highways by far the most favored. After these three factors, taxes were mentioned most frequently, ranked in the top three by 32.5 percent of the respondents. Nearly 22 percent mentioned a low tax rate in the three most important locational factors. Given the wording of the question, it is not possible to determine how frequently taxes were thought to be the critical location factor. Since the questions were asked concerning a hypothetical location rather than a specific past decision, it is possible that these traditional market and cost factors were mentioned more frequently than they will actually apply.

Somewhat surprisingly, only two studies have actually asked firms known to have received tax incentives about the relative weight of the incentive in their location decision. Ross (1953) surveyed firms in Louisiana which had asked for and received state property tax exemptions. Dorgan (1980) surveyed firms in North Dakota which received exemption from local property taxation.

Among other questions, the Ross study asked firms directly whether they would have developed their project without the tax exemption, and whether or not they would have located their plant in Louisiana without the exemption. In the absence of the exemption, 15.8 percent of the firms stated that they would not have developed their new plant or expansion. Also, 17 percent stated that they would not have developed their plant in Louisiana without the exemption. Ross also asked about the deciding factor in both the investment decision and the location decision, and discovered significant inconsistencies in the replies. Thus, while only 5.4 percent of all respondents indicated that the tax exemption was the deciding factor in undertaking their investment, 15.8 percent, when asked in a separate portion of the survey, indicated that they would not have undertaken the investment without the subsidy. Similarly, while only 3.1 percent stated that the exemption was the deciding factor in locating their investment in Louisiana, 17 percent indicated that they would not have located in

Louisiana without the subsidy. These discrepancies are probably a good measure of the willingness of firms to overestimate the influence of incentives in answering the questions. Ross concluded that approximately 7 percent of the dollar value of the investments would have been lost to the state if the subsidy program was not in effect. The remainder received windfall benefits from the tax reductions.

Dorgan did not include such specific questions, and only asked firms for the "major" factors in their location decision. As seen in Table 16, ten of the 125 firms responding to the survey indicated that the tax incentive was a major factor in their location decision. However, for some of the ten firms, a "major" influence need not have been the deciding or marginal influence. Thus the results should be interpreted as saying that no more than ten out of the sample would not have located in North Dakota, with the real number somewhat less (a more precisely worded question would have been valuable). However, there were significant differences in effect among types of firms, with 75 percent of the large agricultural products processing cooperatives reporting a major factor, 15.4 percent of the out-of-state headquarters firms reporting a major factor, and only 3.2 percent of the North Dakota-based firms indicating a major effect.

Table 16

Response of Firms to North Dakota Property Tax Incentives

	Number of Firms Receiving Incentives	Number of Firms Where Incentive Was a Major Factor in Location
Firms based out of state	26	4 (15.4%)
North Dakota firms	95	3 (3.2%)
Large regional cooperatives	4	3 (75.0%)

SOURCE: Table A, "North Dakota's New Industry Tax Exemption: Economic Incentive or Tax Giveaway?", Bryon Dorgan, North Dakota State Tax Commissioner, January 1980.

Summary of Evidence from Surveys and Interviews   Taking into account the wide diversity of techniques, types of respondent companies, and geographical areas, the consistency of findings from surveys and interviews is striking. Even disregarding the existence of reasons to overestimate the importance of business taxes and incentives, businesses themselves agree that the fiscal considerations and incentives are of relatively little importance in their location decision. It is quite rare for more than 10 percent of respondents to indicate that taxes were of any significance in a location decision, with the majority of studies showing significantly ***209*** less that 10 percent. Unfortunately, most of the studies ask the wrong questions if the intent is to determine the marginal effect of incentives and changes in tax structures. Thus, even the 10 percent finding should be considered an upper bound.

EVIDENCE FROM STUDIES ATTEMPTING TO MEASURE THE PUBLIC RETURN

Only two studies have attempted to determine the public rate of return or ratio of benefits to costs for industrial location subsidies. Conceptually, such studies should follow the public investment framework discussed in Chapter Three, in identifying those investments which were affected and the accompanying flow of income which should be counted at the relevant state or local level. No study has attempted to analyze incentives from the national perspective.

The most detailed study was performed by Rinehart (1962) in a series of case studies of industrial firms subsidized by small towns in the rural South during the late 1950s. Rinehart attempted to estimate the direct payroll resulting from a new factory, and included indirect and induced income effects. He subtracted out the wages lost when workers left other jobs which then went unfilled. Unemployed workers were assumed to have placed no value on leisure. The costs included were tax abatements, cash grants, the value of physical improvements, and a variety of other informal inducements provided to the firm. No attempt was made to determine whether unused capacity existed in local public services (such as schools) or whether new capacity (and hence new costs) were required. After discounting both incremental income and costs at an assumed social opportunity cost of 6 percent, Rinehart converted this net present value to a level stream of perpetual income, and calculated the rate of return. Rinehart *assumed* that no investment would have occurred without the subsidies, and evaluated the rate of return from the perspective of the local community—not the state or the nation. Thus the rates of return calculated are far higher than broader analyses. The analysis was done under three different assumptions:

1. the firm produces the same income stream perpetually (no failure);
2. the firm leaves the community at the end of the study period (thus not collecting the portion of subsidy not yet granted, such as the remaining tax abatements); and
3. the firm leaves the community at the end of the study period, and the community loses the full amount of the subsidy (intended to be a worse case).

210   Under the assumptions, Rinehart discovered extraordinarily high rates of return (see Table 17 below). With the most optimistic assumption, the rate of return on individual subsidies ranged from 87 percent per year to 8,195 percent per year. When weighted by the amount of public subsidy, the average annual return was 492.8 percent. Under Rinehart's second assumption, the weighted average annual return dropped to 263.2 percent. It was not possible to calculate the weighted return for Rinehart's third assumption, but if the same ratio held between the unweighted and weighted as in the other case, it would be around 40 percent annually.

Table 17

Estimated Annual Rate of Return on Local Subsidies to Industry

Firm	Case 1	Case 2	Case 3
A	246%	153%	74%
B	311	178	55
C	559	169	26
D	1,506	992	375
E	181	99	28
F	87	70	18
G	220	191	32
H	1,030	665	162
I	665	380	99
J	483	459	88
K	959	810	113
L	139	154	14
M	334	221	17
N	1,373	1,000	25
O	1,116	739	216
P	515	450	52
Q	8,195	3,595	362
R	473	N/A	71
S	340	N/A	21
T	432	N/A	15
U	5,293	N/A	727
V	673	N/A	24
Unweighted Average Return	1,221.0%	613.0%	94.7%
Weighted Average Return	492.8%	263.2%	40.0%

SOURCE: Derived from information on each firm from "Rates of Return on Municipal Subsidies to Industries," Rinehart, J.R. unpublished Ph.d. dissertation, University of Virginia, 1962.

A first reaction to these returns would be that some mistake was made in arithmetic. However, upon reflection, it is clear that they provide insight into the powerful forces inducing local (not state) governments to provide incentives. For the most part, the reasons the returns are high are that it is assumed that all of the incremental income can be assigned to the public subsidy, and the fact that in many cases the subsidy was quite small, perhaps involving a small undeveloped parcel of land or a break on sewer costs. The rate of return on a one dollar public subsidy would indeed by quite high if it induced a large plant to locate in a rural Southern town. Since most officials will assume that their subsidy was the deciding factor, the local return appears extremely high. Of course, the literature reviewed above clearly indicates that these assumptions are not justified.

It is possible to adjust Rinehart's figures to take into account the possibility that some of the firms did not locate in the town because of the inducement. The critical policy question is what percentage needs to be influenced for the public subsidies to be a good investment for the community. Rinehart assumed the social opportunity cost at the time to be 6 percent. As shown in Table 18 below, it is possible to calculate the break-even probability for each firm by determining the percent of benefits used by Rinehart necessary to result in a 6 percent rate of return (although the existence of true uncertainty should dictate a significantly higher discount rate, which would necessitate a correspondingly higher breakeven rate). For the optimistic case one, the probability on average needs only to be 1.22 percent. Under the more conservative assumptions of case two, the break-even probability is still only 2.28 percent. That is, if the community believed that at least 2.28 percent of the benefits were actually induced by the subsidies, it should consider the subsidies minimally acceptable public investments.

Morgan and Hackbart (1974) used a similar conceptual framework to determine the conditions under which state-allowed local property tax abatements were acceptable public investments. They obtained estimates of the tax-exempt industrial investment made in seven states from the state development agencies for the period 1958 to 1961. They estimated the cost of the subsidies by using an average state assessment ratio and average state property tax rate, since they did not have information on the locations of the investment by individual towns. On the income side, they developed an estimate of an incremental capital/output ratio and of a state income multiplier to assess the increase in income derived from the exempted investment. They then used a variety of assumptions about the proportion of the income which was incremental (this was to account for wage losses in the jobs left by new employees as well as immigration by out-of-state residents). *212* They then calculated the expected benefit-cost ratio for different

Table 18

Break-even Percentage of Investment Induced by Subsidies

Firm	Case 1	Case 2	Case 3
A	2.48%	3.92%	8.11%
B	1.93	3.37	10.91
C	1.08	3.55	23.08
D	.40	.61	1.60
E	3.31	6.06	21.43
F	6.90	8.57	33.33
G	2.73	3.14	18.75
H	.58	.90	3.70
I	.90	1.58	6.06
J	1.24	1.31	6.82
K	.63	.74	5.31
L	4.32	1.11	42.86
M	1.80	2.72	35.29
N	.44	.61	24.00
O	.54	.81	2.78
P	1.17	1.33	11.54
Q	.07	.17	1.66
R	1.27		8.45
S	1.77		30.00
T	1.39		40.00
U	.11		.83
V	.89		25.00
Weighted Break-even Percentage	1.22%	2.28%	16.47%

SOURCE: Derived from Table 17.

probabilities corresponding to the chance that a given investment was actually induced by a subsidy. They did not attempt to determine the actual influence of the subsidies. Their results appear in Table 19 below.

The results of Morgan and Hackbart are generally consistent with our manipulation of Rinehart's findings. If only 1 percent of the investment is actually induced, no set of assumptions can render the subsidies a good public investment. However, if the percent induced rises to 5 percent, and both direct and indirect benefits are counted, only 25 percent of the extra income needs to be incremental to render the benefit cost ratio above one. The basic result is that only a small percentage of subsidized investment needs to be actually induced for the subsidy to be an acceptable public investment.

Table 19

Comparison of Benefits and Costs of Tax Exemption Programs

Definition of Benefits	Induced Investment as a Percentage of Total Tax Exempt Investment		
	.01	.05	.10
Benefits = 100% of Value Added			
Direct and Indirect Benefits Discount rate of .10	.88	4.38	8.77
Direct Benefits Only Discount rate of .10	.59	2.94	5.88
Benefits = 50% Value Added			
Direct and Indirect Benefits Discount rate of .10	.44	2.19	4.39
Direct Benefits Only Discount rate of .10	.29	1.47	2.94
Benefits = 25% of Value Added			
Direct and Indirect Benefits Discount rate of .10	.22	1.10	2.10
Direct Benefits Only Discount rate of .10	.15	.74	1.47
Benefits = 10% of Value Added			
Direct and Indirect Benefits Discount rate of .10	.09	.44	.88
Direct Benefits Only Discount rate of .10	.06	.29	.59

SOURCE: Table 1, "An Analysis of State and Local Industrial Tax Exemption Programs", Morgan, W. and Hackbart, M., Southern Economic Journal, October 1974.

Summary of Rate of Return Studies

A very limited amount of empirical work reviewing subsidies during the late 1950s indicates that if even a small proportion of subsidized investment is affected, the state or local subsidy is a good investment. However, the available evidence from surveys and empirical work is insufficient to determine whether or not a very small percent (perhaps 1 to 5 percent) of the total subsidized investment was actually induced. Since it is certain that all states and communities providing subsidies tremendously overestimate the importance of their subsidies, it is easy to understand why state and local governments offer an ever-increasing number of subsidies.

SUMMARY OF EMPIRICAL RESEARCH

For a field that has existed amidst public controversy for several decades, relatively little progress has been made in finally resolving the value of tax incentives for industrial investment when applied at the state level. While very difficult to measure business tax burdens between states in an appropriate manner, it is clear that many firms face interstate tax differentials that are a significant portion of their pretax income. There exists, however, near consensus from studies using surveys and interviews that tax differences or tax incentives play at best a small role in location decisions for most firms. Unfortunately nearly all of these surveys contain flaws of design.

Yet, it is also clear that from a state or local perspective, if only a relatively small share of subsidized firms are actually influenced by the tax incentive, the public investment is an acceptable one. This makes it all the more important to have empirical techniques which can identify relatively small shifts in investment or employment in response to tax differences. Unfortunately, because of the measurement problem for tax burdens, and the relatively small samples used in most econometric investigations, it is difficult to exclude the possibility of a small (but nonetheless sufficient) response.

A review of the literature must include a statement of sympathy for researchers in the field. For the most part, research must rely on unpublished data (and frequently involves the collection of primary date) and use as a key variable a state and local tax burden which is difficult to define conceptually and for which there is substantial disagreement about methodology. Nonetheless, it appears that there remains room for improvement in both survey methods and econometric investigations.

FOOTNOTES TO CHAPTER 3

[1] A significant portion of this section will rely on some familiarity with basic statistical and econometric concepts. For readers without such a background, the summary of the section should provide an adequate picture of the results of previous statistical work in the area.

4

DESCRIPTION OF
NEW EMPIRICAL RESEARCH

While there is clearly no shortage of areas in which additional information is needed, the literature review should make it clear that substantial obstacles are involved in any new eimpirical research on the effects of tax incentives. For purposes of this study, new empirical research was undertaken in four areas in which it appeared there was a reasonable prospect of obtaining useful results:

1. a rough estimation of the initial direct revenue losses to selected states as a result of automatic state tax incentives;
2. a mail survey to manufacturing firms starting or expanding in states which offer automatic income tax incentives;
3. an econometric estimation of equations designed to predict the share of new capital investment in a state for a number of two-digit manufacturing industries, using such factors as business taxes, wages, productivity, unionization, and other factors as independent variables; and
4. a benefit-cost analysis of tax incentives using the results of the mail surveys and econometric investigations.

ESTIMATION OF INITIAL REVENUE LOSSES
To place the issue of state tax incentives into some perspective, it is useful to have some estimate, however rough, of the associated initial revenue loss. This section attempts to provide an order of magnitude estimate. The tax incentives it includes are those which are provided for through a state's corporate income tax, and are available in all parts of the state. Thus, the estimates exclude all state authorized but locally administered property tax incentives (which are certain to be quite substantial), inventory and sales tax exemptions, incentives for research and development or pollution control, and all wage incentives aimed at specific classes of workers. The estimates assume that all eligible firms took advantage of the incentives, although it is likely that some of the smaller firms did not. Thus, these estimates are an upper bound on the cost of the specified incentives, but exclude many state tax incentives from any consideration.

The base for calculation of all of the revenue losses was gross investment in manufacturing in 1977 as reported in the Preliminary
Census of Manufacturers for 1977. Where the incentive is available

only for machinery and equipment, and not for plant and structures, it is assumed that 74.03 percent of the gross investment was in machinery and equipment, as was the case nationwide in 1976 (no comparable figures for 1977 are available).

Some states provide broad-based employment or wage incentives. In this case, the starting point remains the gross investment estimate, and it is assumed that a new job is created for each $25,000 of gross investment. This is necessarily a very crude estimate, and neglects interstate variation in capital intensity and interstate variation in the division of gross investment in terms of new investment and modernization, which have substantially different employment effects. Where the incentive is based on a percentage of new wages, it is assumed that each new employee works at an average wage equal to that prevailing among manufacturing employees in the relevant state in 1977.

While the investment figures are taken from 1977 (since no more current figures are available), all states which had legislated tax incentives as of December 1980 are included. However, in some cases the incentives legislated are not fully in place (for example, Tennessee's tax credit will not be fully implemented until 1984). Nonetheless, if passed, it is assumed that the full tax incentive was available in 1977, and applied to the 1977 investment estimate. Thus, it should be clearly understood that the estimates developed here are not estimates of the actual revenue losses incurred by states in 1977.

The estimates presented in Table 20 below are only an indication of the initial revenue loss. They do not take into account additional revenue to the state in other taxes due to possible increased activity if the incentives are effective in inducing industrial expansion. They should not be interpreted as the *net* cost to the states.

Given the assumptions, the first year revenue loss is nearly $173 million. In some states, there would be continuing losses for an additional ten years (Kansas, West Virginia). This is certainly a substantial public expenditure deserving of evaluation. Of the total revenue loss, about 92 percent is for capital subsidies and only about 8 percent is labor subsidies. Of the capital subsidies, about 87 percent is accounted for by New York and Massachusetts, due to a large share of investment and large incentives. Of the labor incentives, about 81 percent is accounted for by Louisiana and Missouri. These quite substantial sums indicate clearly that state incentives represent a large public program—one of sufficient size to merit serious evaluation.

MAIL SURVEYS The only way to obtain information about particular business investment decisions is to survey or interview business officials directly involved in recent location choices. Personal interviews are very time consuming *217*

Table 20

Estimates of the Initial Revenue Loss
from Selected State Tax Incentives

State	1977 Investment	Investment Incentives	Job Incentives	Total
Delaware	$ 154,000,000	$ 284,000	$ 462,000	$ 746,000
Colorado	447,400,000	223,700	894,000	1,117,700
Kansas	349,300,000	174,650	698,600	873,250
Montana	97,500,000		511,720	511,720
New York	2,715,600,000	108,624,000		108,624,000
Rhode Island	160,000,000	3,202,000		3,202,000
Massachusetts	978,300,000	29,340,000		29,340,000
New Mexico	100,800,000	2,798,334		2,798,334
North Dakota	52,900,000		242,599	242,599
West Virginia	370,100,000	3,701,000		3,701,000
Louisiana	2,167,000		8,668,000	8,668,000
Oklahoma	497,700,000	2,488,500		2,488,500
Missouri	885,800,000	664,350	2,657,400	3,321,750
Tennessee	963,200,000	7,130,570		7,130,570
		$ 158,631,104	$ 14,134,319	$ 172,765,423

SOURCE: 1977 investment figures represent estimates of gross new depreciable investment taken from the preliminary 1977 Census of Manufacturers. The tax incentives, as described in Table 9, were applied to the investment estimates as described in the text.

and limit the number of firms included in the study. Mail surveys impose difficulties in obtaining adequate response rates, but are far less expensive. For this study, the direct mail approach was taken to reach firms that had made investments in states offering automatic tax incentives. The goals of the mail survey carried out for this study were to determine answers to four general questions:

1. the extent to which firms searched for sites among more than one state;
2. the relative importance of different characteristics of competing states in influencing the choice among states;
3. the degree to which businesses were aware of state tax incentives; and
4. the effect of the tax incentive on either the location of an investment or the amount of the investment.

The survey instrument and procedures used in this study were designed to avoid many of the problems in previous surveys (the survey instruments and a detailed discussion of methodology and results are available in Appendix II.) In particular, attention was paid in the following areas:

1. New firms, new expansion investments, and new branch plants were analyzed separately. The survey instrument for expansion investments contained several additional factors not found for the other firms. These categories were used for several reasons. First, the research of Birch (1979) indicates that the majority of employment growth results from employment changes in new manufacturing firms and expansion investments, rather than new branch plants. In contrast, most state development efforts are focused on new branch plants. In addition, previous research by Oster (1979) and Schmenner (1978) indicates that there are differences in the way in which these types of firms make location choices, and in the relative weight they place on characteristics of competing states.
2. Major attempts were made to ensure that the appropriate decision-maker received the survey instrument. Unless someone directly involved in the actual decision answers the questions, it is impossible to evaluate the results. In almost all cases, the surveys were mailed to a specific person who was very likely to have been directly involved in the location decision.
3. The survey questions were specifically created assuming that location decisions were made in stages. The questions used were directed at choices among states, rather than the selection of a specific site. Firms were asked to identify important *differences* among states rather than important factors required for any state selected.
4. Survey questions were directed at specific, named investments, rather than hypothetical investments about which factors should be considered.
5. Survey questions were directed to investments made recently, so that the relevant factors were recallable. Thus, each of the new firms surveyed were started during 1979, while the new branch plants and expansions were also made during 1979.
6. Firms were asked whether or not state tax incentives existed in the state of their actual investment. They could answer yes, no, or don't know. This question appears to be unique among surveys on location choices. Only firms investing in states which actually had tax incentives during 1979 received surveys. This question allowed answers to be interpreted in light of whether or not the firms actually made a decision having known about incentives.   *219*

7. Specific questions were asked about the marginal effect of the incentive. Rather than relying on a general ranking of the influence of a tax incentive among a collection of factors, respondents were asked directly whether the tax incentive affected the location or amount of their investment.
8. The survey asked questions to differentiate the effect of a tax incentive on the location of investment from the amount of investment. It is possible that incentives simply move investment around without affecting its amount, or that investment is not moved around but is increased at the location it would have been made at in any case.
9. The survey was structured to identify strategic (that is, intentionally misleading) answers which might serve to overestimate the importance of incentives. Businesses have an incentive to overstate the importance of tax subsidies since they might believe that the surveyor would use the information to influence future tax policies.

The mail survey provided results which will be summarized in five categories (extensive detail is available in Appendix II): the degree to which firms seriously considered other states, the relative importance of state characteristics in location choices, knowledge of tax incentives, the effect of the incentives on location, and the effect of the incentives on the amount of investment. To make it easy to compare the answers among new firms, expansions, and new branch plants, they will be presented within the same section, rather than repeat the results for each category or firm.

Proportion of Firms Considering Other States There were substantial differences among the categories of firms in their answers to the question "Did you seriously consider locating this investment in any other state?" In no category did more than half of the firms seriously consider other states as possible locations. As shown in Table 21 below, 26.7 percent of the new firms, 28.0 percent of the expansions, and 43.8 percent of the new branch plants considered other states. In general, the expansions and new branch plants were larger firms than the new companies, which may have influenced their search behavior.

Relative Importance of State Characteristics in Location Choices Only those firms that seriously considered locating in another state were asked to indicate the relative importance of a number of factors in choosing among states. They could describe each factor as "Deciding Positive Influence," "Moderate Negative Influence," "Insignificant Influence," or "Moderate Negative Influence." They were not asked about deciding

Table 21

Percent of Respondents Considering Location in Another State

State	New Firms	Expansions	New Plants
New York	22.9%	20.0%	54.5%
Delaware	55.5	100.0	
Colorado	20.3	20.0	0
New Mexico	40.0	0	0
Montana			0
Massachusetts	34.4	30.0	33.3
Kansas	30.4	30.8	37.5
Rhode Island	33.3	25.0	50.0
Maine		0	100.0
West Virginia	33.3	66.7	100.0
North Dakota	33.3		
Total	**26.7%**	**28.0%**	**43.8%**

NOTE: Blanks represent states where no firms responded in the appropriate category.

negative influences because if they existed, they would not have located in the state. The responses, tabulated separately for new firms, expansions, and new branch plants, are shown in Tables 22, 23, and 24 below, respectively. There are clear differences in relative importance, as determined by the proportion describing each factor by level of importance, among the different types of firms.

New firms are very concerned with the size of their markets, with access to a growing market and current customers most important. Personal reasons of management are also very frequently mentioned. After these factors, a number of "supply" factors are considered to be important: access to raw materials, availability of capital, supply of skilled labor, and transportation are frequently mentioned. Familiarity with the local economy is considered quite important as well. Business taxes are of only modest importance, as are personal taxes. The political climate and air quality regulations, which are frequent topics of political discussion, are rarely considered by new businesses.

Based on the research of Schmenner (1978), a number of factors *221*

Table 22

Relative Importance of Location Factors for
New Firms Making Interstate Location Choices

Factor	Percent of Respondents Who Consider Factor to be of:				
	Deciding Positive Influence	Moderate Positive Influence	Insignificant Influence	Moderate Negative Influence	No Answer
Availability of capital	30.0%	23.3%	36.7%	4.4%	5.6%
Supply of skilled labor	24.4	31.1	36.7	3.3	4.4
Cost of skilled labor	16.7	31.1	42.2	4.4	5.6
Supply of unskilled labor	13.3	31.1	44.4	4.4	6.7
Cost of unskilled labor	15.6	24.4	47.8	6.6	5.6
Union activities	13.3	15.6	51.1	14.4	5.6
Supply of fuel and electricity	7.8	17.8	58.9	5.6	10.0
Cost of fuel and electricity	6.7	18.9	56.7	11.1	6.7
Climate	10.0	27.8	48.9	10.0	3.3
Personal reasons of management	41.1	27.8	21.1	2.2	7.8
Transportation network	24.4	34.4	32.2	5.6	3.3
Political climate	8.9	15.6	56.7	12.2	6.7
Familiarity with economy	26.7	37.8	26.7	2.2	6.7
Air quality regulation	1.1	7.8	73.3	11.1	6.7
Business tax structure	14.4	30.0	33.3	18.9	3.3
Personal tax structure	15.6	16.7	41.1	22.2	4.4
Access to raw materials	33.3	18.9	36.7	6.7	4.4
Access to present customers	52.2	23.3	20.0	1.1	3.3
Access to growing market	50.0	20.0	25.6	2.2	2.2
Land costs	17.8	16.7	47.8	11.1	6.7

SOURCES: Responses from mail survey.

peculiar to expansion investments were included in the list of factors to be evaluated by firms having made expansions in 1979. Some of these—achieving economies of scale, maintaining an intact labor force, and ease of expanding on-site—were the most frequently mentioned reasons for making investment at the present site. Market factors—both access to current customers and to a growing market—were also considered quite important. The political climate and personal reasons of management were rated quite high, as were nontraditional factors, while access to raw materials was the most important supply factor. Business taxes were the least important factor considered by those deciding on the location of expansion investments.

For new branch plants, labor market concerns—particularly the supply of both skilled and unskilled labor—were deemed most important. In addition, the presence of unions was seriously considered. In contrast to both new firms and expansions, the state business tax structure was considered generally important. Somewhat

Table 23

Relative Importance of Location Factors for Expansions Making Interstate Location Choices

Percent of Respondents Who Consider Factor to be of:

Factor	Deciding Positive Influence	Moderate Positive Influence	Insignificant Influence	Moderate Negative Influence	No Answer
Availability of capital	21.4%	28.6%	50.0%	0.0	0.0
Economies of scale realized with expansion on-site	42.9	21.4	21.4	7.1	7.1
Supply of skilled labor	21.4	50.0	28.6	0.0	0.0
Cost of skilled labor	14.3	42.9	28.6	14.3	0.0
Supply of unskilled labor	7.1	28.6	50.0	7.1	7.1
Cost of unskilled labor	7.1	35.6	42.9	14.3	0.0
Union activities	21.4	14.3	28.6	35.7	0.0
Maintain intact labor force	42.9	35.7	21.4	0.0	0.0
Supply of fuel and electricity	21.4	21.4	42.9	14.3	0.0
Cost of fuel and electricity	14.3	28.6	35.7	21.4	0.0
Climate	7.1	28.6	64.3	0.0	0.0
Personal reasons of management	28.6	21.4	42.9	7.1	0.0
Product line or production process not easily divided	14.3	42.9	35.7	7.1	0.0
Transportation network	14.3	42.9	42.9	0.0	0.0
Political climate	28.6	7.1	42.9	21.4	0.0
Familiarity with economy	7.1	14.3	78.6	0.0	0.0
Air quality regulation	0.0	14.3	71.4	14.3	0.0
Ease of expanding on-site	42.9	28.6	28.6	0.0	0.0
Business tax structure	0.0	50.0	28.6	21.4	0.0
Personal tax structure	14.3	21.4	42.9	21.4	0.0
Access to raw materials	28.6	35.7	35.7	0.0	0.0
Access to present customers	28.6	28.6	42.9	0.0	0.0
Access to growing market	21.4	21.4	57.1	0.0	0.0
Land costs	7.1	35.7	42.9	14.3	0.0

SOURCE: Reponses from mail survey.

surprisingly, market factors—either access to a growing market or to current customers—were seen as relatively unimportant.

Knowledge of State Tax Incentives State tax incentives can be an effective development tool only if business decisionmakers are aware of them. As shown in Table 25 below, most firms are not aware of incentives. Among new firms, less than a fifth of the firms were aware that incentives existed in the state of their actual location. Among expansions, 36 percent were aware of the incentives. Since such firms did not generally consider other states with any more seriousness than new firms, this higher proportion may reflect the somewhat larger size of the firms. Among **223**

Table 24

Relative Importance of Location Factors for New Branch Plants Making Interstate Location Choices

Percent of Respondents Who Consider Factor to be of:

Factor	Deciding Positive Influence	Moderate Positive Influence	Insignificant Influence	Moderate Negative Influence	No Answer
Availability of capital	21.4%	42.9%	35.7%	0.0%	0.0%
Supply of skilled labor	64.3	14.3	14.3	0.0	7.0
Cost of skilled labor	21.4	64.3	7.1	7.1	0.0
Supply of unskilled labor	35.7	7.1	42.9	0.0	14.0
Cost of unskilled labor	7.1	28.6	42.9	7.1	14.0
Union activities	35.7	14.3	28.6	14.3	7.0
Supply of fuel and electricity	14.3	28.6	42.9	0.0	14.0
Cost of fuel and electricity	14.3	21.4	42.9	7.1	14.0
Climate	7.1	14.3	57.1	14.3	7.0
Personal reasons of management	28.6	28.6	35.7	0.0	7.0
Transportation network	28.6	21.4	35.7	7.1	7.0
Political climate	21.4	21.4	35.7	7.1	14.0
Familiarity with economy	0.0	28.6	57.1	0.0	14.0
Air quality regulation	0.0	21.4	64.3	0.0	14.0
Business tax structure	35.7	7.1	50.0	0.0	7.0
Personal tax structure	7.1	21.4	35.7	21.4	14.0
Access to raw materials	21.4	28.6	50.0	0.0	0.0
Access to present customers	14.3	28.6	50.0	7.1	0.0
Access to growing market	14.3	7.1	57.1	7.1	14.0
Land costs	21.4	35.7	35.7	0.0	7.0

SOURCE: Responses from mail surveys.

new branch plants, half of the firms were aware of state tax incentives (90 percent of the firms in New York), which probably reflects the more intense comparison of states by those considering new branch plants. Among new firms and expansions, more firms claimed that tax incentives did not exist (they could have indicated that they did not know) than correctly stated that they did.

Effect of the Tax Incentives on Location Decisions Those firms which correctly indicated that state tax incentives were available were asked whether they would have located in another state if no incentive had been available. A number of firms which indicated that they would have located elsewhere had previously stated that they did not seriously consider other states—a clearly strategic set of answers. After eliminating these and similar answers, 3.3 percent of the new firms, 224 none of the expansions, and 6.3 percent of the new branch plants

Table 25

Knowledge of Tax Incentives Among
New Firms, Expansions, and New Plants by State

State	New Firms	Expansions	New Plants
New York	28.2%	70.0%	90.0%
Delaware	22.2	100.0	
Colorado	20.3	20.0	0
New Mexico	20.0	50.0	
Montana	0		0
Massachusetts	13.3	0	0
Kansas	8.7	38.5	50.0
Rhode Island	14.8	25.0	50.0
Maine	*	0	50.0
West Virginia	0	66.7	0
North Dakota	0		
Total	**19.6%**	**36.0%**	**50.0%**

*New firms were not surveyed in Maine because they are not generally eligible for the available tax incentives

NOTE: Blanks represent cases where there were no responses.

indicated that they would have located in another state in the absence of tax incentives.

Effect of the Tax Incentives on the Amount Invested In contrast to the all or none aspect of a location decision, some firms might have changed their amount of investment—but not location—in response to a tax incentive. The change in amount may reflect either a change in the capital/labor ratio or simply a scale change in the overall project. In contrast to the prior question on location of investment, it was not possible to structure the amount question to detect misleading answers, since it is perfectly possible for a firm not have considered other locations but to respond to a tax incentive by changing the amount of investment. Thus, including any possible strategic answers, 7.7 percent of the new firms, 12 percent of the expansions, and 21.9 percent of the new plants indicated that they would have reduced their investment in the absence of a tax incentive. These proportions must be considered as upper bounds, and it is likely that the real figures are somewhat lower. However, simply knowing the proportion of firms which would have reduced their investment does not indicate how **225**

much they would have reduced their investment, and a specific question asking for such estimates was not asked.

Summary of the Results For the most part, the results of the mail
of the Mail Survey survey correspond to common sense.
More branch plants consider locating in another state than new firms or expansions, but for the most part, less than half of all new investments are made as a result of a multistate search for a new location. There are differences among firms in the relative importance of state characteristics for location decisions, but only among new branch plants do business taxes assume any major importance. A majority of firms are unaware of state tax incentives, with many firms incorrectly asserting that no tax incentives are available. New branch plants are most likely to be aware of incentives, perhaps because they search more widely and are most courted by state and local development organizations. Only a very small portion of firms change their location choices because of state tax incentives, but a larger proportion of businesses claim to have increased their investment (although in an unknown amount).

ECONOMETRIC It is quite clear that many factors influence
INVESTIGATIONS the location decision for most manufac-
turing investments. The survey method relies upon the personal interpretation of business executives to assign relative weights to each factor. An alternative method is to observe actual patterns of investments among states, and attempt to relate those patterns to interstate differences in location factors. The standard methodology used in such an exercise is to use multiple regression techniques to estimate an equation which relates the value of a "dependent" variable, such as investment, to the values of "independent" variables as they vary across states. In general, if there are enough variables (that is, if the researcher has identified most of the factors which affect the outcome) and sufficient observations (one observation is never enough), and the underlying relationships among variables are reflected in the form of the equation (that is, only the relative weights are at issue), it is possible to make reasonable estimates of the impact of changes in the value of independent variables on the dependent variable.

As noted above, the end result of a multiple regression analysis is an equation relating the dependent variable to the independent variables. For each independent variable, the statistical technique estimates a "coefficient," which describes the magnitude of the effect of changes in the independent variables on the value of the dependent variable. To understand this, consider the following example. In an equation in which the dependent variable is employment, measured in millions, average wage rates might be included as an independent variable. If the estimated coefficient was −2.0, it means that if average wages increased by one unit, say from $4.00 to $5.00, the number of jobs would decrease by two million.

Statistical significance is a concept needed to interpret the results of multiple regression analysis. It allows the researcher to determine the validity of the estimated coefficients. Typically, an estimated coefficient is considered either significant or insignificant, which is shorthand for saying whether the researcher has sufficient confidence that the true coefficient is different from zero (and thus considered insignificant). In cases where a coefficient is statistically significant, the estimated value of the coefficient is the best "guess" of the true relationship between the independent and dependent variables. In cases where the coefficient is statistically insignificant, the best assumption is that the value of the coefficient is zero, which implies that the independent variable in question has no impact on the dependent variable.

General Methodology   In the investigations reported here, the dependent variable used was a state's share of total national gross investment in a particular industry during 1977. At issue is whether the share of national investment made in a given state is systematically influenced by such factors as the business or personal tax burdens, wage levels, labor productivity, or other similar factors. The statistical techniques employed calculated coefficients for each variable, which can be used to estimate the relative importance of different location determinants. In particular, we were interested in whether or not the coefficients calculated for different measures of the business tax burden are significant, and if so, in their sign and magnitude.

Equations were estimated for thirteen manufacturing industries at the two-digit SIC level of detail: Food and Kindred Products; Textiles; Paper and Allied Products; Chemicals; Petroleum and Coal Products; Rubber and Miscellaneous Plastic Products; Stone, Clay, and Glass; Primary Metals; Fabricated Metal Products; Nonelectrical Machinery; Electrical Machinery; Transportation Equipment; and Instruments.

A number of different variables were used in each equation. Some variables had different values for each industry in every state: two measures of the business tax burden, two measures of labor productivity, the average wage rate, and the state's share of national employment. A number of variables varied among states but had the same value for each industry within the state: temperature, the growth rate of union membership, the proportion of the labor force in unions, personal tax burden, the growth rate of population, population *227* density, per capita personal income, the growth rate of personal income, energy costs, and the proportion of personal income used for welfare programs. Precise descriptions of each of the variables are available in Appendix III.

Since they are the critical variables for this study, the two measures of business tax burden require some explanation. For purposes of the econometric analyses (and discussion here), the measures were designated TAXLOAD and ORDERST. TAXLOAD generally is the actual dollar value of the state and local taxes paid by a hypothetical corporation in a given industry in various states (the concept underlying the tax burden estimates presented in Table 5). In contrast, ORDERST is a measure of the rank of a given state in an ordering of all of the states by industry tax burden. In using ORDERST, it is assumed that more confidence should be placed in the ranking of states by business tax burden than on the specific number calculated and used for TAXLOAD.

In some cases, previous research and economic theory would predict that increases in the value of a variable should increase a state's share of national investment: measures of labor productivity, population growth, per capita income, and income growth. In other cases, previous research would predict that increases in the value of a variable should lead to a decrease in investment share: wage rates, population density (as proxy for land costs), and welfare costs. For the various business and personal tax measures, it is theoretically impossible to predict the direction of influence since benefits and costs must be balanced, but anecdotal evidence indicates that it should be negative for both business and personal taxes.

A major caveat is in order before examining the results. Only one year of investment data was used for the analysis due to the major task of calculating tax burdens. Ideally, the analysis would incorporate the experience of more years, and the results of the current investigation should be interpreted with caution.

Presentation of Results By testing a number of combinations of variables, a large number of different equations (and thus coefficients) were estimated. Because the focus of this research is on the effect of business taxes, only results for business taxes will be presented in the text (with more detailed results shown in Appendix III). These results are presented in Table 26 below, reporting the significance and elasticities of TAXLOAD and ORDERST in the best equations. Frequently, the primary difference between the equations was a simple substitution of ORDERST for TAXLOAD.

For the most part, the single most important determinant of current investment in an industry is the current location of employment. This

228 result holds regardless of the measure used for business tax burden,

Table 26

Summary of Significance and Elasticities for Business Tax Measures*

Industry	TAXLOAD Significance	TAXLOAD Elasticity	ORDERST Significance	ORDERST Elasticity
Food: 20	insignificant		insignificant	
Textile: 22	insignificant		insignificant	
Paper: 26	insignificant		insignificant	
Chemicals: 28	insignificant		.094	−.020
Petroleum	insignificant		.067	−.013
Rubber: 30	.009	−.176	.007	−.004
Stone: 32	insignificant		insignificant	
Primary Metals: 33	insignificant		insignificant	
Fabricated Metals: 34	insignificant		.035	−.002
Machinery: 35	insignificant		insignificant	
Electronics: 36	insignificant		insignificant	
Transportation: 37	.087	+.176	.061	+.001
Instruments: 38	insignificant		insignificant	

*Where the coefficient is insignificant, no elasticity is reported because the best estimate of the coefficient is zero.

SOURCE: Derived from the tables reporting regression results for each industry in Appendix Three.

and is generally consistent with the finding of the mail survey that most firms did not seriously consider locating in other states.

There is substantially more diversity among industries in the relative importance of the business tax measures. For each industry and each measure of tax burden, two results are presented: the level of statistical significance and the estimated elasticity of the share of new investment with respect to the tax measure. In most statistical studies, a variable is considered statistically significant only below the .10 level of confidence (or frequently, the more restrictive .05 level). As seen in Table 26 below, TAXLOAD is significant at the .10 level for only two industries—Rubber (significant at the .05 level) and Transportation. However, contrary to conventional wisdom, the results indicate that increases in TAXLOAD result in increases in investment share for Transportation. In both industries, the elasticity is quite small, at negative .176 for Rubber and positive .176 for Transportation. This should be interpreted as follows: a 1 percent increase in business taxes on the Rubber industry by a given state will result in a .176 percent loss of investment share and conversely for Transportation.

However, when ORDERST is used as a measure of business tax burden, it is statistically significant in five industries: Chemicals, Petroleum, Rubber, Fabricated Metals, and Transportation. Except for Transportation, an increased business tax burden leads to a *229* decrease in investment share. However, the elasticity of investment share is very small, ranging from -.002 to -.020. While it is not possible to directly translate this into a reflection of change of taxes (because ORDERST is a measure of the rank of a state, not the actual taxes), this in general is a very low elasticity.

The econometric results should not be taken as definitive, given the very serious problems with using only one year for an investment study. However, it is reasonable to interpret them as providing additional support for the hypothesis that for most firms, interstate differences in business taxes play a minor role in investment decisions, and that relatively large changes in relative tax burdens are required to significantly affect investment patterns. However, these results, or those of the mail survey, do not indicate that tax incentives represent poor public policy. That determination requires a weighing of the benefits—in terms of increased income—against the revenue loss.

EVALUATING THE PUBLIC RETURN TO STATE TAX INCENTIVES

When viewed as a public investment, a tax incentive should be provided when its expected return exceeds the return available on alternative investments. To determine the rate of return requires an estimation of the initial investment (the cost of the tax incentive), the annual return (the new income generated), and the probability that the new investment was induced by the tax incentive. This section will use the results of both the mail survey and the econometric investigations to explore the possible rate of return on state investment tax incentives.

Interpreting Results of the Mail Survey

The mail survey provided estimates of the proportion of firms whose location decisions were influenced by state tax incentives. These estimates can be used as part of the evaluation of tax incentives as public investments.

For the average manufacturing firm, each dollar of new investment in depreciable assets generates about $1.44 in annual income, including payroll, profits, and interest payments (see Appendix IV for details on the methods used in this section). This is the relevant stream of benefits to be used in a benefit-cost analysis if all of the new income remains within the state (that is, all employees initially resided in the state, all owners reside in the state, and all lenders are located in the state). The cost—or initial public investment—is the dollar cost of the investment tax credit.

This information can be used to estimate the annual return on the revenue loss. For example, the largest investment tax credit is that of New York at 4 percent. Thus, each dollar of investment in depreciable assets generates a first year, one-time cost of $.04, and a continuing stream of income of $1.44. If all of this new income can be attributed to recipients within the state, the annual rate of return on investment is 3590 percent. Of course, this tremendously exaggerates the value of the tax incentive because it implicitly assumes that all new investment is due solely to the subsidy. The results need to be adjusted to take into account the fact that only a proportion of new investment is actually induced by the incentive. If the public discount rate, or opportunity cost of its funds, is 10 percent, what proportion of the investment needs to have been due to the subsidy for the adjusted return to just equal 10 percent? Only .26 percent of total investment is required to have been affected if 10 percent is the "threshold" rate of return.

However, this example assumes away a number of factors which would serve to increase the proportion of investment affected in order for the tax incentive to be acceptable public investment. First, in many cases it is unlikely that all of the new income—payroll, profits, and interest—should be attributed to the state. Particularly for new branch plants, additional workers are imported from out of state, and owners and lenders are located elsewhere. For the most part, small firms and expansions are more likely to use local labor and be locally owned and financed. Second, a new manufacturing facility may call forth new public investment, such as roads, sewers, or schools, unless there is appropriate underutilized public capacity. If this is the case, the cost of the infrastructure should be added to the direct cost of the tax incentive in evaluating the rate of return. Again, it is more likely that new branch plants will require additional infrastructure than the start-up and expansion of firms in the area will. Third, given the tremendous uncertainty surrounding the actual return to be achieved, the opportunity cost—or discount rate—on the use of public funds should be increased. Just as private investors demand higher returns for risky investments, the public sector should demand higher returns on very uncertain investments. One illustrative set of assumptions about these factors is that half of the income flows out of state or to new immigrants, that infrastructure equal to 25 percent of private depreciable investment is called for, and that uncertainty results in an increase in the discount rate from 10 percent to 20 percent. Under this set of assumptions, the "break-even" probability rises from only .26 percent to 8.1 percent.

This example was based on the largest state tax incentive. A smaller tax incentive would be a desirable public investment at a lower probability of inducing investment because the initial costs are lower. The survey results allow the comparison of states with different levels of subsidy, and while extremely tentative, such a comparison does not indicate that a smaller subsidy reduces the effectiveness in influencing firms. Maintaining the optimistic assumptions that all income remains in-state, that no other public infrastructure is required, and that the *231* discount rate is only 10 percent, the required "break-even" probability drops from .28 percent for the largest tax credit down to only .007 percent for the smallest subsidy. However, with such a small subsidy, any additional public infrastructure completely dominates the calculation of rate of return (because it is equivalent to a 25 percent tax credit in the first year). Under the alternative assumptions of half of the income remaining within the state, an additional 25 percent public infrastructure, and a 20 percent discount rate, the break-even probability increases to 7 percent.

The results clearly indicate that, given equal chances of influencing investment, tax incentives will be a better public investment where there is underutilized public infrastructure, labor, and capital, so that public costs are lower and a higher proportion of income remains within the state. The results from the mail survey indicate actual probabilities of influencing the location of investment somewhat in the required range under the alternative assumptions—3.3 percent of new firms, none of expansions, and 6.3 percent of new branch plants. A final determination of the value of tax incentives must rest on the specific circumstances of each state and the new private investments undertaken. It is possible that tax incentives are appropriate public investments.

Interpreting Results the Econometric Investigtions A somewhat different approach must be used to examine the return to tax changes using the econometric results. The two measures of state tax burdens on business—TAXLOAD (the actual dollar value of tax burdens) and ORDERST (a measure of the rank of the state for a given industry)—do not incorporate the effect of temporary tax incentives. Instead, the results indicate the level of sensitivity of investment to relative tax burdens among states. The form of the equations—with share of national investment the dependent variable—assumes that interstate tax changes influence the location of investment but not the national total (a constant-sum game). In determining the rate of return to state tax changes from these results, the key measure is the elasticity of investment share with respect to relative tax burden. The elasticity measure can be used to determine the amount of induced investment as a result of a 1 percent change in a state's average tax burden, which can then be used to determine the stream of benefits. The cost in lost revenues is a continuing cost when an overall reduction is used rather than a limited tax incentive.

When TAXLOAD—the absolute dollar amount of average business tax burden—is used in the equation, the only industry showing a statistically significant negative response is Rubber and Miscellaneous Plastic Products. In that industry, the elasticity of investment share is

232

.176, indicating that a reduction of 1 percent of average business tax burden should lead to an increase of .176 percent of that state's share of total industry investment. In the Rubber industry, this represents an increase of only $58,930 in new investment (for details of the methodology used in this section, see Appendix IV). With each dollar of new depreciable investment resulting in $1.44 of new income, this results in an annual income increase of $84,623. The cost of this new investment is the 1 percent reduction in tax revenues applied to all the new Rubber investment (note that applying the reduction to all new investment is still far more targeted than applying to all Rubber business income). This represents an annual loss of about $30,135. Thus, new income exceeds annual costs, and the annual return is about 281 percent. Even if it is assumed that only half of the new income can be attributed to the state, and that additional public infrastructure is required (equal to 25 percent of the induced new investment), the annual return is still far above the 20 percent required for a risky public investment.

However, these results hold only if the general tax reduction can be targeted solely to the Rubber industry. No other industry exhibited a significant negative response to tax burdens as measured by TAXLOAD. Unless the tax reduction was targeted, all new manufacturing investment would receive the reduction, substantially increasing the lost revenue but not increasing the amount of new investment. Rubber and Miscellaneous Plastics accounted for only 3.8 percent of overall manufacturing investment in 1977. If only the new Rubber investment produced new income, this would reduce the rate of return substantially. With all income assumed to remain within the state, the return would drop to 10.7 percent, or only 5.4 percent if half of the income remained within the state. It would drop even more if additional public infrastructure was required. Using 20 percent as the desired return on public investments with uncertain return, across-the-board reductions in the tax burden on new manufacturing investment are not acceptable public investments. For each state, the actual returns would depend on the mix of new investment. In states where the Rubber industry is significantly larger than the national average, an across-the-board reduction may be an acceptable public investment. In states where it is less than the national average, the returns will be quite small and sometimes negative.

It is more difficult to interpret the econometric results based on equations containing ORDERST as a measure of business tax burden, because ORDERST represents a ranking of state tax burdens rather than the actual taxes paid. Thus, any estimates of elasticity of investment share represent the response to a change in the order statistic of 1 percent and not a change in the business tax burden. However, it is possible to make some reasonable assumptions and interpret the results, although they should be treated with the greatest *233* of caution.

With about fifty states in the ranking, and if the amount of difference between each state was approximately equal, a change of 1 percent in the order statistic would correspond to about half of a rank change. Since there would be a 100 percent change from the lowest to highest state in the ranking, this change of half of a rank would correspond to a 1 percent change in the underlying tax burden if the ranks are fairly evenly distributed.

ORDERST, as a measure of tax burden, resulted in slightly better results than TAXLOAD—a significant coefficients in five industries and slightly higher R^2 values. For Chemicals, Petroleum, Rubber, and Fabricated Metals, negative elasticities of -.020, -.013, -.004, and -.002, respectively, were estimated. These are substantially lower than the estimates found using TAXLOAD. For the highest elasticity—Chemicals—the annual gain in new income is substantially less than the annual loss in tax revenue from a 1 percent reduction in tax burden, even with the most optimistic assumptions about the distribution of new income and the need for public infrastructure investment. For lower elasticity industries, including Rubber, the disparities between new income and lost revenues increase. Thus, the results using ORDERST indicate that even targeted reductions in business taxes are inappropriate. Untargeted reductions to new manufacturing investment would fare extremely poorly.

Summary of the Public Return Discussion A clear-cut conclusion on the value of business tax reductions is not possible given this evidence. For states with very small tax incentives, only a tiny fraction of new investment needs to have been induced for the incentive to have been an appropriate public investment. For states with the largest tax incentives, the required proportion of induced investment, given reasonable assumptions about the distribution of income, the public discount rate, and the need for new infrastructure investment, lies in the general range found from the survey results. Further clarification requires much more detailed information on the hiring and ownership structures of firms receiving incentives, as well as on their need for supporting public infrastructure.

The regression results point to a more clear-cut conclusion. Given the estimates of the elasticity of investment share with respect to overall tax changes, untargeted business tax reductions are very poor public investments even if applied only to new investment. In only one industry—the Rubber industry—and with one of the two measures of tax burden, the evidence indicates that a targeted reduction in business taxes would be an appropriate public investment. Using the alternative measure, even targeting tax reductions to those sectors where a significant effect on investment was detected is found to be inappropriate.

SUMMARY OF THE RESULTS OF THE NEW EMPIRICAL RESEARCH

A substantial amount of progress has been made in the research reported in this chapter toward resolving some of the issues surrounding the value of state tax incentives. While methodological problems dictate that caution is required in interpreting the results, the most important conclusions of the research include the following:

- The initial foregone revenues for states, taken as a whole, are substantial, and deserving of evaluation.
- Most firms making new investments do not even consider locating in any state other than their final choice.
- Most firms making new investments in states with tax incentives are unaware that the incentives exist.
- Only a very small proportion of firms making investments claim that they would have located in another state in the absence of tax incentives.
- In most industries, the general level of business taxation has an undetectable effect on investment patterns.
- In those industries where an effect can be detected, it is quite small.
- When evaluated as a public investment, specific tax incentives may have an acceptable rate of return, particularly if targeted to areas of high unemployment and unused public infrastructure.
- Overall business tax reductions, even if targeted to sensitive industries, do not appear to be acceptable state tax policy for stimulating investment.

5

A GUIDE FOR THE PERPLEXED: POLICY DIRECTIONS

In a great many choices faced by public policymakers, reasonably careful analytical work is unable to transform messy, confused issues into simple, clear cut choices between "good" and "bad" public policy. The issue of state tax incentives, and the analysis contained in this study, is not an exception. In such cases, empirical work should strive to eliminate extreme claims, and leave the tough choices to political figures.

Two extreme claims should be immediately discarded. First, it is not true, as some have claimed, that business tax incentives influence a substantial number of firms to locate in a given state. Second, it is also false that no firms are influenced by tax incentives or interstate tax differentials. Tax incentives do appear to influence some firms, but very few. For the great majority, the reduced taxes represent a pleasant windfall. Given the small size of most state tax incentives, it is probably true that some of the firms who changed their location due to the subsidy made an irrational decision.

There appear to be two quite distinct strategies open to states which choose to employ tax incentives. First, states can assume that the incentives are generally ineffectual, but are indicative of the state's interest in new business development. Alternatively, they can assume that sufficiently large subsidies do influence some firms and should be designed to reduce the number of windfalls. The adoption of either strategy leads to quite different use of incentives. In either case, the results of the mail survey, which found substantial differences among new firms, expansions, and new branch plants, should influence the final subsidy strategy.

THE "CHEAP" SIGNALING STRATEGY For the state which assumes that tax incentives are quite weak in their ability to influence location decisions, but act to either influence the seriousness of the search process or simply fool some irrational firms, the smallest possible incentives should be employed. This seems to be the strategy of those states offering incentives as small as $50 per $100,000 investment. It is quite difficult to construct scenarios in which such a small incentive could act to offset tax or nontax differentials among competing states. Its only purpose can be to cause those firms which

236

look to alternative states to more seriously investigate those with tax incentives, or to make business decisionmakers feel wanted. In these cases, the tax incentives should probably be widely advertised among out-of-state firms. The availability of the tax incentive, in practice, should be limited by imposing minimum investment or employment requirements. The combined strategy of advertising plus minimum size requirements will increase the information value of the incentive while severely restricting the revenue loss. Such small incentives should then be evaluated relative to other advertising and outreach strategies rather than on the basis of their ability to directly influence location decisions.

THE SERIOUS SUBSIDY APPROACH For those states which choose to take tax incentives as a direct means of seriously influencing location, the study contains a number of important policy conclusions. First, incentives appear to affect a larger proportion of investments made by new firms and new branch plants than by new expansions. Second, the effect of taxes on the share of investment appears to vary among industries, with Rubber, Chemicals, Petroleum, and Fabricated Metal Products more responsive than other sectors. Third, benefit-cost studies indicate that the return on the subsidies is higher if local residents and capital sources are used in the project, and if underutilized public infrastructure can be used. Such conditions are more likely to be attained if new firms and expansions, rather than out-of-state branch plants, are subsidized.

These considerations indicate that it may be very desirable to target tax incentives to firms whose characteristics indicate responsiveness and to areas of labor pools whose nature serves to increase the public rate of return. Such a targeted approach is certain to be more appropriate than an across-the-board reduction in business taxes and probably more attractive than tax incentives available to all new investment. Given that targeting is desirable, a classical choice in public policy arises: the use of legislative change in the tax code to provide automatic tax incentives to all firms which meet certain criteria versus administrative selection of investment projects to receive tax incentives or direct grants. The former method—automatic tax incentives—substantially reduces the public overhead cost of maintaining a staff to make individual determinations, but almost certainly acts to increase the proportion of subsidies which are windfalls to recipients.

Some states already provide targeted incentives through existing tax codes. For example, Oregon provides tax incentives to manufacturing firms locating in depressed areas. Maine limits its tax incentives to firms undertaking quite large investments (so much so that to date only one firm has taken advantage of the subsidy). The Commerce Clearing *237*

House *State Tax Review* frequently reports special exemptions from sales taxes or a portion of property taxes for very specific industries in some states. However, it is not clear that these forms of targeting are the most appropriate. It is unlikely that simple geographical criteria—such as unemployment rate in a country—are sufficient to ensure that firms investing in lagging areas primarily hire local residents, or rely upon surplus public infrastructure. In some states, targeting the stage of investment—whether new firms, expansions, or new branch plants—may be unconstitutional on the basis of discriminating among forms of investment. Finally, targeting tax incentives to specific industries through legislation should require constant fine tuning and has the potential to reflect political influence rather than expected return on a public investment. In addition to these general problems, the temptation to target tightly through an inflexible tax code should be partially constrained by the realization that some firms outside of targeted areas, targeted sectors, or targeted stage of investment may be influenced by the incentives and provide net benefits. If incentives are provided through the tax code on an automatic basis, a reasonable case can be made for not targeting them.

The alternative subsidy device is to provide public employees with the discretion to provide cash grants or negotiated incentives to firms making new investments. This approach is widely pursued in Europe, and has parallels in the United States in the Urban Development Action Grant (UDAG) program and the formal and informal ability of some local tax assessors and city councils to provide negotiated reductions in property tax rates.

In theory, public officials should make case-by-case determinations on the likely net benefits of each subsidy. This would include judgments about whether the firm would have made the investment without the subsidy. To increase net benefits, subsidies might be made contingent on hiring local unemployed workers or locating in areas with underutilized public infrastructure. The level of subsidy could vary from case to case, reflecting judgments about the level needed to influence a location decision and the magnitude of net benefits from the investment (in contrast, all automatic tax incentives are mandated as a certain percent of eligible investment or wages). Where cash grants are made, ideally the development officials will seek to maximize the net benefits given the annual allocation of funding.

The discretionary grants are simultaneously more subject to public oversight and less desirable political influence than automatic tax incentives are. They will be subject to annual budget review and are exercised at the discretion of development officials rather than private investors. However, depending on the level of independence of the negotiators, they can also be held hostage by legislators seeking subsidies for constituents.

The relative attractiveness of discretionary incentives depends largely on the ability of the public negotiators to determine whether or not an investment would have been made in any case. If a substantial number of windfall subsidies can be eliminated, the discretionary program is probably a superior policy. If sufficient discrimination is not possible, the program will serve to provide subsidies to firms with superior political influence and the ability to penetrate the inevitable obstacle course of applications and hearings.

For those states which choose to provide subsidies, it may be desirable to provide both an automatic and a discretionary subsidy program. The automatic subsidy would be quite small, but heavily advertised to out-of-state firms. The discretionary subsidies would be budgeted each year, with each award subject to legislative veto. Negotiators would have broad flexibility in choosing firms and projects, including the ability to impose both hiring and location requirements.

CONCLUSIONS

The preceding remarks should not be interpreted as support for the provision of tax incentives. To the contrary, in many ways the provision of tax incentives represents a significant obstacle to sound development policy. Even if tax incentives are a good public investment, meeting the conditions discussed in Chapter Four, they will influence only a tiny proportion of new investment in any state. While the evidence is unclear about whether or not targeted incentives are a *good* policy, it is unequivocal about whether or not incentives are a *significant* policy. They are not. The evidence provides little support for those who believe that poor states, or stagnating states, can stimulate their economies in any significant way by a heavy reliance on either targeted tax incentives or across the board reductions in business taxes. Even where the evidence indicates that incentives are potentially a good public investment, they could be eliminated with almost an unnoticeable effect on a state's economy. In contrast, if the amount of time state legislatures spend debating tax incentives and the effect of taxes on investment was redirected toward other areas, substantial progress might be made. Tax incentives are clearly not a substitute for state initiatives in labor markets, capital markets, transportation, regulation, and the quality of life. Too often it is easier to pass a tax incentive, and widely advertise it, than to deal with more fundamental problems. To ignore the problems and factors which influence the great majority of investment decisions is to doom a state's development policy to marginal influence.

BIBLIOGRAPHY

1. Advisory Commission on Intergovernmental Relations (1980). "Regional Growth: Interstate Tax Competition," Report A–76 (Washington, D.C.)

2. Advisory Commission on Intergovernmental Relations (1980). *Significant Features of Fiscal Federalism:* 1979–1980 Edition. Report M–123 (Washington, D.C.).

3. Birch, D. (1979). *The Job Generation Process.* MIT Program on Neighborhood and Regional Change, Cambridge, Massachusetts.

4. Buchanan, J. and Moes, J. (1960). "A Regional Countermeasure to the Minimum Wage," *American Economic Review,* June.

5. Campbell, A. (1965). "State and Local Taxes, Expenditures, and Economic Development," in *State and Local Taxes on Business,* Tax Institute of America (Princeton, New Jersey).

6. Carlton, D. (1979). "Why New Firms Locate Where They Do: An Econometric Model," Working Paper Number 57, Joint Center for Urban Studies of MIT and Harvard (Cambridge, Massachusetts).

7. Cornia, G., Testa, A., and Stocker, F. (1978). "State-Local Fiscal Incentives and Economic Development," Urban and Regional Development Series Paper Number 4, Academy for Contemporary Problems (Columbus, Ohio).

8. Daniels, B. and Kieschnick, M. (1979). *Development Finance: A Primer for Policymakers.* The National Rural Center (Washington, D.C.).

9. Dorgan, B. (1980). "North Dakota's New Industry Tax Exemption: Economic Incentive or Tax Giveaway," A Study for Presentation to the State Board of Equalization and the North Dakota State Legislature, North Dakota State Tax Commission (Fargo, North Dakota).

10. Genetski, R. and Chin, Y. (1978). "The Impact of State and Local Taxes on Economic Growth," *Harris Economic Research Office Service,* Harris Bank (Chicago, Illinois).

11. Harrison, B. and Kanter, S. (1978). "The Political Economy of State Job Creation Incentives," *Journal of the American Institute of Planners,* October.

12. Hodge, J. (1978). "A Study of Industries' Regional Investment Decisions," unpublished paper, Federal Reserve Bank of New York (New York, New York).

13. *Inc.* Magazine (1980). "Buildings and Site Selection" (Boston, Massachusetts).

14. Jusenius, C. and Ledebur, L. (1977). "The Migration of Firms and Workers in Ohio: 1970-1975," Academy for Contemporary Problems (Columbus, Ohio).

15. Kanter, S. (1977). "Another Look at State Business Subsidies," a paper presented at the Seventieth Annual Conference on Taxation, National Tax Association-Tax Institute of America.

16. Moes, J. (1961). *Local Subsidies for Industry.* University of North Carolina Press (Chapel Hill, North Carolina).

17. McMillan, T. (1969). "Why Manufacturers Choose Plant Locations Versus Determinants of Plant Locations," *Land Economics,* August.

18. Morgan, W. (1964). "The Effects of State and Local Taxes and Financial Inducements on Industrial Location," unpublished PhD dissertation at the University of Colorado.

19. Morgan, W. and Hackbart, M. (1974). "An Analysis of State and Local Industrial Tax Exemption Programs," *Southern Economic Journal,* October.

20. Mueller, E. and Morgan, J. (1962). "Location Decisions of Manufacturers," Papers and Proceedings of the 74th Annual Meeting of the American Economics Association.

21. Oster, S. (1979). "Industrial Search for New Locations: An Empirical Analysis," *Review of Economics and Statistics,* May.

22. Price Waterhouse & Co. (1978). *State Tax Comparison Study* (St. Louis, Missouri).

23. Reigeluth, G., Wolman, H. and Reinhard, R. (1979). "The Fiscal Consequences of Changes in a Community's Economic Base: A Review of the Literature," The Urban Institute (Washington, D.C.).

24. Rinehart, J. (1962). "Rates of Return on Municipal Subsidies to Industries," an unpublished PhD dissertation, University of Virginia.

25. Rinehart, J. and Laird, W. (1972). "Community Inducements to Industry and the Zero Sum Game," *Scottish Journal of Political Economy,* February.

26. Ross, W. (1953). "Tax Exemption in Louisiana as a Device for Encouraging Industrial Development," *The Southwestern Social Science Quarterly,* February-March.

27. Sacks, S. (1965). "State and Local Finances and Economic Development," in *State and Local Taxes on Business,* Tax Institute of America (Princeton, New Jersey).

28. Schmenner, R. (1978). "The Manufacturing Location Decision: Evidence from Cincinnati and New England," a paper prepared for the Economic Development Administration, (Washington, D.C.).

241

29. Stafford, H. (1974). "The Anatomy of the Location Decision: Content Analysis of Case Studies," in *Spatial Perspectives on Industrial Organization and Decision-making,* ed. F.E. Ian Hamilton (John Wiley, New York).

30. Struyk, R. (1967). "An Analysis of Tax Structure, Public Service Levels, and Regional Economic Growth," *Journal of Regional Science,* Winter.

31. Thompson, W. and Mattila, J. (1959). *An Econometric Model of Postwar State Industrial Development,* Wayne State University Press (Detroit, Michigan).

32. Vasquez, T. and deSeve, C. (1977). "State/Local Taxes and Juridictional Shifts in Corporate Business Activity: The Complications of Measurement," *National Tax Journal,* September.

33. Vaughan, R. (1977). *The Urban Impacts of Federal Policies: Volume 2, Economic Development.* R–2028–KF/RC. The Rand Corporation (Washington, D.C.).

34. Vaughan, R. (1980). Abscam paper, unpublished.

35. Williams, W. (1967). "A Measure of the Impact of State and Local Taxes on Industry Location," *Journal of Regional Science,* Summer.

36. Wolman, H. (1979). "Components of Employment Change: A Review of the Literature," The Urban Institute (Washington, D.C.).

37. Zubrow, R. (1961). "Some Difficulties with the Measurement of Comparative Tax Burdens," National Tax Association Proceedings, 54th Annual Conference.

APPENDIX I

METHODOLOGY FOR CALCULATING STATE AND LOCAL TAX BURDENS ON BUSINESS

This appendix provides an explanation of the methods used to calculate the tax burdens displayed in Table 5. The most important point to understand is that the taxes are calculated on the basis of *hypothetical* balance sheets and income statements—not those of specific corporations operating in each state. For the All Manufacturing category, the following financial figures were used:

Balance Sheet		Income Statement	
Total Assets	$8,728,000	Sales	$6,919,920
Inventory	1,803,000	Operating Income	958,560
Machinery and Equipment	1,974,400		
Plant and Structures	693,680		
Land	354,000		
Capital Stock	1,065,000		
Retained Earnings	3,354,000		

These figures were derived largely from the Federal Trade Commission's *Quarterly Financial Report*. Each quarter, the FTC reports the total balance sheet and income statement for the U.S. manufacturing sector. To arrive at financial information for an average firm, the 1979 Third Quarter results were divided by the number of manufacturing corporations reporting income to the Internal Revenue Service in 1974 (the last year available from the IRS). The third quarter of 1979 was used to avoid distortions due to the 1980 recession.

To arrive at the tax burden for each state, the tax rates of each state (as reported in the *All States Handbook* published by Prentice-Hall) were applied to the hypothetical corporation. The only taxes considered were property taxes, corporate income or franchise taxes, capital value taxes, and sales taxes on purchases by manufacturing firms. In the case of property taxes, the average rate reported by Prentice-Hall *243* was used, although this necessarily ignores a good deal of intrastate variation in some cases. Not included in the comparison were unemployment insurance or workmen compensation taxes, which do vary among states, but are largely experience rated, making it almost impossible to provide reasonable estimates of interstate differences. For purposes of simplicity and to avoid problems of allocating income among states, it was assumed that all assets, employees, and sales of the firm occur within the state in question. The results should be interpreted as representing the taxes paid by a firm in different states, with the firm in question operating in some state—not in its initial years. This allows special tax credits to be ignored. For the most part, such credits are very small, and only apply early in the life of a particular investment or hiring expansion.

Similar results were obtained for thirteen other industry classifications, and are available from the author. The same methodology was used to calculate state and local tax burdens for 1977, which were used in the investment equations discussed in Chapter Four. These results are also available from the author.

APPENDIX II

METHODOLOGY AND DETAILS ON THE MAIL SURVEY

DESCRIPTION OF
METHODOLOGY
All corporations surveyed had actually made a manufacturing investment in 1979. Only firms which had invested in a state which automatically offers, through its tax code, specific investment and or employment incentives, were included in the sample. These states were New York, Massachusetts, Montana, Kansas, Delaware, New Mexico, Colorado, Rhode Island, West Virginia, Maine, and North Dakota. Because the filing date for tax returns in these states had already passed at the time of the survey, it is likely that the tax incentive had already been exercised unless the firm was not profitable and had no state tax liability.

Three different kinds of manufacturing investment decisions were analyzed through the surveys: the creation of a new company, the creation of a new branch plant of an existing company, and the expansion of an existing plant. The identities of companies for the survey were obtained from two sources. For new companies, a listing of all manufacturing companies established during 1979 in the eleven states was purchased from Dun and Bradstreet, which maintains such records for credit-rating and marketing purposes. For the new branch plants and expansions, listings were taken from 1979 issues of *Industrial Development* magazine, published by the Industrial Development Research Council, which attempts to identify and publish all investments in excess of $500,000.

Determining the appropriate recipient of the survey is quite important, since the ideal respondent would have participated directly in the decision and have been in a position to have weighed a variety of factors in choosing. For the new companies, this represented no obstacle, since the records purchased form Dun and Bradstreet included the name of the president of the firm, and all of the companies involved were extremely small. For the branch plants and expansions, however, considerable difficulties were involved. There is a great deal of variation among large firms in the way in which they organizationally structure the decision about plant location and expansion. *Industrial Development* periodically surveys corporations **245** to identify the executive in charge of process, and publishes the results. When identified for the companies in the sample, these executives were used. When not identified, the next alternative, for publicly held corporations, involved obtaining a recent annual report and attempting to identify an executive with the title of vice-president for facility planning, real estate, or corporate planning. If not available, the chief executive officer was used. For firms which were not publicly held, the headquarters of the company was telephoned, and a name obtained.

RESULTS FOR NEW COMPANIES Surveys were sent to all of the 1,821 new companies identified in the Dun and Brad street files. Seventy six were returned unopened, usually labeled "Moved—no forwarding address" by the Postal Service. A reasonable assumption is that these firms had failed after they were entered in the Dun and Bradstreet file. A significant number of new firms are undoubtedly not in the data base yet. However, almost all firms seeking outside credit from suppliers or lenders would be in the file. It is reasonable to assume that those excluded were generally smaller and operated largely on a cash/personal checking account basis. Such firms are probably less sophisticated in many aspects of business decisionmaking, and less likely to have considered a location in another state.

Three hundred and thirty-seven usable survey forms were returned. This is a response rate of 19.3 percent among the sample, taking out those returned by the Postal Service. Table 2-1 compares the distribution of responses with the sample in terms of state of origin, while Table 2-2 compares the distribution of responses with the sample in terms of two-digit SIC classification.

Interpretation of Relative Importance of Location Factors for New Firms Table 22 in the text presents the results of the survey question asking about the relative importance of differences among states in making location choices. There are a number of ways to interpret such survey answers. A number of ways of ranking the importance of the various factors are shown in Table 2-3 below. The first column focuses solely on those factors mentioned most frequently as a deciding positive influence. This method, however, completely discards the information that is contained in the other answers. Thus, the second column simply adds the responses of those who found a factor of deciding importance and those who found it of moderate positive influence. Another way to combine these two answers is shown in the third column, where those who rank a factor of deciding positive influence receive double the weight of those who rate a factor of

246

Table 2-1

Distribution of Sample and Responses by State: New Firms

	Sample		Responses		
State	Number	Percent	Number	Percent of Responses	Response Rate
New York	906	49.8%	131	38.9%	14.5%
Delaware	25	1.4	9	2.7	36.0
Colorado	227	12.5	59	17.5	26.0
New Mexico	33	1.8	5	1.5	15.2
Montana	45	2.5	10	3.0	22.2
Massachusetts	303	16.6	61	18.1	20.1
Kansas	105	5.8	23	6.8	21.9
Rhode Island	119	6.5	27	8.0	22.7
West Virginia	38	2.1	9	2.7	18.4
North Dakota	20	1.1	3	.9	15.0
	1,821		337		

The Chi-square test for differences between the distribution by state for the responses and the sample indicates that the responses differ significantly from the sample. The primary difference between the responses and the sample is the underrepresentation of new companies from New York and the overrepresentation of new companies from Colorado.

moderate positive influence. The fourth column is the ranking of factors found to be a moderate negative influence.

While there is no single correct way of interpreting the results, there is substantial consistency in the different rankings. With all five methods, access to current customers, access to a growing market, and personal reasons of management are the top three factors. With the exception of the inverse negative ranking, the least important factors are political climate, the supply of fuel and electricity, the cost of fuel and electricity, and air quality regulations. The two tax factors are consistently in the lower half of the rankings (except for the negative ranking).

SELECTED RESULTS FOR EXPANSION INVESTMENTS

As noted in the text, expansion investments in eligible states were identified through various issues of *Industrial Development*. Surveys were sent to firms which had made 143 expansion investments. Usable survey results were received from fifty firms, for an overall response rate of 35 percent. One letter was received from a firm which had made four separate expansion investments in 1979, and chose to describe the factors relevant to those investments without using the *247*

Table 2-2

Distribution of Sample and Responses by Sector: New Firms

Sector	Sample Number	Sample Percent	Responses Number	Percent of Responses	Response Rate
20	94	4.2%	18	5.3%	19.1%
21	1	.1	0	0	0
22	68	3.7	8	2.4	11.8
23	290	15.9	25	7.4	8.6
24	110	6.0	19	5.6	17.3
25	82	4.5	17	5.0	20.7
26	36	2.0	6	1.8	16.7
28	58	3.2	14	4.2	24.1
29	6	.3	1	.3	16.7
30	72	4.0	13	3.9	18.1
31	41	2.3	8	2.4	19.5
32	67	3.7	18	5.3	26.9
33	40	2.2	7	2.1	17.5
34	204	11.2	52	15.4	25.5
35	256	14.1	56	16.6	21.9
36	111	6.1	21	6.2	18.9
37	0	0	0	0	0
38	76	4.2	21	6.2	27.6
39	209	11.5	33	9.8	15.8
	1,821		**337**		

The Chi-square with eighteen degrees of freedom is 33.13, indicating that the response distribution is significantly different than the sample distribution. This largely reflects the underrepresentation of Sector 23 (the Apparel industry), and the overrepresentation of Sectors 32 (Stone, Clay, and Glass) and 38 (Instruments). Because Sector 23 is heavily concentrated in New York, the primary distortion appears to be due to the low response rate from the New York City Apparel industry, which is well known for its dependence on illegal aliens and attempts to avoid any public probing.

---

survey form. The pattern of response is compared to the pattern of the sample in terms of geographical and sectoral distribution in Tables 2-4 and 2-5 below.

Interpretation of Relative Importance of Location Factors for Expansions

Table 2-6 uses a number of ways to interpret the survey responses from expansion firms. As with the new firms, the most important location factors are identified consistently through any of the ranking methods, with economies of scale, maintaining an intact labor force, the ease of expanding on-site, and access to raw materials consistently the most influential. After the top four, the rankings are much less consistent, largely reflecting the volatility of a ranking procedure when

Table 2-3

Ranking of the Importance of Location Factors for New Firms

FACTORS	Deciding Mentions	Deciding + Moderate	Deciding + .5 Moderate	Inverse Negative Ranking
Access to current customers	1	1	1	1
Access to growing market	2	2	2	2
Personal reasons	3	3	3	3
Access to raw materials	4	8	5	11
Availability of capital	5	7	6	6
Familiarity with economy	6	4	4	4
Supply of skilled labor	7	6	8	5
Transportation	8	5	7	10
Land costs	9	14	12	15
Costs of skilled labor	10	9	9	7
Personal taxes	11	15	14	20
Cost of unskilled labor	12	12	13	12
Business taxes	13	11	10	19
Supply of unskilled labor	14	10	11	8
Union activities	15	16	16	18
Climate	16	13	15	13
Political climate	17	19	18	17
Supply fuel/electricity	18	17	17	9
Cost of fuel/electricity	19	18	19	14
Air quality	20	20	20	16

SOURCE: derived from Table 22

Table 2-4

Distribution of Sample and Responses by State: Expansions

State	Sample Number	Sample Percent	Responses Number	Percent of Responses	Response Rate
New York	41	28.7%	10	20.0%	24.4%
Delaware	4	2.8	1	2.0	25.0
Colorado	11	7.7	5	10.0	45.4
New Mexico	3	2.1	2	4.0	66.7
Montana	0	0	0	0	0
Massachusetts	32	22.4	10	20.0	31.3
Kansas	26	18.2	13	26.0	50.0
Rhode Island	8	5.6	4	8.0	50.0
Maine	3	2.1	2	4.0	66.7
West Virginia	15	10.5	3	5.6	20.0
North Dakota	0	0	0	0	0
Total	**143**		**50**		**35.0%**

Table 2-5

Distribution of Sample and Responses by Sector: Expansions

Sector	Sample		Responses		
	Number	Percent	Number	Percent of Responses	Response Rate
20	8	5.6%	1	2.0%	0.0%
21	0	0.0	0	0	0.0
22	1	0.7	1	2.0	100.0
23	2	1.4	1	2.0	50.0
24	1	0.7	0	0.0	0.0
25	0	0.0	0	0.0	0.0
26	5	3.5	3	6.0	60.0
28	14	9.8	3	6.0	21.4
29	4	2.8	2	4.0	50.0
30	8	5.6	2	4.0	25.0
31	2	1.4	2	4.0	100.0
32	1	0.7	0	0.0	0.0
33	7	4.9	1	2.0	14.3
34	8	5.6	6	12.0	75.0
35	18	12.6	6	12.0	33.3
36	18	12.6	8	16.0	44.4
37	7	4.9	6	12.0	85.7
38	6	4.2	2	4.0	33.3
39	1	0.7	1	2.0	100.0
Unidentified	32	22.4	5	10.0	15.6
Total	**143**		**50**		**35.0%**

The Chi-square test indicates that the responses differ significantly from the sample in both the distribution of firms by state and sector. The Chi-square is relatively smaller for the distribution by states, and primarily reflects underrepresentation of New York and overrepresentation of Kansas, Maine, and New Mexico. The distribution by sector is distorted primarily by overrepresentation in SIC 37 (Transportation) where six of the seven firms in the sample responded, SIC 34 (Fabricated Metal Products), and significant underrepresentation among firms whose SIC could not be identified.

there are relatively few responses (so that a shift of one or two answers can move a ranking several places).

SELECTED RESULTS FOR NEW BRANCH PLANTS

New branch plants, as parts of existing firms, were selected from listings in *Industrial Development*. It is possible that a very small number of new branch plants were actually new firms with an initial investment of over $500,000. However, there was no overlap between firms identified as new companies through the Dun and Bradstreet listings and those identified as new branch plants by *Industrial Development*. Survey forms were sent to 101 new plants.

Table 2-6

Ranking of Importance of Location Factors for Expansions

FACTORS	# Deciding	Deciding + Moderate	Deciding + .5 Moderate	Inverse Negative
Economies of scale	1	4	3	12
Maintain labor	1	1	1	1
Ease of expanding	1	2	2	1
Raw materials	4	4	4	1
Present customers	4	6	6	1
Political climate	4	18	12	20
Personal reasons	4	10	7	12
Growing market	7	13	12	1
Supply of fuel	7	13	12	16
Union activities	7	18	15	24
Supply skilled	7	2	4	1
Capital	7	10	8	1
Cost skilled labor	13	6	8	16
Cost of fuel	13	13	15	20
Product line	13	6	8	12
Transportation	13	6	8	1
Personal taxes	18	18	17	20
Supply unskilled	18	18	21	12
Cost unskilled	18	13	17	16
Climate	18	18	21	1
Familiarity	18	23	23	1
Land costs	18	13	17	16
Air regulation	23	23	24	1
Business taxes	24	10	17	20

SOURCE: Derived from responses in Table 23

Usable responses were received from thirty two firms, a response rate of 31.7 percent. The distribution of the sample and the responses by state and sector are displayed in Tables 2-7 and 2-8 below.

Interpretation of Relative Importance of Location Factors for New Branch Plants As with the new firms and expansion investments, it is possible to interpret the answers to the survey question about the relative importance of interstate differences in a number of ways. As shown in Table 2-9 below, the supply of skilled labor is consistently ranked as the first or second most important factor by all methods. When the number of "deciding" and "moderate" mentions are added together, the cost of skilled labor becomes the most important factor. Business taxes are generally considered fairly important with each method. Overall, those factors ranked in the first half of the rankings by one method are in the first half in the other rankings, with the significant *251*

Table 2-7

Distribution of Sample and Responses by State: New Plants

State	Sample Number	Sample Percent	Responses Number	Responses Percent of Responses	Response Rate
New York	40	39.6%	11	34.4%	27.5%
Delaware	8	7.9	0	0.0	0.0
Colorado	10	9.9	3	9.4	30.0
New Mexico	3	3.0	0	0.0	0.0
Montana	2	2.0	2	6.3	100.0
Massachusetts	9	8.9	3	9.4	33.3
Kansas	14	13.9	8	25.0	57.1
Rhode Island	10	9.9	2	6.3	20.0
Maine	3	3.0	2	6.3	66.7
West Virginia	2	2.0	1	3.1	50.0
North Dakota	0	0.0	0	0.0	0.0
Total	**101**		**32**		**31.7%**

The Chi-square test indicates that the response is significantly different than the sample. This primarily reflects underrepresentation of Delaware and New Mexico, and overrepresentation of Kansas.

---

exception of the "inverse negative" ranking, in which union activities are frequently mentioned. As with the expansion investments, these rankings are quite sensitive to the shift of even a single firm's answers, given the relatively small number of responses.

Table 2–8

Distribution of Sample and Responses by Sector: New Plants

	Sample			Responses	
Sector	Number	Percent	Number	Percent of Responses	Response Rate
20	9	8.9	0	0.0	0.0
21	0	0.0	0	0.0	0.0
22	0	0.0	0	0.0	0.0
23	3	3.0	0	0.0	0.0
24	1	1.0	0	0.0	0.0
25	3	3.0	2	6.3	66.7
26	1	1.0	0	0.0	0.0
28	2	2.0	0	0.0	0.0
29	5	5.0	2	6.3	40.0
30	9	8.9	2	6.3	22.2
31	1	1.0	1	3.1	100.0
32	2	2.0	0	0.0	0.0
33	4	4.0	0	0.0	0.0
34	5	5.0	0	0.0	0.0
35	13	12.9	10	31.3	76.9
36	8	7.9	3	9.4	37.6
37	7	6.9	3	9.4	42.9
38	2	2.0	0	0.0	0.0
39	6	5.9	2	6.3	33.3
Unidentified	20	19.8	7	21.9	35.0
Total	**101**		**32**		**31.7**

The Chi-square test indicates that the distribution of responses is significantly different than the distribution of the sample.

Table 2-9

Ranking of the Importance of Location Factors for New Branch Plants

FACTORS	Deciding	Deciding + Moderate	Deciding + .5 Moderate	Inverse Negative
Supply of skilled labor	1	2	1	1
Supply of unskilled labor	2	9	6	1
Union activities	2	6	3	18
Business taxes	2	9	6	1
Personal reasons	5	4	3	1
Transportation	5	6	6	1
Raw materials access	7	6	10	1
Political climate	7	9	11	10
Cost skilled labor	7	1	2	10
Land costs	7	4	6	1
Capital availability	7	3	3	1
Present customers	12	9	12	10
Growing market	12	18	16	10
Cost of fuel	12	14	14	10
Supply of fuel	12	9	12	1
Cost unskilled labor	16	14	15	10
Climate	16	18	18	18
Personal taxes	16	16	16	20
Familiarity w/economy	19	16	18	1
Air quality regulation	19	18	20	1

SOURCE: Derived from Table 24.

COUNCIL OF STATE PLANNING AGENCIES LOCATION SURVEY
CONFIDENTIAL

In answering the questions in this survey, please refer only to the circumstances relevant in choosing the location for your recent new plant.

1. Did you seriously consider locating this new plant in any other state? Yes __ No __ (If you answered "No", please skip question 2 and go on to question 3, 4, and 5.)

2. In choosing among states, please think about the factors which led you to choose your final choice. Focus on *differences* between the state you actually chose and those you considered. For example, if *all* of the states you considered had an ample supply of skilled labor, then this had a insignificant effect in choosing between states. Please look over the list of factors below, and indicate how they influenced you by checking the appropriate column.

Factor	Deciding Positive Influence	Moderate Positive Influence	Insignificant Influence	Moderate Negative Influence
Availability of capital				
Supply of skilled labor				
Costs of skilled labor				
Supply of unskilled labor				
Cost of unskilled labor				
Union activities				
Supply of fuel and electricity				
Cost of fuel and electricity				
Climate				
Personal reasons of management				
Transportation network				
Political climate				
Familiarity with economy				
Air quality regulation				
Business tax structure				
Personal tax structure				
Access to raw materials				
Access to present customers				

(Continued on following page) **255**

Access to growing market				
Land costs				

3. Some states offer special tax incentives—such as investment tax credits—for new and expanding firms. Did the state tax code of your final choice include a special tax incentive?
   Yes __ No __ Don't Know __
   If such an incentive was available, please consider the effect of this tax incentive on your location decision.
4. If the tax incentive was *not* offered, would you have located your new plant in another state?
   Yes __ No __
5. Without the tax incentive, would you have reduced the *amount* of your investment?
   Yes __ No __

   Please return to: Council of State Planning Agencies

COUNCIL OF STATE PLANNING AGENCIES LOCATION SURVEY
CONFIDENTIAL

In answering the questions in this survey, please refer only to the circumstances relevant in choosing the location for your recent business start-up.

1. Did you seriously consider locating this new business in any other state? Yes __ No __ (If you answered "No", please skip question 2 and go on to question 3, 4, and 5.)

2. In choosing among states, please think about the factors which led you to choose your final choice. Focus on *differences* between the state you actually chose and those you considered. For example, if *all* of the states you considered had an ample supply of skilled labor, then this had a insignificant effect in choosing between states. Please look over the list of factors below, and indicate how they influenced you by checking the appropriate column.

Factor	Deciding Positive Influence	Moderate Positive Influence	Insignificant Influence	Moderate Negative Influence
Availability of capital				
Supply of skilled labor				
Costs of skilled labor				
Supply of unskilled labor				
Cost of unskilled labor				
Union activities				
Supply of fuel and electricity				
Cost of fuel and electricity				

(Continued on following page)

Climate

Personal reasons of management

Transportation network

Political climate

Familiarity with economy

Air quality regulation

Business tax structure

Personal tax structure

Access to raw materials

Access to present customers

Access to growing market

Land costs

3. Some states offer special tax incentives—such as investment tax credits—for new and expanding firms. Did the state tax code of your final choice include a special tax incentive? Yes __ No __ Don't Know __
If such an incentive was available, please consider the effect of this tax incentive on your location decision.
4. If the tax incentive was *not* offered, would you have located your new business in another state? Yes __ No __
5. Without the tax incentive, would you have reduced the *amount* of your investment? Yes __ No __

Please return to: Council of State Planning Agencies

COUNCIL OF STATE PLANNING AGENCIES LOCATION SURVEY CONFIDENTIAL

In answering the questions in this survey, please refer only to the circumstances relevant in choosing the location for your recent expansion

1. Did you seriously consider expanding by locating a new plant in any other state than your actual expansion? Yes __ No __ (If you answered "No", please skip question 2 and go on to question 3, 4, and 5.)

2. In choosing among states, please think about the factors which led you to choose your final choice. Focus on *differences* between the state you actually chose and those you considered. For example, if *all* of the states you considered had an ample supply of skilled labor, then this had a insignificant effect in choosing between states. Please look over the list of factors below, and indicate how they influenced you by checking the appropriate column.

(Continued on following page) **257**

Factor	Deciding Positive Influence	Moderate Positive Influence	Insignificant Influence	Moderate Negative Influence
Availability of capital				
Economies of scale realized with expansion on-site				
Supply of skilled labor				
Costs of skilled labor				
Supply of unskilled labor				
Cost of unskilled labor				
Union activities				
Maintain intact labor force				
Supply of fuel and electricity				
Cost of fuel and electricity				
Climate				
Personal reasons of management				
Product line or production process not easily divided				
Transportation network				
Political climate				
Familiarity with economy				
Air quality regulation				
Ease of expanding on-site				
Business tax structure				
Personal tax structure				
Access to raw materials				
Access to present customers				
Access to growing market				
Land costs				

3. Some states offer special tax incentives—such as investment tax credits—for new and expanding firms. Did the state tax code of your final choice include a special tax incentive? Yes __ No __ Don't Know __

(Continued on following page)

If such an incentive was available, please consider the effect of this tax incentive on your location decision.

4. If the tax incentive was *not* offered, would you have located your new plant in another state?
   Yes __ No __

5. Without the tax incentive, would you have reduced the *amount* of your investment?
   Yes __ No __

   Please return to: Council of State Planning Agencies

APPENDIX III

DETAILS ON ECONOMETRIC METHODOLOGY AND RESULTS

This appendix serves to provide additional description of the methodology used, the variables, and results for a number of equations. A great deal more information is available from the author—means and standard deviations for each of the variables and correlation coefficient matrices. In addition to the equations presented in this Appendix, a number of additional equations were tested, and results from those experiments are also available.

DESCRIPTION OF THE VARIABLES

SHARNEWK: The share of new gross investment in depreciable manufacturing assets in a single state for a selected industry in 1977, as reported in the preliminary reports of the Census of Manufacturers 1977. Where a state had no reported investment, its share is represented as zero. For investment in states where disclosure was a problem, the state is not included in the estimated equation because it is impossible to estimate the actual investment.

TAXLOAD: For each industry, a hypothetical average corporation with balance sheets and income statements for 1977 was constructed from IRS and FTC financial reports. For each hypothetical firm, an average tax burden for each state was constructed including corporate profits or franchise taxes, property taxes, capital value taxes, and sales taxes, where applicable. The variable is the dollar amount of taxes paid by the hypothetical corporation in that state. See Appendix I for methodological details as applied to 1980 estimates.

TEMP: For each state, the average annual temperature for the state's largest three cities was calculated. This serves in part as a proxy for weather, and has been found significant in other research.

UNIONGRO: For each state the cumulative rate of growth or decline in the share of the private nonagricultural work force in unions over the period 1970 to 1977 was calculated.

UNION77: Share of the work force in 1977 in unions.

PRODWAGE: For each industry in each state, this variable is the dollar amount of value added divided by the dollar amount of wages paid to production workers. In states with no industry, the national average was substituted.

PRODHOUR: For each industry in each state, this variable represents the dollars of value added divided by the hours worked by production workers. PRODHOUR and PRODWAGE do not appear in the same equation. Same procedure for missing values.

WAGERATE: Wages paid divided by hours worked by production workers. For missing values, the average wage paid by other manufacturing sectors in the state is substituted.

TPPI77: Total state and local taxes with an initial impact on individuals per $1,000 of personal income in 1977.

POPCHANG: For each state, the cumulative rate of growth or decline of population over the period 1970 to 1977 was calculated.

DENSITY: Population per square mile in 1977 for each state, used as a proxy for land costs, which are not recorded by state.

PCPI77: For each state, per capita personal income in 1977, used as a measure of local final consumption demand.

INCCHANG: For each state, cumulative rate of growth or decline of total personal income (not per capita) for the period 1970–1977.

ENERGY: For each state, the dollar cost per million BTU of fuel or electricity actually used in the state in 1976.

SHARHOUR: For each industry in each state, the share of national

261

hours of production worked is used as a measure for the share of the industry already in the state.

WELFARE: For each state, the dollars from state and local revenue sources (Federal welfare was excluded) per $1,000 of personal income expended on general welfare programs.

ORDERST: An alternative measure of business tax burden. Basically, this measure is based on the possibility that it is possible to place business tax burdens in the correct order among states, but have relatively little confidence about the exact number (and hence differences between states which are close in ranking). It was assumed that the actual tax burden by a firm varied with a normal distribution around the estimated figure based on hypothetical balance and income statements. The ranking of states was used to draw a number (in effect) from a table of "order statistics." Because the variance of the normal distribution is not known, it is impossible to use the coefficients to define an elasticity, but the procedure does ensure that the other coefficients are not biased.

EXPECTED SIGNS OF THE COEFFICIENTS Theory and previous empirical research provides some guide to the expected signs for these variables. A positive coefficient indicates that an increase in the value of the variable is associated with an increase in the share of new capital expenditures, while a negative coefficient indicates the converse.

TAXLOAD: Theoretically no prediction because it depends on the services "purchased" with taxes. Anecdotally, the sign should be negative.

TEMP: Increased temperature is usually thought to be an indication of good weather and thus fewer work interruptions. Previous research has found positive coefficients.

UNIONGRO: Available research indicates that unions are generally successful in increasing wages and that increased labor productivity frequently follows. Theoretically, no prediction. Anecdotally, negative.

UNION77: Same discussion as for UNIONGRO.

PRODWAGE: Increased production per dollar of wages should yield a positive coefficient.

PRODHOUR: Positive.

WAGERATE: Theoretically no prediction is possible, since it depends on productivity. Anecdotally, negative.

TPPI77: As with business tax burden, no theoretical prediction is possible, since it depends on the value of services received. Anecdotally, should be negative.

POPCHANG: Increased labor supply and markets for goods should be an inducement. Positive.

DENSITY: If density increases land costs, should serve as a deterrent. Negative.

PCPI77: As an indicator of the magnitude of final demand, should be positive.

INCCHANG: If used as a predictor of future market growth, positive.

ENERGY: As a cost of production, should be negative.

SHARHOUR: With adjustment costs needed for films starting new locations, the coefficient should be positive.

WELFARE: As a redistributive expenditure with no direct benefits for businesses, should have a negative coefficient.

ORDERST: As with business tax burden, theoretically no prediction, but anecdotally should be negative.

PROCEDURES USED
The equations for each industry were estimated using the ordinary least squares option within the Statistical Package for the Social Services (SPSS). While a large number of different regressions were run, only a small proportion are shown here (the remainder are available on request from the author). The two business tax burden variables—TAXLOAD and ORDERST—were used as alternates, with the results from running both equations presented here. Because of the very large number of variables tested, and the small number of observations, it was unreasonable to expect statistical significance at normal levels of confidence (usually the .05 level) in very many instances. SPSS has an option which allows the researcher to select some predetermined level of confidence, allowing all variables with a level of significance lower than that determined to be excluded from the final *263*

form of the equations. The higher the level of confidence required, the fewer variables that typically remain. The cost of excluding variables, even with a low level of significance, is to bias the coefficients estimated for the remaining variables. This cost becomes more serious if the criterion used is quite strict. In this case, however, the criteron used was only that variables whose level of significance was at least .50 were retained in the equation. This means that, given certain statistical assumptions, there is a probability of at least 50 percent that the actual coefficient for a variable is different than zero.

PRESENTATION OF RESULTS

Empirical results are shown for each of thirteen industries examined. For each industry, there are potentially two sets of results—one each for equations using TAXLOAD or ORDERST. Where both business tax burden measures are excluded from the final equation, there is no difference among results, and only one table is presented for the industry. For each regression, three summary statistics are provided: adjusted R^2, the overall F statistic, and the level of significance of the overall F statistic. For each independent variable included in the final equation, the coefficient, standard error, significance, elasticity, and contribution to R^2 (note: not to adjusted R^2, which is typically somewhat lower) are displayed.

SIC 20: Food and Kindred Products

Neither TAXLOAD nor ORDERST exert a significant influence on the investment patterns in the food industry. The existing location of the industry, as represented by SHARHOUR, dominates all other factors. However, with an adjusted R^2 of .570, a substantial portion of interstate variation remains unexplained. The most likely excluded factor of importance is the location of agricultural output.

Table 3-1
Food and Kindred Products
(TAXLOAD and ORDERST Excluded)

Adjusted R^2: .570		*Overall F Statistic: 32.16*		*Significance: .000*	
Independent Variable	*Coefficient*	*Standard Error*	*Significance*	*Elasticity*	*R^2 Contribution*
SHARHOUR	.881	.111	0	.881	.576
TPP177	-.176E-03	.150E-03	.247	-.647	.013
Constant	.160E-01	.113E-01	.166		

SIC 22: Textile Mill Products

While TAXLOAD is included in the equation with a negative coefficient, its coefficient is not significant. At the .05 level of significance, only SHARHOUR is significant, and dominates the equation in terms of contribution to R^2. At the .10 level of significance, ENERGY is also significant, but with an unexpected positive coefficient. Its contribution to R^2 is quite small.

With ORDERST substituted for TAXLOAD, the results are quite similar. The adjusted R^2 is identical, and the overall F statistic very similar. ENERGY becomes significant at the .05 level, while INCCHANG becomes significant at the .10 level, with a positive coefficient and high elasticity. SHARHOUR continues to account for almost all of the R^2. ORDERST is negative, but insignificant.

Table 3-2
Textile Mill Products
(TAXLOAD Included)

Adjusted R^2: .972   Overall F Statistic: 157.854   Significance: .000

Independent Variable	Coefficient	Standard Error	Significance	Elasticity	R^2 Contribution
SHARHOUR	.987	.322E-01	0	.985	.971
TEMP	.190E-03	.195E-03	.336	.471	.001
ENERGY	.567E-02	.297E-02	.065	.584	.001
INCCHANGE	.341E-01	.206E-01	.106	1.332	.001
UNIONGRO	-.101E-01	.135E-01	.459	.053	.001
WAGERATE	-.164E-02	.142E-02	.255	-.336	.001
PCP177	.316E-05	.215E-05	.150	.974	.001
UNION77	-.333E-03	.227E-03	.152	-.322	.000
TAXLOAD	-.858E-08	.658E-08	.201	-.054	.001
POPCHANG	-.261E-03	.211E-03	.225	-.107	.001
Constant	-.561E-01	.294E-01	.064		

SIC 26: Paper and Allied Products

SHARHOUR and WAGERATE are the the only significant variables. SHARHOUR accounts for over 40 percent of the interstate variation while WAGERATE accounts for nearly 20 percent. Both coefficients are positive. The adjusted R^2 is .684, and would probably be increased if a variable reflecting forest acreage were included. TAXLOAD is excluded from the truncated equation.

ORDERST, in contrast, is included in the final equation when substituted for TAXLOAD. Otherwise, the results are very similar, with only SHARHOUR and WAGERATE significant and dominating the determination of R^2.

265

Table 3-3
Textile Mill Products
(ORDERST Included)

Adjusted R^2: .972   Overall F Statistic: 141.748   Significance: .000

Independent Variable	Coefficient	Standard Error	Significance	Elasticity	R^2 Contribution
SHARHOUR	.977	.341E-01	0	.974	.971
TEMP	.101E-03	.239E-03	.674	.251	.001
ENERGY	.626E-02	.303E-02	.047	.645	.001
INCCHANGE	.429E-01	.230E-01	.071	1.676	.001
UNIONGRO	-.143E-01	.136E-01	.299	-.075	.001
WAGERATE	-.212E-02	.145E-02	.155	-.433	.001
PCP177	.284E-05	.212E-05	.189	.875	.001
UNION77	-.332E-03	.226E-03	.150	-.321	.000
ORDERST	-.240E-02	.178E-02	.187	-.002	.001
POPCHANG	-.253E-03	.215E-03	.247	-.104	.001
TPP177	.919E-04	.112E-03	.418	.321	.000
Constant	-.644E-01	.366E-01	.087		

Table 3-4
Paper and Allied Products
(TAXLOAD Excluded)

Adjusted R^2: .684   Overall F Statistic: 13.198   Significance: .000

Independent Variable	Coefficient	Standard Error	Significance	Elasticity	R^2 Contribution
SHARHOUR	.868	.145	0	.862	.432
WAGERATE	.878E-02	.188E-02	.000	2.149	.197
WELFARE	-.109E-01	.781E-02	.172	-.453	.065
PCP177	-.272E-05	.306E-05	.379	-.839	.015
TEMP	.265E-03	.370E-03	.479	.649	.009
UNIONGRO	.260E-01	.208E-01	.220	.130	.005
ENERGY	-.470E-02	.403E-02	.251	-.494	.077
PRODWAGE	-.164E-03	.198E-03	.413	-.062	.005
Constant	-.207E-01	.292E-01	.483	-.062	.005

SIC 28: Chemicals and Allied Products   The variables included in the equations for the chemical industry account for just over half of the variation in investment shares among states. TAXLOAD is excluded from the truncated equation. As with the paper industry, SHARHOUR and WAGERATE enter with a significant, and positive coefficient. UNION77 is almost significant at the .10 level with a negative coefficient, and accounts for over 9 percent of the R^2.

Table 3-5
Paper and Allied Products
(ORDERST Included)

Adjusted R^2: .689   Overall F Statistic: 13.488   Significance: .000

Independent Variable	Coefficient	Standard Error	Significance	Elasticity	R^2 Contribution
SHARHOUR	.859	.142	0	.854	.438
WAGERATE	.862E-02	.187E-02	.000	2.374	.197
WELFARE	-.109E-01	.715E-02	.135	-.454	.065
PCP177	-.240E-05	.304E-05	.436	-.739	.015
ORDERST	-.254E-02	.240E-02	.296	-.004	.011
PRODWAGE	-.215E-03	.186E-03	.255	-.081	.005
UNIONGRO	.246E-01	.206E-01	.241	.123	.005
ENERGY	-.466E-02	.400E-02	.251	-.490	.009
Constant	-.731E-02	.208E-01	.728		

With ORDERST substituted for TAXLOAD, the business tax measure does enter the final equation, and is significant at the .10 level. While its coefficient is negative, the elasticity of investment share with respect to ORDERST is quite small, at -.020, indicating that an increase in the value of ORDERST of 1 percent would reduce a state's share of investment by .02 percent of the average investment share. UNION77 becomes significant at the .05 level, with a quite high negative elasticity. This does not indicate a search for low wages, as WAGERATE remains significant and has a quite high positive elasticity. ENERGY becomes significant at the .05 level, and has a negative coefficient. However, variation in energy prices only accounts for about 3 percent of variation in investment shares.

Table 3-6
Chemicals and Allied Products
(TAXLOAD Excluded)

Adjusted R^2: .515   Overall F Statistic: 7.819   Significance: .000

Independent Variable	Coefficient	Standard Error	Significance	Elasticity	R^2 Contribution
SHARHOUR	.960	.253	.001	.958	.288
WAGERATE	.243E-01	.861E-02	.003	7.203	.132
UNION77	-.141E-02	.853E-03	.106	-1.359	.094
UNIONGRO	.869E-01	.546E-01	.120	.443	.021
ENERGY	-.163E-01	.976E-02	.104	-.173	.035
PRODWAGE	.485E-03	.371E-03	.198	.266	.011
TEMP	.866E-03	.904E-03	.344	2.146	.010
Constant	-.132	.817E-01	.115		

Table 3-7
Chemicals and Allied Products
(ORDERST Included)

Adjusted R^2: .536		Overall F Statistic: 7.505		Significance: .000	
Independent Variable	Coefficient	Standard Error	Significance	Elasticity	R^2 Contribution
SHARHOUR	.940	.246	.000	.937	.288
WAGERATE	.227E-01	.758E-02	.005	6.724	.132
UNION77	−.163E-02	.715E-03	.028	−1.570	.094
ORDERST	−.982E-02	.572E-02	.094	−.020	.024
PRODWAGE	.570E-03	.357E-03	.119	.312	.018
UNIONGRO	.839E-01	.517E-01	.113	.428	.016
ENERGY	−.262E-01	.125E-01	.042	−2.758	.030
DENSITY	.435E-04	.379E-04	.259	.306	.014
Constant	−.544E-01	.588E-01	.361		

SIC 29: Petroleum and Coal Products The equations for the petroleum industry explain less than half of the variation in investment shares. This may reflect access to port facilities and air quality laws, which are difficult to capture in variables. SHARHOUR and WAGERATE dominate the results, each with positive coefficients. WAGERATE contributes slightly more than SHARHOUR to R^2, and has a substantially higher elasticity. TAXLOAD is excluded from the final equation. PRODWAGE is positive and significant at the .10 level, but contributes less than 3 percent to R^2.

The results change somewhat when ORDERST is substituted for TAXLOAD. ORDERST enters the equation with a negative coefficient significant at the .10 level. The response of investment share, however, is quite inelastic. Variations in business tax burden account for about 4 percent of variation in investment share. PRODWAGE ceases to be significant, while UNION77, with a negative coefficient, becomes significant at the .10 level.

SIC 30: Rubber and Miscellaneous Plastic Products The equations explain over 95 percent of the variation among states in investment shares. SHARHOUR, TAXLOAD, ENERGY, INCCHANG, POPCHANG, and DENSITY are each significant at the .05 level, while UNIONGRO is significant at the .10 level. SHARHOUR dominates the results accounting for over 90 percent of the R^2. TAXLOAD, as expected from anecdotal evidence, has a negative coefficient, but accounts for less than 1 percent of R^2. ENERGY, somewhat surprisingly, has a positive coefficient. INCCHANG has a positive coefficient, but

Table 3-8
Petroleum and Coal Products
(TAXLOAD Excluded)

Adjusted R^2: .431   Overall F Statistic: 5.860   Significance: .000

Independent Variable	Coefficient	Standard Error	Significance	Elasticity	R^2 Contribution
SHARHOUR	1.599	.355	.000	1.584	.199
WAGERATE	.300E-01	.661E-02	.000	9.308	.227
PRODWAGE	.184E-02	.106E-02	.089	.789	.027
TEMP	.875E-03	.148E-02	.559	2.167	.023
UNIONGRO	.190	.114	.104	-1.025	.012
UNION77	-.198E-02	.152E-02	.202	-1.895	.024
TPPI77	-.504E-03	.678E-03	.461	-1.775	.007
Constant	-.177	.125	.165		

Table 3-9
Petroleum and Coal Products
(ORDERST Included)

Adjusted R^2: .459   Overall F Statistic: 6.462   Significance: .000

Independent Variable	Coefficient	Standard Error	Significance	Elasticity	R^2 Contribution
SHARHOUR	1.500	.347	.000	1.486	.199
WAGERATE	.319E-01	.642E-02	.000	9.883	.227
ORDERST	-.180E-01	.958E-02	.067	-.013	.042
PRODWAGE	.155E-02	.102E-02	.137	.663	.021
UNIONGRO	.144	.117	.223	.778	.011
UNION77	-.267E-02	.146E-02	.075	-2.563	.034
DENSITY	.432E-04	.488E-04	.382	.300	.009
Constant	-.173	.469E-01	.001		

accounts for less than 1 percent of R^2. POPCHANG and DENSITY each have negative coefficients, and contribute trivially to R^2. It is conceivable that POPCHANG has a negative coefficient due to the possible effects of pollution from the industry on the residential choices of residents.

When ORDERST is substituted for TAXLOAD, the results are quite similar. Adjusted R^2 remains the same, and no variables change from significant to insignificant, or vice versa.

SIC 32: Stone, Clay, and Glass Products

Both TAXLOAD and ORDERST are excluded from the equation due to lack of significance. SHARHOUR dominates the 269

Table 3-10
Rubber and Miscellaneous Plastic Products
(TAXLOAD Included)

Adjusted R^2: .958   Overall F Statistic: 118.800   Significance: .000

Independent Variable	Coefficient	Standard Error	Significance	Elasticity	R^2 Contribution
SHARHOUR	.996	.371E-01	0	.993	.931
TAXLOAD	-.650E-07	.237E-07	.009	-.176	.009
UNION77	-.223E-03	.134E-03	.106	-.222	.004
ENERGY	.953E-02	.215E-02	.000	1.016	.004
INCCHANG	.377E-01	.135E-01	.008	1.503	.008
UNIONGRO	-.155E-01	.868E-02	.082	.080	.004
POPCHANG	-.332E-03	.153E-03	.036	-.134	.002
DENSITY	-.129E-04	.593E-05	.036	-.091	.003
PCP177	-.158E-05	.133E-05	.243	.498	.001
Constant	-.525E-01	.187E-01	.008		

Table 3-11
Rubber and Miscellaneous Plastic Products
(ORDERST Included)

Adjusted R^2: .959   Overall F Statistic: 120.922   Significance: .000

Independent Variable	Coefficient	Standard Error	Significance	Elasticity	R^2 Contribution
SHARHOUR	.997	.368E-01	.000	.994	.931
ORDERST	-.263E-02	.913E-03	.007	-.004	.011
ENERGY	.934E-02	.214E-02	.000	.996	.004
INCCHANG	.348E-01	.136E-01	.015	1.390	.008
UNIONGRO	-.155E-01	.860E-02	.079	.080	.006
DENSITY	-.124E-04	.589E-05	.042	-.088	.002
POPCHANG	-.308E-03	.149E-03	.047	-.124	.002
PCP177	.149E-05	.132E-05	.266	.470	.001
UNION77	-.208E-03	.133E-03	.125	-.207	.001
Constant	-.533E-01	.184E-01	.006		

equation, with a positive coefficient, and a contribution to R^2 of over 80 percent. TEMP is the only other significant coefficient, and as expected is positive. However, it accounts for less than 3 percent of interstate variation in investment shares.

SIC 33: Primary Metal Industries Both TAXLOAD and ORDERST are excluded from the equation due to lack of significance. Only SHARHOUR is significant at the .05 level, and contributes over 80 percent of R^2. This may

Table 3-12
Stone, Clay, and Glass Products
(TAXLOAD and ORDERST Excluded)

Adjusted R^2: .863   Overall F Statistic: 43.150   Significance: .000

Independent Variable	Coefficient	Standard Error	Significance	Elasticity	R^2 Contribution
SHARHOUR	.876	.660E-01	.000	.875	.837
TEMP	.479E-03	.211E-03	.029	1.236	.026
DENSITY	-.121E-04	.743E-05	.112	-.086	.007
PRODWAGE	.215E-02	.335E-02	.525	.353	.003
UNION77	-.306E-03	.210E-03	.152	.309	.003
PCP177	.272E-05	.218E-05	.220	.874	.003
POPCHANG	-.246E-03	.221E-03	.272	-.106	.004
Constant	-.383E-01	.182E-01	.041		

Table 3-13
Primary Metal Industries
(TAXLOAD and ORDERST Excluded)

Adjusted R^2: .841   Overall F Statistic: 29.523   Significance: .000

Independent Variable	Coefficient	Standard Error	Significance	Elasticity	R^2 Contribution
SHARHOUR	.807	.772	.000	.783	.820
TPPI77	-.244E-03	.158E-03	.133	-.820	.017
WAGERATE	.160E-02	.163E-02	.331	.464	.013
TEMP	.484E-03	.319E-03	.138	1.148	.003
PCPI77	.489E-05	.352E-05	.103	1.709	.003
DENSITY	-.287E-04	.153E-04	.070	-.184	.005
POPCHANG	-.426E-03	.343E-03	.212	-.169	.005
ENERGY	.504E-02	.468E-02	.290	.501	.004
Constant	-.553E-01	.331E-01	.104		

reflect the lack of net new investment in the industry, with most investment occurring at existing locations for maintenance. DENSITY is significant at the .10 level, with a negative coefficient.

SIC 34: Fabricated Metal Products   The equation accounts for almost all of interstate variation in investment shares, with an adjusted R^2 of .978. SHARHOUR accounts for almost all of the variation. WAGERATE has a positive influence, and is significant at the .10 level, while UNION77 has a negative influence, significant at the .10 level. Surprisingly, PRODWAGE has a negative influence, significant at the .10 level. *271*

WAGERATE, UNION77, and PRODWAGE each account for only about 1 percent of R^2. While TAXLOAD is included in the final equation, its coefficient is insignificant.

With ORDERST substituted for TAXLOAD, the overall F statistic increases substantially, although there is little change in R^2. SHARHOUR continues to dominate the equation, accounting for almost all of the interstate variation. ORDERST has a negative coefficient, and is significant at the .05 level. However, the associated elasticity is extremely low. UNION77 and PRODWAGE retain their negative coefficients, but become significant at the .05 level.

Table 3-14
Fabricated Metal Products
(TAXLOAD Included)

Adjusted R^2: .978   Overall F Statistic: 225.337   Significance: .000

Independent Variable	Coefficient	Standard Error	Significance	Elasticity	R^2 Contribution
SHARHOUR	1.016	.323E-01	.000	1.016	.975
ENERGY	-.134E-02	.122E-02	.278	-.143	.003
WAGERATE	.318E-02	.181E-02	.086	.844	.001
UNION77	-.212E-03	.107E-03	.055	-.209	.001
PRODWAGE	-.951E-04	.507E-04	.069	-.027	.001
TPPI77	-.622E-04	.558E-04	.272	-.224	.000
TEMP	-.206E-03	.134E-03	.134	-.520	.001
TAXLOAD	-.264E-07	.293E-07	.373	-.053	.000
WELFARE	.398E-03	.535E-03	.462	.020	.000
Constant	.628E-02	.154E-01	.681		

Table 3-15
Fabricated Metal Products
(ORDERST Included)

Adjusted R^2: .980   Overall F Statistic: 321.130   Significance: .000

Independent Variable	Coefficient	Standard Error	Significance	Elasticity	R^2 Contribution
SHARHOUR	1.025	.310	.000	1.024	.975
ENERGY	-.159E-02	.109E-02	.154	-.169	.003
WAGERATE	.287E-02	.170E-02	.099	.763	.001
UNION77	-.223E-03	.101E-03	.030	-.225	.001
PRODWAGE	-.104E-03	.486E-04	.039	-.030	.001
ORDERST	-.189E-02	.866E-03	.035	-.002	.001
TEMP	-.261E-03	.120E-03	.051	-.661	.002
Constant	.640E-02	.139E-01	.648		

SIC 35: Machinery,
Except Electrical
Only SHARHOUR is significant, and accounts for over 90 percent of variation in investment shares. This is the only industry, in which TAXLOAD is included in a final equation, while ORDERST is excluded. However, TAXLOAD, with a positive coefficient, is statistically insignificant.

SIC 36: Electric and
Electronic Equipment
With TAXLOAD included, 95 percent of the variation in investment shares is explained. However, TAXLOAD is insignificant. SHARHOUR dominates the equation, accounting for about 90 percent of R^2. As frequently discussed in the industry, WAGERATE and DENSITY exert negative influences on investment, with WAGERATE exerting a larger relative negative influence. Somewhat surpris-

Table 3-16
Machinery, Except Electrical
(TAXLOAD Included)

Adjusted R^2: .912		Overall F Statistic: 70.589		Significance: .000	
Independent Variable	Coefficient	Standard Error	Significance	Elasticity	R^2 Contribution
SHARHOUR	1.064	.613E-01	0	1.063	.905
POPCHANG	.277E-03	.204E-03	.183	.120	.010
TEMP	.294E-03	.186E-03	.122	.759	.004
PCPI77	.263E-05	.202E-05	.200	.844	.001
UNION77	-.181E-03	.202E-03	.374	-.183	.001
TAXLOAD	.106E-07	.100E-07	.297	.061	.001
INCCHANGE	.131E-01	.160E-01	.401	.532	.001
Constant	-.458E-01	.244E-01	.068		

Table 3-17
Machinery, Except Electrical
(ORDERST Excluded)

Adjusted R^2: .913		Overall F Statistic: 100.148		Significance: .000	
Independent Variable	Coefficient	Standard Error	Significance	Elasticity	R^2 Contribution
SHARHOUR	1.075	.603E-01	.000	1.074	.905
POPCHANG	.272E-03	.199E-03	.179	.118	.010
TEMP	.262E-03	.178E-03	.149	.676	.004
PCPI77	.210E-05	.189E-05	.273	.674	.001
UNION77	-.178E-03	.200E-03	.378	-.180	.001
Constant	-.284E-01	.162E-01	.088		

ingly, WELFARE exerts a positive influence, although it contributes little to R^2. PCPI77, perhaps as a measure of the availability of skilled labor rather than market demand, exerts a positive influence, although it accounts for less than 1 percent of R^2. The results are almost identical when ORDERST is substituted for TAXLOAD.

SIC 37: Transportation Equipment SHARHOUR, UNION77, WELFARE, WAGERATE, INCCHANG, and PCPI77 are all significant at the .05 level, while

Table 3-18
Electric and Electronic Equipment
(TAXLOAD Included)

Adjusted R^2: .950		Overall F Statistic: 95.500		Significance: .000	
Independent Variable	Coefficient	Standard Error	Significance	Elasticity	R^2 Contribution
SHARHOUR	1.118	.567E-01	0	1.114	.906
WAGERATE	-.758E-03	.154E-03	.000	-.219	.030
DENSITY	-.182E-04	.619E-05	.006	-.124	.005
PCPI77	.353E-05	.164E-05	.038	1.086	.003
TEMP	.313E-03	.198E-03	.123	.777	.005
WELFARE	.906E-02	.350E-02	.014	.372	.007
UNION77	-.275E-03	.173E-03	.121	-.267	.001
UNIONGRO	.106E-01	.111E-01	.345	-.056	.001
TAXLOAD	-.103E-07	.145E-07	.483	-.067	.001
Constant	-.351E-01	.178E-01	.057		

Table 3-19
Electric and Electronic Equipment
(ORDERST Included)

Adjusted R^2: .950		Overall F Statistic: 95.752		Significance: .000	
Independent Variable	Coefficient	Standard Error	Significance	Elasticity	R^2 Contribution
SHARHOUR	1.121	.571E-01	.000	1.117	.906
WAGERATE	-.753E-03	.155E-03	.000	-.217	.030
DENSITY	-.181E-04	.620E-05	.006	-.123	.005
PCPI77	.348E-05	.165E-05	.041	1.071	.003
TEMP	.290E-03	.213E-03	.181	.720	.005
WELFARE	.906E-02	.349E-02	.014	.371	.007
UNION77	-.285E-03	.177E-03	.116	-.277	.001
UNIONGRO	.111E-01	.110E-01	.321	-.059	.001
ORDERST	-.112E-02	.150E-02	.459	-.001	.001
Constant	-.349E-01	.177E-01	.057		

TAXLOAD and TPPI77 are significant at the .10 level. SHARHOUR, with a positive coefficient, dominates the equation, accounting for over 90 percent of R^2. Only WELFARE, with a negative coefficient, accounts for more than 1 percent of R^2 among the remaining significant variables. TAXLOAD, for the first time, is significant and *positive* although it accounts for only .2 percent of interstate variation. In contrast, personal taxation, as represented by TPPI77, has a negative coefficient, while also contributing very little to R^2.

The results are quite similar when ORDERST is substituted for TAXLOAD. No variables change sign or alter in significance with the substitution. ORDERST, while still positive, remains a very minor contributor to R^2.

Table 3-20
Transportation Equipment
(TAXLOAD Included)

Adjusted R^2: .964   Overall F Statistic: 98.853   Significance: .000

Independent Variable	Coefficient	Standard Error	Significance	Elasticity	R^2 Contribution
SHARHOUR	1.034	.443E-01	0	1.009	.930
UNION77	.101E-02	.285E-03	.001	.855	.009
WELFARE	-.134E-01	.642E-02	.046	-.481	.015
POPCHANG	-.336E-03	.394E-03	.401	-.094	.007
WAGERATE	.418E-02	.139E-02	.005	1.041	.003
INCCHANG	-.470E-01	.215E-01	.038	-1.512	.001
PCPI77	-.682E-05	.285E-05	.024	-1.765	.002
TAXLOAD	.102E-07	.573E-08	.087	.176	.002
TPPI77	-.310E-03	.175E-03	.088	-.895	.002
PRODWAGE	.699E-04	.493E-04	.167	.843	.002
Constant	.690E-01	.313E-01	.036		

SIC 38: Instruments and Related Products The equation, with TAXLOAD included, accounts for nearly 90 percent of interstate variation. SHARHOUR accounts for nearly all of this, with an elasticity greater than one. Among the remaining variables, only WAGERATE is significant and has a positive coefficient. WAGERATE contributes less than 2 percent to R^2. TAXLOAD, while included in the truncated equation, is insignificant. PCPI77, with a surprising negative coefficient, is significant at the .10 level, but contributes little to R^2.

When ORDERST is substituted for TAXLOAD, the results are very similar. ORDERST has a negative coefficient but is insignificant, while SHARHOUR continues to dominate the equation. *275*

Table 3-21
Transportation Equipment
(ORDERST Included)

Adjusted R^2: .964   Overall F Statistic: 101.081   Significance: .000

Independent Variable	Coefficient	Standard Error	Significance	Elasticity	R^2 Contribution
SHARHOUR	1.024	.437E-01	0	1.00	.930
UNION77	.948E-03	.277E-03	.001	.834	.009
WELFARE	-.134E-01	.635E-02	.045	-.480	.015
POPCHANG	-.314E-03	.389E-03	.426	-.088	.007
WAGERATE	.450E-02	.141E-02	.004	1.119	.003
ORDERST	.369E-02	.189E-02	.061	-.001	.001
PCPI77	-.705E-05	.248E-05	.019	-1.823	.001
INCCHANG	-.461E-01	.212E-01	.038	-1.483	.002
TPPI77	-.326E-03	.174E-03	.073	-.939	.002
PRODWAGE	.787E-04	.490E-04	.120	.048	.002
Constant	.741E-01	.313E-01	.026		

Table 3-22
Instruments and Related Products
(TAXLOAD Included)

Adjusted R^2: .898   Overall F Statistic: 43.008   Significance: .000

Independent Variable	Coefficient	Standard Error	Significance	Elasticity	R^2 Contribution
SHARHOUR	1.387	.946E-01	0	1.350	.876
WAGERATE	.899E-02	.318E-02	.008	1.943	.016
UNION77	-.471E-03	.409E-03	.257	-.414	.010
TAXLOAD	-.708E-07	.507E-07	.172	-.284	.008
TPPI77	.167E-03	.194E-03	.395	.556	.002
PCPI77	-.513E-05	.300E-05	.096	-1.465	.003
PRODWAGE	-.310E-03	.276E-03	.269	-.106	.001
UNIONGRO	.198E-01	.201E-01	.332	-.006	.002
POPCHANG	.308E-03	.360E-03	.399	.118	.002
Constant	-.134E-01	.206E-01	.518		

SUMMARY OF ECONOMETRIC RESULTS

As previously discussed, the strength of these results is limited by reliance on a single year's cross sectional data. However, even with this constraint, the results appear quite striking.

For the most part, the single most important determinant of current investment in an industry is the current location of employment. Only

Table 3-23
Instruments and Related Products
(ORDERST Included)

Adjusted R^2: .897   Overall F Statistic: 42.818   Significance: .000

Independent Variable	Coefficient	Standard Error	Significance	Elasticity	R^2 Contribution
SHARHOUR	1.390	.947E-01	0	1.352	.876
WAGERATE	.902E-02	.319E-02	.008	1.948	.016
UNION77	-.462E-03	.409E-03	.267	-.407	.010
ORDERST	-.393E-02	.293E-02	.188	-.001	.007
TPPI77	.163E-03	.194E-03	.407	.543	.002
PCPI77	-.520E-05	.300E-05	.092	-1.486	.004
PRODWAGE	-.312E-03	.267E-03	.267	-.107	.001
UNIONGRO	.198E-01	.202E-01	.335	-.106	.002
POPCHANG	.292E-03	.365E-03	.430	.112	.002
Constant	-.193E-01	.216E-01	.379		

a portion of this can be interpreted as resulting from expansion or rehabilitation of existing plant. This result holds regardless of the measure used for business tax burden. For the most part, the elasticity of investment share with respect to employment share is in the close neighborhood of one, meaning that a 1 percent increase in employment share is generally accompanied by a 1 percent increase in investment share.

APPENDIX IV

PROCEDURES USED IN THE BENEFIT-COST ANALYSIS OF TAX INCENTIVES

This Appendix describes in more detail the methods used to develop the benefit-cost estimates of Chapter Four. The goal of those estimates was to determine whether or not tax incentives were reasonable public investments. This appendix does not duplicate the general discussion of public investment principles which appears in Chapter Two, nor does it present all of the calculations involved in estimating the rate of of return on tax revenues foregone. Instead it focuses on showing how certain critical figures were derived. In particular, it explains:

1. the estimate of new income generated by manufacturing investment;
2. the estimate of new investment generated by a cut in overall business tax burden; and
3. the tax loss associated with a reduction in overall tax burden.

ESTIMATING NEW INCOME GENERATED BY MANUFACTURING INVESTMENT
In the public investment analysis, benefits are defined as the new income arising out of the manufacturing investment which accrues to state citizens. Since the various investment tax credits are usually based on depreciable investment, it is useful to relate income to depreciable investment. Income has three components: payroll, pretax profits, and interest. The payroll figure was obtained by calculating the ratio of payroll to value of shipments (a close proxy for sales) for all manufacturing industries from the 1977 Preliminary Census of Manufacturers. This ratio was then applied to the sales total from the aggregate income statement for manufacturing firms available by summing the quarterly figures reported in the *Quarterly Financial Reports* of the Federal Trade Commission. This resulted in an estimate of payroll for the aggregate income statement, which could be directly compared to net depreciable assets for the parallel aggregate balance sheet. The ratio of pretax profits to net depreciable

278

assets was more straightforward, relying solely upon those aggregates from the 1977 FTC reports. The ratio of interest payments to net depreciable assets was obtained by assuming that the average interest rate on all liabilities in 1977 was 7 percent. This interest rate resulted in an estimate of total interest payments, which could then be compared to net depreciable assets. When rounded to two decimal places, this procedure resulted in the following estimates of income for each dollar of net depreciable investment: $.97 of payroll, $.36 of pre-tax profits, and $.11 of interest or a total of $1.44 of annual income per dollar of initial depreciable investment. This ratio will naturally vary among industries, states, and individual projects.

ESTIMATING THE NEW INVESTMENT GENERATED BY A GENERAL BUSINESS TAX CUT

The econometric results were used to analyze the effects on specific sectors of a lasting reduction in the overall tax burden, as opposed to a specific investment tax credit. The analysis was carried out for both the TAXLOAD and ORDERST tax burden variables. The critical figure in the analysis was the estimate of elasticity generated by the regression analysis. The elasticity of investment share in the Rubber industry was estimated to be $-.176$, meaning that for the mean state, a reduction of 1 percent of tax burden would result in an increase in investment share of .176 percent (note: not .176 percentage points). Thus, a state lowering its business taxes on future income and assets in the Rubber industry should expect its share of national investment to increase to 1.00176 times its current share. For the Rubber industry in 1977, with national investment of $1573.7 million, this represents only $58,930 in new investment for the mean state. To this amount of new investment, the previously determined ratio of new income to investment can be applied to estimate benefits. The same methodology is used when elasticities based on ORDERST are used.

ESTIMATING THE TAX LOSS ASSOCIATED WITH A REDUCTION IN TAX BURDEN

Since it was assumed that the tax reduction would go to income and assets from new investment only, the tax loss should be calculated by estimating some ratio of total state and local tax payments to depreciable investment. For the average manufacturing firm in 1977, 9.04 percent of depreciable investment went to state and local taxes, based on comparing the net depreciable assets in an average manufacturing firm with the average tax burden for the average manufacturing firm. The cost of the new investment must be the tax loss due to the lower tax rates on income and assets from all new investments, not just the induced investment. For the *279* mean state, a reduction of 1 percent in taxes resulting from the new investment would be only $30,135.

INDEX

CONTRIBUTORS

Michael Barker is Executive Director of The Gallatin Institute, an economic policy research group based in Washington, D.C., and Editor of *Politics & Markets*, a monthly newsletter. He was formerly Director of Policy Studies at The National Governors' Association's Council of State Planning Agencies, where he was responsible for advising the nation's governors on the development of alternative economic policies. From 1975 to 1978 he was an aide to Massachusetts Governor Michael Dukakis. Mr. Barker is Editor of the twelve-volume *Studies in State Development Policy*, published by The National Governors' Association. He has written widely on industrial policy, financial regulation, business finance, and economic and community development. He has also been an economic policy adviser to The National Urban Coalition, The Democratic National Committee, and numerous federal and state officials.

Michael Kieschnick is Senior Editor of *Politics & Markets*, a monthly newsletter, and Chairman of The Working Assets Fund, a money market fund based in San Francisco, California. He was formerly Director of the State of California's Office of Economic Policy, Planning, and Research, and an aide to former California Governor Jerry Brown. He has also taught at the University of California, Berkeley, and worked as a consultant to the U.S. Environmental Protection Agency, The U.S. Economic Development Administration, The National Governors' Association, The National Center for Economic Alternatives, and The National Rural Center. He is the author of *Theory and Practice in the Design of Development Finance Innovations* and *Development Finance: A Primer for Policymakers*. Dr. Kieschnick is a graduate of Stanford University, and received a Ph.D. in Public Policy from the Kennedy School of Government, Harvard University.

Roger J. Vaughan is a Senior Fellow at The Gallatin Institute in Washington, D.C., and Senior Editor of the of the monthly newsletter, *Politics & Markets*. He has been an aide to former New York Governor Hugh Carey, an assistant vice-president in Citibank's economics department, and an urban economist at the Rand Corporation. He is a frequent economic policy adviser to Members of Congress, and has been a consultant to the Democratic National Committee. A graduate of Oxford University, Dr. Vaughan received a Ph.D. in economics from the University of Chicago. He writes regularly on industrial policy, employment training, federal tax policy, and infrastructure finance. Under the sponsorship of The Twentieth Century Fund, Dr. Vaughan is currently completing a study of the impact of public policy on innovation and entrepreneurship in the U.S. economy.

About the Council of State Planning Agencies: The Council, formed in 1965 as an affiliate of the National Governors' Association, is a membership organization comprised of the policy and planning staff of the nation's governors. Through its Washington office, the Council provides technical assistance to governors' offices and state officials on a wide spectrum of policy issues. From time to time, the Council also performs both policy and technical research on state and national policy.